Don Bloch, born in New Y...  ...e
novels, *Arising, Little Frien*... ...*n
Wind* and *Face Value*. Edu... ...e
has travelled widely in the... ...ll
as in Africa. He now make...

DON BLOCH

Passing Through

Stories

PALADIN
GRAFTON BOOKS
A Division of the Collins Publishing Group

LONDON GLASGOW
TORONTO SYDNEY AUCKLAND

Paladin
Grafton Books
A Division of the Collins Publishing Group
8 Grafton Street, London W1X 3LA

Published in Paladin Books 1988

First published in Great Britain by
William Heinemann Ltd 1986

ISBN 0-586-08674-9

Printed and bound in Great Britain by
Collins, Glasgow

Set in Baskerville

For Bobby

Contents

Pembantu[2]

Imagine a boy climbing a coconut palm. A slip of a child, barefoot. No slow shinnying; confident, lithe ascension, up and up. Even for his thirsty friends on the ground, heads back, shading their eyes, the pack laughing, urging him on, how quickly the height grows dizzying. The cluster of young green nuts, *kelapa muda*, is within reach. One hand stretches out – and then the impossible happens. The boy loses hold. Slowly at first but with gathering speed, he falls. On impact the right arm is crumpled beneath his twisted body, the left is flung up over his head – grasping still for the fatal prize. That is what the province of North Sulawesi looks like on the map, with Manado, the provincial capital, a small bulge at the left wrist.

I

The climate of Manado is killing. Hot and damp past endurance. It is an unpleasant town in other respects as well – crowded, dirty, noisy. Garbage in great stinking mounds is dumped in and along the sluggish, liver-colored river that winds through the city to empty into a polluted harbor. While the rich occupy hillside villas, gaudy bunkers behind locked gates and thick, sturdy walls, the poor – and there are many more of these – live in the *kampungs* below. Once these were marshland, now they are festering urban slums with open sewers.

To call Manado overcrowded is euphemistic. People live so close together that to drown out their neighbors' breathing they have to turn their radios up. And I wouldn't be at all surprised if in a few generations the notorious Manado mosquito is born without wings.

What's more, from the day we arrived in Manado, everywhere Koert Jan and I looked we saw people in uniform. Likely as not they were dangerously bored. I had never been fingerprinted before. The authorities soon made up for that. Immigration, labor, health, security, traffic police – they all trotted out their little black absorbent pads. Does it do something to your dreams, I wonder, to fall asleep with ink in the whorls of your fingertips?

No, Manado meant waiting, false smiles, nerves shining, pettiness, sweat, extreme politeness. All things considered we'd be happier living somewhere else.

When a rumor reached us that an American missionary couple, the Pressmans, were abandoning their house in Tomohon, Koert Jan and I hurried to enquire. Although Tomohon was only about an hour from Manado, inland, up in the mountains, at night it would be cold enough for us to sleep under a blanket. We found the Pressman house down a quiet side lane. Towering fir trees lined the property in front. The house itself was built on the model of a 1950's American suburban ranch home. At the foot of the garden was an active volcano, the Lokun. Later we discovered that the Lokun's looks deceived: when it belched great spider-large flakes of ash which settled in our yard, these came not from the summit of the steep, symmetrical cone, but from a vent half-way up one side.

Koert Jan and I had to fight our way up the front walk against a current of excited Indonesian ladies, their arms full of parcels and packages. Lavish clusters of bougainvillaea, purple and pink, flowered over the front door which was propped open

2

with an old car battery. We walked smack into the midst of a 'total sale'. The large living room was cluttered with goods. Gimmicks, gew-gaws and canned soups were displayed, china-ware; tools, embroidered cushions, towels, hair-curlers – everything imaginable and more – including a four-foot plastic Christmas tree complete with tangled tresses of tinsel and yards and yards of electric candles. Various well-groomed Indonesian matrons, short and plump, clearly dressed for the occasion, were poking through the jumble of treasures, barely able to conceal their excitement.

Louise Pressman, thin, pinched even, was keeping a watch on things like a hawk. 'I'd ask you all to sit down,' she said, 'but our last chair just went out the door.' In the setting her southern drawl was remarkable. So was her hair: blonde of an artificial sheen, arranged in careful curls and waves. 'No, dear,' she gently chided one of her buyer-guests, 'that thermometer is for sticking into meat.'

Reverend Foster Pressman was out back. We found him using the top of a tin can to scrape a patch of blue-green fungus off the gnarled branch of a sour-sop tree. Eyes inches from the bark – he wore glasses in wire frames on a beaded chain – he was totally absorbed in his task. Behind him terraced *sawah*s stretched into the distance. A bullock was plowing the near fields. Beyond, women, bent double, up to their thighs in the paddy beds, were planting out young rice shoots of an electric green. They'd tucked their dresses up into their belts, old and young alike, thighs wet and glistening, daubed, too, with mud. As they worked the women chatted away while dark birds darted among them in profusion, skimming close across the surface of the irrigation water.

'It's real nice, that vista,' the Rev. Pressman said. 'Always changing.'

With little waste of time on preliminaries, Koert Jan explained that we wanted to rent the house for two years.

'Well,' Foster Pressman grinned slowly, 'I think that can

3

be arranged.' He snapped off a number of dead twigs from the sour-sop tree, shook his head. A dumpy figure, whose freckles with age had grown into splotches, Foster didn't once look us straight in the eyes. 'Fact is, God sent you right on time.'

Architect and builder of the house turned out to be none other than Foster Pressman himself. It was, however, the property of the American-based soul-saving outfit, the Assemblies of God. Inside the ambiance was hardly Indonesian. Yet the place was practical and comfortable, light and spacious beyond anything we had dared hope to find. A separate servants' annex complete with washroom, storage space and workshed receded at right angles to the residential unit. The driveway ended in a carport with a low side wall lined with potted plants. There was even a study one entire wall of which was lined with bookshelves, empty now, to which plastic labels of the kind shot from a letter gun were affixed: Original Sin, Redemption, Superstition, Recipes, etc.

'It's Sugar's ticker,' Pressman said, 'needs a valve job.' Then he put a finger to his lips. After serving the Assemblies of God for twenty-three years in Indonesia, the last eight of them in Tomohon, they were pulling out head over heels because Mrs Pressman had to have heart surgery.

Louise – at her third request we began to call her by her Christian name – told a different story. A short time ago on the eve of her birthday, while she and Foster slept in the back bedroom – pink walls, pink curtain, pink bedspread – their bedroom door as always ajar, thieves had ransacked the house, top to bottom. First the thieves had poisoned the Pressmans' German shepherd watchdog, tossing him a chunk of bad meat. Then they had cut out a small window above the kitchen sink. Probably the first to slip in was a child who unlocked the door for the rest. 'They opened every cupboard in the place, every last drawer. In the morning there were burnt matchsticks on the floor just everywhere. Foster and me slept right through it

4

all, thank God.' And nothing was missing – except hundreds of cookies baked for the birthday celebration the next day.

Across the road from the house, our house, through the row of fir trees, stood a pentecostal school complex. It was closed, ostensibly because the pitched sheet-iron roof leaked. Louise Pressman, however, chose to see her husband and herself as victims of political oppression. The Indonesian government, she explained, was leaning rather heavily on Christian 'elements'. Then she went ahead to predict the ruin of the church if it ever fell into Indonesian hands. 'Oh, these people love to pray, to shout and testify and carry on' – she nodded and Foster nodded, so we nodded – 'but when it comes to leading a Christian life, I'll tell you honestly I'm afraid that's too much to ask.' Louise's sense of defeat couldn't have been good for her heart.

We were able to reach a rental agreement right away, without dickering. Then we asked the Pressmans, first thing, if they could recommend any household help. Two men alone, especially when our work would take us into the field so much of the time, were going to need someone to look after things, wash clothes, market and prepare meals.

'Reta's just what you need, really,' Louise said. 'She's a darling, a doll.' Drifting silently but conspicuously among the dwindling remains of the Pressmans' worldly goods – they were to spend the last night in their home of so many years sleeping on the tile floor with only a quilted sleeping-bag thrown over them – there was a tall girl who had lost practically all of her hair – and both eyebrows. Only a few long pale puffs of hair remained, straggling down from random spots on the crown. Erect, strong, alert, Reta, whom I guessed to be in her mid-twenties, had lived with, and worked for the Pressmans seven years.

'The hair's nothing to worry about,' Louise said promptly. 'Hereditary, some kind of illness not uncommon in the area.'

Reta's cooking, apparently, was out of this world. She was

better than Louise with an iron, and a needle. What's more, if Reta washed your floor, we were assured, you could eat off it.

'Girl's a real Martha,' Foster added.

'Best of all' – here Louise spoke loud enough for Reta to hear – 'Reta is honest. A hundred per cent. And around here that doesn't grow on trees.

'Unfortunately,' Louise shrugged, 'Reta's already been promised to the Davidsons.' A thin hand and bony wrist hung with a silver charm bracelet pointed out across the glittering *sawah*s. 'Dorothy's found out that girl of theirs has been feeding her whole family from the kitchen. Sugar in her pockets, that kind of thing. Morris is with the theology school up the hill. Protestant,' Louise added with a patronising smile. 'They've bought our GE washing-machine. Eighteen years old and runs like new.'

II

Along with a *pembantu*, we were looking for a driver. We could not expect to drive ourselves over the often tortuous roads to reach remote villages and then be collected enough to interview and observe effectively. Also, in the event of an accident, whatever the reason, a westerner behind the wheel might be pulled out by a mob, beaten or even stoned and his car fired on the spot. A few days on the roads had taught us traffic was a life and death affair. The road from Manado to Tomohon, for example, wound sharply up a steep hill. At every turn new spectacular views of the sea and nearby islands unfolded. There were few places going in either direction where it was safe to pass but that didn't faze local drivers. Fatal crashes were marked with large upright wreaths of purple and white paper flowers. These markers could be a road hazard in themselves.

Tenny, the driver we engaged, had extensive experience. For

6

almost three years he had been driving a group taxi, his father's Colt, along the Manado-Tomohon route. *Dari sini ke sana* it was called, From Here to There. On a good day Tenny fitted in five return journeys, waiting at the end terminals for enough passengers to trickle aboard so he could set off nearly full. Not exactly waiting – for hustling fares, competing with dozens of other vehicles, plucking at potential riders' sleeves, shouting jingles, shouldering parcels – that was all part of the job. As a rule such taxis were grossly overloaded, people stacked on top of each other, roof racks bulging. What couldn't be crammed on top, baggage, produce, furniture, would be lashed to back or sides. The taxis would be top-heavy, frequently careening on two wheels as they sped into bends or swerved to avoid gaping potholes. Where there was the slightest gap, a glimpse of daylight, drivers tried to pass, glorying in idiotic stunts, riding their horns. It was generally accepted etiquette to tap the horn every time a chicken at roadside so much as flapped a wing, so all the constant honking came to mean nothing.

During Tenny's job interview with us he said a bare minimum. Most of the time he sat squeezing his hands between his knees, squirming, biting his lower lip. He grinned a lot and looked up at the ceiling. When he gave answers, his voice was barely audible. Anes, an older brother, had heard we were looking for a driver and brought Tenny to the house. Anes kept up a loud, boastful, rather disagreeable and overenthusiastic monologue: Tenny wanted to stop driving his father's taxi; he was the best on the road but the job was ruining his health; a doctor at the provincial hospital in Manado had diagnosed an ulcer; to get better Tenny needed to eat regularly, something which the stop-and-go life style of taxi drivers didn't allow.

When we went out together to look at our new Toyota canvas-top jeep, it was clear at once that Tenny loved and revered machines. He may have had trouble putting together a sentence, but beyond the shadow of a doubt he could dismantle and reassemble an engine in his sleep.

During a test ride Tenny performed well, holding in check the fancy stylish tricks – like steering with crossed arms – that were part of the taxi driver's stock in trade. He was certainly far superior to the other candidates we screened. One, a highly recommended government chauffeur, the father of eleven, nearly got us killed half a dozen times in the course of a brief trial spin. The man was too short to operate the brake effectively and unable to shift gears without momentarily disappearing under the dashboard. Another boy, sent along kindly by Morris Davidson, one of their gardener's 'brothers', had a wild romantic look about him. Black shoulder-length hair, nails from here to tomorrow, knife in his belt, a glazed, dreamy expression. Although he tried for half an hour he was unable to back the Toyota out of our driveway. All his driving experience, we later learned, had been on a tractor.

Eager to start work, Koert Jan hired Tenny on the spot.

'I don't know,' Tenny said, 'I have to ask my wife.'

'You're married?' Koert Jan asked.

'Three years' – Tenny beamed. 'No children,' he added, without our asking. At the time we didn't fully appreciate his blush of embarrassment.

Koert Jan told Tenny we were looking for a cook and housekeeper. He went on to say we didn't want to separate him from his wife. Perhaps she might consider coming to work for us, too? Tenny nodded but you could see he wasn't sure. Looking at Anes out of the corner of his eye, he explained that Annie had never worked for anyone before. She wasn't from the kind of family that turned their daughters into servants for other people, but he would ask her.

If Annie came to work for us, Koert Jan pointed out, she would in effect run things. There wouldn't be any *nyonya*, lady of the house, breathing down her neck.

The next morning Tenny brought Annie to meet us. For the most part the Minahasa are short and squat, with large heads. There is something distinctly Mongoloid about the way they

8

look. On Java hapless visiting Minahasa have been set upon and clubbed by mistake during anti-Chinese riots and street fighting. Tenny looked Eskimo. Mostly, I suppose, because of the straight, spiky hair in bangs. He had a large mouth, thick, sensuously curved lips, and a broad, flat nose. Annie, three years older, was altogether frog-like. Her eyes bulged, she was slightly stoop-shouldered and her shapeless, sleeveless dress, an unflattering shade of green, came down practically to her ankles. At our house she almost always wore her long hair pulled back into a knob-like bun at her nape, a style suited to someone very much older. Yet when Annie spoke, which she usually did in a flurry of short phrases, she came alive. The animation made her singularly attractive.

Annie consented to come to work for us. For both parties a trial period of one month was agreed. On days when we would stay at home writing up notes, Tenny would be expected to see to the maintenance of the car, but also to be helpful around the house and garden. And for Annie's sake we promised to try to find another girl or woman to share the work. Not that there was really enough to do for two, but we had been advised that to keep Annie happy a companion was essential. Otherwise, with us away so much of the time, she would soon feel lonely and discontented and wish to return to her village. Everything about our house and living arrangements was new for her and would require getting used to without her having to cope with loneliness as well.

Good help, Koert Jan and I knew, would make a big difference in our lives. We had talked a lot about what it would be like to live with servants. Difficult. Not merely because of our guilt feelings but because the quality of daily life in that far-flung corner of Indonesia was likely to depend in large measure on the kind of easy, goodwill we could achieve in our immediate household. To suppose we could do our work without servants was idiotic. Any attempt of the sort would be a false liberal stunt of the worst order. Nor did we imagine that

9

once we hired help we could ever abolish master-servant distinctions, even if it was wise to try. We would hope for friendship, trust – and take things day by day.

The day Tenny and Annie moved in, they arrived carrying one battered cardboard suitcase and several baskets full of fruit from Tenny's parents' garden. Rich clusters of langsat, crawling with ants – a delicate, translucent fruit, something like lichees. Sweet mangosteens that looked like purple tomatoes. Eating them stained the mouth. And a football-sized fruit with a hard shell and prickly barbs we had never seen before.

'Durian,' Tenny told us and acted out how to pick the fruit he had climbed a durian tree, the oldest, tallest tree in the forest. 'To open,' Tenny demonstrated, 'you have to jump on it.'

The durian split open. We made faces.

'Stink fruit!' Annie squealed and held her nose. With his fingers Tenny gouged loose two pits covered with gooey white flesh. One for Koert Jan, one for me. It was delicious.

'Jakarta,' Tenny spoke with his mouth full, 'hotels, durian forbidden.'

How glad we were to find Tenny was not at all the shy introvert he had seemed in his older brother's presence. Anything but. Already the first morning we learned how expansive a personality he really had. Loud, brash, vulgar – irrepressible is perhaps the best word, vital.

Later the same day Koert Jan called me from the study, and signaling for silence led me to look out from behind the living room curtains. Tenny, stripped to the waist to wash down the car, dripping wet, was blowing soap bubbles on the lawn. Annie, hanging wash out on the back line, stood watching, hands on her hips, laughing. Into a bit of water in his cupped palm Tenny dropped some grains of detergent and then, with utter concentration, lips pursed at the edge of his hand, he blew large iridescent bubbles which rose and drifted to the accompaniment of Annie's screams until they burst among the branches of our avocado trees.

10

Tenny couldn't do enough to be obliging. From the Pressmans we had inherited a double-decker bunk bed. Right away Tenny asked permission to saw through the uprights and make a set of beds that could be pushed together side by side. We had a double mattress made from local kapok – and pillows, a novelty in Tenny and Annie's lives. When our sea freight arrived from Holland, Tenny tore into the crate with the frenzy of a child unwrapping a present. He and Annie had to touch and admire everything. They collected a jar full of the white plastic beads used in packing and kept it by their bedside the way we might seashells.

Most of Tenny's energy, however, went into the Toyota. He washed and polished it to a point of obsession. Even the slightest smudge on the canvas top he would call to Koert Jan's attention immediately. He tinkered with the engine, made adjustments, suggested we buy expensive accessories, including a rotating fan he fixed to the center of the dashboard. '*Gengsi*, Mr Koert, Mr Eric,' Tenny said proudly as he hung a fringe of tassels across the top of the front windshield. *Gengsi* was a word we were to hear more and more often.

During the early days of our work relations and friendship with Tenny and Annie, the language barrier didn't make things any easier. Bahasa Indonesia, the official national language, has no structure to speak of. No declensions, nor conjugations. Context is all. To form the plural of words, you say them twice. People seem to speak as if juggling knives with their lips but in fact these knives are straight-backed consonants which at high speed sound alike. B's like p's, d's, t's and k's. Annie especially made faces at us when we tried to communicate. But grudgingly she concentrated, interpreted, understood. When finally she could decipher a key word mispronounced, she would light up. Annie had a wonderful laugh: her head would snap back, the top half of her body would twist.

Indonesian food was still new to us. Annie's meals bore little resemblance to what was served up as authentic cuisine in

11

Indonesian restaurants in the Netherlands. Anything we didn't recognise at once Annie told us was *RW* – dog – the local speciality. Then Annie howled, laughing her body-rocking laugh when horror glinted in our eyes. 'It's good,' she'd say. 'It's not dog. Try it, try it.'

III

Before the month was out the resourceful Reta came to work for us too. Our luck seemed complete. Reta and Dorothy Davidson had not been able to get along. At the end of each day, Reta, the picture of self-possession when she worked for Louise Pressman, was shattered. Practically in tears, she would slink back through the *sawah*s to our house where for so long she'd lived in security and basked in praise and there she would complain to Tenny and Annie, or to us – to whomever would listen – how stupid Mrs Davidson was. The very first time Dorothy used the Pressmans' indestructible old GE washing-machine, for example, she broke it with an overload of laundry. The Pressmans had stuck to an Indonesian bill of fare, but not Dorothy Davidson. An American housewife to the bone, she clipped recipes from magazines and kept them in a file and wanted Reta to learn new dishes from the West that used such ingredients as marshmallows, rice crispies, instant mashed potato mix, tomato catsup, grape jelly and Gravy Master. And Reta ruthlessly mocked Mrs Davidson's inability after so many years of residence to speak Bahasa Indonesia. Even Lauri, she swore, the Davidson parrot, did better. The Davidsons, we also learned, did not allow Reta free run of the house. Their bedroom was out of bounds. This, I believe, or rather the lack of trust it implied, is what cut most deeply.

At Reta's urging, Koert Jan finally went to speak with Dorothy Davidson. The encounter did not turn out to be as embarrassing as we'd feared. 'For Louise's sake I agreed to have her, but, yes, I think she would be happier with you.' A pause, a pout. 'You know she's so competent I find it terrifying.'

Installed again in familiar surroundings, Reta – or Kojack, as Tenny and Annie called her to her face – demonstrated what a truly extraordinary worker she was. The storage shed out back next to the washroom was easily converted into an extra bedroom. Proud and disciplined, Reta apologised non-stop for her many failings. But there were no failings, none at all.

With her when she came Reta brought a wig, brunette with blonde tips, one the Pressmans had picked up for her in Little Rock, Arkansas during a sabbatical leave. The way it looked the wig might have been plucked from some Woolworth store dummy's head when no one was looking. It fitted so badly that despite a few touches of adhesive material on Reta's crown you couldn't help fearing that the slightest abrupt movement would send it sliding right off. The wig was a kind of poodle cut, short curls. The Pressmans had also given Reta a set of artificial eyelashes. Louise had taught her to pencil in her missing eyebrows with a bold arch. When Reta dressed up to attend Assemblies of God services on Sundays, she would glow with pleasure. She would apply robin's-egg-blue eye make-up and pink lip gloss, too. The total effect was not very godly.

Around the house Reta usually wore a worn, slightly frizzy peach-colored bathrobe and pom-pom slippers, hand-me-downs from Louise. At first glance, with her baldness and strict facial control, she appeared monklike. The contrast was vivid when she put on her wig, her make-up, a fancy dress with rather a plunging V-neckline and high-heeled shoes with fine silver straps criss-crossing her insteps.

In North Sulawesi the morals of household help were of widespread concern, at least to their employers. The challenge apparently was how to keep girls from smuggling boyfriends on to the premises for the night, how to keep them from becoming pregnant and returning to their villages, how to protect them from widespread venereal disease. Well, thanks to the make-up of our household we were, for the time being at least, spared any and all such headaches. Poor Reta had already had her uterus removed, as a consequence, it seems, of a stomach ailment. Here I can only pass along what I was told. Mrs Pressman had nursed her through her serious illness. For a month Reta had been weak as a baby. Rev. Pressman had met all the medical costs, hardly bothering to mention his generosity. When Reta, decked out like a whore, went to pray, we knew, and she knew, that underneath she was a hollow shell.

Once Reta was free to come to work for us, she asked us to do the proper thing: to visit her parents and request their permission. So as soon as possible, together with Annie and Tenny, we visited Reta's home, about a two-hour drive deeper into the mountains. It was one of the neediest we entered during our entire stay. The narrow façade of horizontal wood slats fronted directly on the main road. Everything cried out for paint and repair. The roof beams sagged, well on their way to rot. The earth floor, trampled hard, was uneven. The interior was bare. There was nothing by way of ornamentation except a crucifix and a few wall plaques with citations from the Bible. Chairs for us had to be borrowed from a neighbor. From outside the window openings were soon crammed with the faces of neighborhood children, some scrambling on to the backs of others for a better view. They talked constantly about what they saw – us – as if we weren't there, or couldn't understand a word. Which we couldn't. It was a dialect they spoke. Once there fell a hushed silence and a small boy whose face glowed, obviously the head of his class, called out to us, 'Good morning, madam' at which the others began to hoot and shriek until Reta flapping the skirt of her dress shooed them away.

Reta's father, the victim of a stroke years earlier, did not emerge from his bed in a dark back room. The door was kept open though so he could hear our voices. His mind was unaffected, but his face, Reta told us, looked like it was scarred by lightning. Reta's mother was a nervous and shapeless woman, old and wispy. The pattern of her simple housedress had been washed into oblivion. In her eyes there was only the merest hint of the spirit Reta could display.

During tea, served with home-baked cake which must have cost the family dear, for sugar, butter and eggs were high-priced goods, Reta showed us her picture album, a memorial of the years she spent with the Pressmans. Almost all the photos Reta had of herself were in a wig, and in various of Mrs Pressman's fancy dresses. In some she even wore Mrs Pressman's rope of pearls and pearl earrings. At first Koert Jan and I thought Reta might have been dressing up naughtily, raiding closets in Louise's absence, but, no, Reta assured us, the Pressmans had taken the pictures themselves. There was, how or why I will not try to analyse further, a distinctly pornographic tint to the simple, fully-clothed color portraits. Was Louise the driving force behind the poses? Eye to her viewfinder, weak of heart, did she murmur, 'Beautiful, Reta. A darling, a doll,' until Rev. Pressman would drift out of his study, stand and watch a while as he fumbled to refill his pipe and then reseated back at his typewriter discover he could not resume work on his sermon until the tremor of sexual excitement passed?

As we flipped the pages Tenny and Annie crouched next to us, running their fingers over practically every picture. They were in a conspiratorial frame of mind, sending us sly side glances. Each time Reta appeared in a different outfit, 'Who's that?' Tenny asked.

'That's me,' she answered, unaware she was being teased.

We were not prepared for the last two pages of the album.

'My brother's child,' Reta said. 'Stillborn.'

Were we being called upon to admire snapshots of the infant corpse with wads of cotton stuffed into nostrils and ears?

Before our leavetaking, Reta's mother asked Koert Jan to

lead us all in prayer. He did so in silence, briefly. That apparently was a disappointment. When he looked up and smiled, the woman let fly a rousing pentecostal cry. She called on God to protect her child and watch over us. Tenny and Annie's behavior, passable up to this point, now deteriorated into unsuppressed giggles. Reta looked at her mother with admiration, and clenched the devout woman's hand tightly.

During the ride back to Tomohon, however, Tenny and Annie were sober. The poverty of Reta's home, I suppose, had made a deep impression. In Tinoör, their home village, half-way between Manado and Tomohon, set back in the interior, they already owned a small house of their own, a prefab model made of wood. They had a piece of land, too. Reta, so subdued in her parents' house, now sat in the back of the Toyota, holding hands with Annie and chatting away a blue streak. The road grew dark, the pavement full of ruts and cracks. Tenny drove skilfully. Endless stretches of young clove trees, wealth in the making, lined both sides of the road. At one point we sped downhill and the air turned foul. A rickety bridge of saplings carried us past extensive, steaming sulphur springs. Ascending again we came upon a series of deep caves in towering rock face.

'Japs in there,' Tenny assured us. Soldiers hiding, still unaware that World War II was over, surviving on a diet of insects and water from underground streams.

As we approached Tomohon, traffic accumulated. The streets were muddy from a local cloudburst. Horse carts slithered about. In the glare of lanterns workers were dipping ladles into cauldrons of steaming pitch. Others were busy trying to steer wheelbarrows among pyramids of gravel, still busy at the late hour to bring a petrol station in the center of town to completion in time for the coming *Sidung Raya*, the national council of churches.

We neared home, more and more sights familiar. Even jolts I recognised were comforting, just as when a child, half-asleep in

16

the back of our family car, I always knew when a homewards journey was almost over once we reached a familiar succession of bends and turns, of stops and starts.

With Reta on the premises 'Mrs always did this' or 'Mrs always did that' became refrains we were obliged to live with, explanations, for example, why the curtains had to be drawn at a certain hour every day, or why our mattresses were aired out in one part of the garden and not another, or why underwear had to be sterilised in boiling water. Reta imposed order, sniffing along the side of her nose at those who could abide any disorderliness. At the time we moved in we had found liberal sprinklings of poison everywhere, a white powder lining cupboards, window-ledges, floor mouldings. Louise Pressman had indeed boasted to us that her house was wholly insect-free. Reta did not conceal her surprise when she saw how we had scrubbed away every trace of poison, and that occasional creeping, crawling things failed to throw us into fits of hysteria. What confused her the most, however, was the absence of religion. Koert Jan and I were not church-goers. Nor did we make a habit out of prayer before and after meals.

Out back Annie laughed a great deal with Reta – probably, we felt, about us. We wondered whether Reta didn't intimidate Annie slightly. If she did, however, Annie betrayed no resentment. As cooks – the girls prepared meals on alternate days – Reta was so exceptional that it was not humanly possible to be impartial in our compliments. Koert Jan began to consider redistributing responsibilities so that Reta would cook more often.

IV

The approach to Manado by air tempts belief that the only tree God ever created was the palm. Endless undulations of green sweep right down to the edge of the sea. For ten days Koert Jan and I had been in Jakarta on business. As prearranged Tenny was at the airport to meet our return flight. We were not in good humor after four wind-tossed hours. As usual it was a hassle to claim our baggage. Porters in Manado all seem to have trained in Marx Brothers movies.

As soon as we passed out of the arrivals shed, Tenny led us to a low wall around the corner. 'Look,' he said and pointed out across the landing field. The first thing I saw were large numbers of women and children sitting behind wire fences. They sat in an unnatural silence, staring up at the sky. Then I noticed the men in black, hundreds of them, milling around, spilling on to the edges of the runway. Men with angry faces, faces distorted still further by a heat that came rippling up from the pavement. Many were armed with rifles slung across their backs.

'From Tondano,' Tenny told us as he hurried us away to the Toyota, 'the Wild West.' Further explanation tumbled out as we headed for town. During our brief absence, the Governor of North Sulawesi, a born-again Christian who radically re-formed his dissolute life after his wife died in a car crash, had been deposed by the authorities in Jakarta. Why? He had been seen riding in the front seat of his official vehicle, next to the chauffeur, it was alleged, thus demeaning his office. And he frequented prostitutes. Everyone knew the real reason was his sudden determination to do something about deeply en-trenched corruption. A temporary military governor was due in on the next Garuda flight. The theatrical black clothes of the waiting welcome committee were a sign that they would back their man to the death.

'Bang!' Tenny made six-shooters of his hands on top of the wheel and fired at children carrying buckets of water at the side of the road.

'How's Annie?' we asked.

'She's baking bread.'

'And Reta?'

'Kojack's gone.'

Tenny seemed to drive faster than when we left. Koert Jan told him to slow down. Tenny showed annoyance, but reduced his speed, just.

'Gone?' I asked.

'The missus sent her money to come to Jogja.'

Annie was out on the front walk to greet us, clapping her hands and crying, '*Oleh-oleh, oleh-oleh.*' We paid our help at the going rate. (Other expatriates had impressed upon us the need for solidarity.) We did our best to make up for the low wages with gifts. For Tenny we had a digital wristwatch. For Annie a bolt of elegant batik, enough for a dress. Once given and accepted with a little dance and squeals of appreciation, these *oleh-oleh* disappeared from our sight forever. For Reta we had brought – no matter.

Later in the day Dorothy Davidson turned up. Over a neighborly cup of tea, a bit smugly, she filled us in on the events leading up to Reta's departure. It appeared the change of scene had done wonders for Louise Pressman's heart. Foster saw fit to accept a post for a year at an Assemblies of God school in Jogjakarta. For Mrs Pressman a condition for her agreeing to stay was reunion with Reta. She simply couldn't begin to train new help from scratch. To pay back the travel expenses of her transport to Java, Reta would work for the Pressmans for no wages. Upon their departure from Indonesia the Pressmans hoped to hand Reta over to their son Frederick and his family, currently completing his missionary training in Arkansas. The principal difficulty in this neat scheme for Reta had been her father, his ill health. It was likely he would die during her absence. Still, knowing how the Pressmans had tended his daughter during her illness, and with a photo album by his bed, he had not withheld consent.

To pick up the money that the Pressmans wired for her plane ticket, Reta apparently wheedled Tenny into driving her to Manado. He had taken the car out a second time to bring her away to the airport. Tenny in fact fidgeted nervously describing Reta's going because we had forbidden him ever to use the project vehicle for private purposes. One joy ride and it would be his last. He was very apologetic and we could see how there were extenuating circumstances.

Something like a month later a long letter from Reta arrived. The letter was in character, full of self-vituperation and expressions of feelings of unworthiness. Reta, whose hand was predictably meticulous and even, begged our forgiveness. The Missus had needed her. Otherwise she would have been more than happy to stay with us. We weren't stupid like Dorothy Davidson.

Reta sent greetings to Tenny and Annie. She hoped we didn't mind Tenny's driving her on two trips to Manado. She had paid him for all the petrol he said it took and for new oil, just as he asked.

Clearly letters, the possibility, were not part of Tenny's world.

V

At the installation of the new governor, the Minister of the Interior came from Jakarta to see everything went smoothly. He announced that the former governor who had resigned because of ill health had, alas, not recovered sufficiently to attend the ceremony. The affrontery of this flim-flammery was too much for the born-again Christian fuming in the wings. He summoned the press to his home overlooking the sea. Practically flexing his muscles to prove his point, he boasted that he had never felt better in his life. He had been invited to the inaugural ceremony and he had refused to attend. First the Minister would have to point out even one small thing he had done wrong in office.

For a few weeks, from time to time, small groups of men in

black could be seen drinking in Manado, standing about in the streets. As far as we could find out, however, their rebellion never amounted to more than grumbling and an occasional warning shot fired at the moon. Whatever tension may have lingered finally broke with the announcement that the good ex-governor was marrying a rich Sumatran widow and moving to Medan to raise a second family and maybe some race-horses.

These were halcyon days for us. After Reta pulled out, Annie thrived. As eager as she had been for a companion, and as much fun as she and Tenny had milked from having Reta around, now Annie was once again sole mistress of the house. Her cooking improved. When she did laundry, she now washed and dried our clothes first, Tenny's and hers afterwards. Out back she cleared a patch of land to start a garden, planting groundnuts, beans and maize. Every day she clipped fresh flowers and set them in vases to surprise us, the way Reta had done.

It was during this time, too, that we got to know Annie and Tenny's families. Annie's father had been shot during *Promesta*, the bloody civil war that raged in North Sulawesi in 1959. Local guerrilla elements who believed in self-determination fought with diehard nationalists. Some families split into mortally opposed factions. There were wounds, we were told, that hadn't healed yet. Annie's father, committed to the cause of local independence, had been gunned down in the woods behind Tinoör, either betrayed to enemy fighters by an infiltrator, or possibly murdered by his own comrades who had been misled into distrusting him. No one knew where, or even in fact whether he lay buried. For Indonesians, even good Christians, this was a harrowing uncertainty. There is no end to the mischief that a restless spirit can wreak on the living.

Some few years later Annie's mother shed her widow's weeds to marry a colonel in the Indonesian army. A small, pretty man, Javanese. She bore him six children, four of them survivors. From her mother's first marriage, Annie was the only child who lived. Originally Annie's mother came from the same village as Tenny's parents, Tinoör, but after remarriage she had moved to Matani some few kilometers beyond Tomohon. Here her army husband rented a ramshackle house on cement piles. You could stick your arm through cracks in the wooden walls and floor. An attempt was made to cut down the draught by pasting up old calendars everywhere and stuffing seams with newspaper. In fact half the panes of glass in the windows were cracked or shattered and the roof leaked like a sieve. Yet the house was, without fail, festive.

The first time we went to Annie's parents, her mother, young-looking still, teeth flashing gold, came down into the dirt yard to greet us. All the dogs in the neighborhood began to bark. Annie's younger brothers hauled in their kites – that year many apparently harmless small kites became entangled with overhead electric wires, sparking short circuits and even on occasion fires. We were escorted to the porch and served a proper formal tea. The ancient porcelain cups and teapot made Koert Jan's mouth water.

Annie's half-brothers and -sisters huddled back in the smoke of the kitchen to stare and giggle at us. The youngest girl eventually ventured out to run her fingers along my forearm and feel the hair growing there. In Annie's siblings the stature of their mother and the facial perfection of their father prevailed. They were lean and beautiful, with large, lambent eyes, as different as different can be from Annie. Still they treated her with special deference. When she barked commands they obeyed and she smiled shyly at us.

Throughout tea Annie's mother stood with her back against the edge of the door, swaying slightly back and forth with her hips thrust forward. 'It's terrible,' she said, patting the obvious bulge of her stomach, 'I've had enough children. Maybe you can tell me how to stop?'

Annie's step-father, with his faint moustache and fine dandy-like features, a handsome figure out of place among the Minahasa, laughed at our acute embarrassment. Then Annie's mother's face sobered. 'Annie is a good girl,' she said, 'except she doesn't have any children.'

Annie crossed her arms and looked indignant. She puffed her lips but didn't speak. Clearly this wasn't the first time she'd been subjected to such rallying, and in public.

Two days after this first social call, Annie's father sent one of his sons to our house with some sweet potatoes for us. Ferry came roaring into our driveway, barefoot, on his father's motorcycle. The crash helmet he wore was so large it came half-way down his nose. Ferry also brought a request. Annie's father wanted to borrow our Toyota the next day to report to army headquarters.

Koert Jan met the request with a firm, friendly no. Perhaps the request was a joke at the same level as Annie's mother's pretended pregnancy? Ferry heard Koert Jan's refusal without any sign of a reaction. After that he went with Tenny to the school grounds across the road and together they laid out a badminton court for us, splicing bamboo to make the boundary lines, shoveling away cow pies, trimming the grass.

In any event relations with Annie's parents remained cordial. We met off and on. At family funerals, weddings and baptisms. At Kinnilow, a warm natural spring that was a favorite local swimming hole, we taught Annie's brothers, and Tenny, to swim. The first day they were terrified of the water. It was remarkable how quickly they overcame their fear. Koert Jan did most of the teaching. First he coaxed them not to fight the water. Then he showed them how to do the dead man's float. They would lie prone in his arms and relax. I envied Koert Jan his physical ease with them.

Sometimes Annie would come along and stand on a shelf of rock at the edge of the water shrieking happy insults at the boys while they thrashed about. 'Swim,' she would say, 'swim.' Or she would point at the bedraggled underpants they wore and slap both her thighs.

One day Tenny snuck up behind Annie and pushed her, dress and all, into the water. 'Koert Jan!' I cried. From where I sat high up on the rocks writing letters there was no way I could reach Annie in time. I expected her to sink like a stone, and sink she did. Such stupid little jokes have a way of turning into tragedy.

As I started to scramble down to the water, Annie rose to the surface, sputtering and laughing! Instead of climbing out, she slicked her hair back and began to swim in earnest, feet pointed, fingers together. Her dress eddied on the surface as she moved. All the boys cheered. Tenny covered his mouth with two hands, giddy with pride.

Annie's mother continued to be very friendly. Yet as we grew to know her better a strange fact emerged: she never told the truth gratuitously. Most of the time she spoke in the same short bursts of sentences which Annie, too, preferred. She stamped and gesticulated like her daughter. And I doubt a single occasion passed when we met without her teasing Annie about her barrenness. And Annie never once answered her mother back.

Soon we were on even closer terms with Tenny's parents. Tinoör, where they lived, was an ingrained enclave with its own language and traditions. Near the beginning of the dirt track that wove inland to the village from the main Manado – Tomohon road, Tinoör was erecting a Protestant church. An enormous, ghastly thing, a monstrosity. At a cost of a hundred million rupiah – Tinoör was especially rich in cloves – the church was to be the largest in the province, the community's grand gesture to win *gengsi*. When we left Indonesia, the church, described as almost ready when we first drove past it, was still unfinished. Years added to the expense. Cement speculators made securing supplies next to impossible. Heavy rains and erosion – the site had perhaps been unwisely selected

24

– threatened the very church foundation. Louise Pressman, for one, would have been gratified, and rolled her eyes in thanks to heaven.

The whole time, moreover, Tinoör had no reliable water supply. The bamboo aqueduct which carried fresh stream water down from a rock source several kilometers above the village had been damaged by severe storms and perhaps, too, by wild boars. Yet no funds were diverted from the mammoth church to pay for the necessary repairs. Not that people didn't grumble. At times it seemed to me the villagers could more easily do without drinking water than something to grumble about. Before our departure a story had even begun to circulate that the church stood on bewitched ground – perhaps the site of Annie's father's murder?

Past the massive shell of the church *in nascendi* with its steeply pitched roof, the track to Tinoör dips, circles and climbs through some sparse woods to enter the village proper along a narrow ledge. The entry point passes the office of the *hukum tua*, the village head. It is a small stone building, painted white, one window, one door. A gong hangs outside, the iron rim of an old truck wheel. The gong is used to summon villagers in an emergency. Here the roadway can easily be blockaded, sealing Tinoör off from the outside world. The first time Tenny drove us to Tinoör, he stopped and pantomimed ringing the gong. He also told us a story so we would know what kind of a place we had come to visit.

Apparently for some months before our arrival in North Sulawesi no one could enter Tinoör by day or night without first answering the challenge of a band of armed villagers on watch at the village head's office. The train of events leading up to this embattled situation began a few years ago when a Tinoör woman, Sylvie Mangundap, married a man from the Sangihe Talaud islands, a day's journey by proa to the north. Sylvie Mangundap had a harelip and even though she was a hard, conscientious worker, no one else had been willing to marry

25

her. What's more, Alexander was young and Alexander was handsome.

In general the Minahasa look down on the islanders, classifying them, together with villagers from the backlands of the province, as 'mountain people'. These mountain people, Tenny explained, are primitive. Fit to be servants and climb palm trees. Largely uneducated, their Christianity is a surface affair. They like to drink, and to cheat on their wives. Most important, however, in determining the Minahasas' attitude towards the Sangihe islanders is their skin, so dark! The Minahasa equate fair skin with beauty. The healthy glow of complexions exposed to the sun is a source of snickering. Even Annie when she worked in the garden would pull a plastic bag over her head to keep her face in shade.

Tempering people's scorn for the islanders, however, was their reputation for black magic. Throughout Sangihe Talaud there are *dukun*s, traditional medicinemen, said to be able to pick up a handful of dry leaves, talk to them, and then the leaves would start to chatter like bats and fly away. These *dukun*s were alleged to be as clever in the manipulation of men's souls.

In Tinoör Alexander, the Sangihe husband, was at first welcomed with a show of heartiness. Before long, however, he had a name as a *peracun*, one who kills through poison, one who goes after what he wants by following *cara gelap*, dark practices. Such gossip, it should be said, was by no means rare. Throughout North Sulawesi conflict is endemic and suspicion runs high. No one ever falls ill or dies just like that. Witchcraft is thought to be the underlying cause. Grief is directed at a man by his enemy. In relation to Alexander, whose skin Tenny assured us was black as night, a succession of mysterious deaths in the village soon after his arrival loosened people's tongues. All these deaths had somehow involved land disputes. Meanwhile Alexander just behaved as if he were innocent of any misdoing. He was convivial, generous to guests, expansive with his wife's family. He took an active part in endless

26

conversations speculating about the forces which lay behind the sudden episodes of dying. Gradually, however, he began to appropriate part of his wife's brother's property, an older man with one collapsed lung. He replanted boundary markers, a little at a time. On and on and on. Sylvie's brother did his best to set the matter straight in an informal, amiable manner, but to no avail. Bit by bit Alexander kept gnawing away at his land.

At last the matter was brought before the local authorities. A court case was held in the regency capital. According to the judge's ruling, Sylvie's brother won. It was then that the Sangihe man, fired by a sense of injury, made the mistake of openly disclosing his identity as *peracun*. Like someone forced to swallow food he found distasteful, Alexander was having a difficult time accepting the verdict of his guilt. Outside the courtroom when his wife's brother, the gloating victor, went to climb on his motorcycle, in the presence of many witnesses, Alexander called out a warning that the man would never reach Tinoör alive.

For the first miles of the homeward journey, through the Tondano lake basin and up into the fertile ridges surrounding Tomohon, everything went just as usual. Then, however, at the point where the descent towards Tinoör began, near Kinnilow, the victorious brother found himself forced to dismount from his vehicle. His head hurt and he couldn't walk straight but instead he went spinning in circles like a chicken. Here both Tenny and Annie laughed. We were standing in the dirt yard in front of their house. Tenny stuck out both arms wide and whirled around until he lost his balance and collapsed.

An uncle who had been a witness in the court was following the brother in a car. He picked the man up and brought him at once to Rumah Sakit Bethesda, the Protestant hospital in Tomohon, where the victim was pronounced dead on arrival. Early the next day the wife's brother returned to Tinoör in a casket. His people said he wasn't dead yet, only in a coma, 'still breathing'. Twenty-four hours later though he was seen to cry

27

in the coffin and that was before he really died. There was an argument that if only the uncle had taken the brother to a *dukun* right away, and not to the modern hospital, his life could have been saved.

During this time Alexander was staying with members of his Sangihe family in Manado. After news of his victim's death arrived, he boasted that he was going back to Sylvie in Tinoör. When he returned, at the narrowing of the road, he met the village head who invited him to come into his office. While they were inside, a large crowd gathered, including police from Tomohon with rifles. Alexander pretended not to be afraid. When he came outside, the crowd attacked. Police fired into the air, but that didn't help. One officer had his face cut, so the rest didn't interfere further. As for the *peracun*, he was beaten to death and his clothes were ripped right to shreds.

Koert Jan asked whether anyone was ever punished for this act of mob violence. Tenny recounted that at first the army leaders called in a hundred people from Tinoör. This number was reduced to thirteen who were held responsible. Thirteen had to report to the *camat*, the district military executive. Finally, however, no action was taken against them.

After a temporary absence, Sylvie Mangundap herself returned to Tinoör. She went about her business as if nothing had happened. Her maize harvest was early. When she spread the corn out to dry in front of her house, children came and threw handfuls to the wind. She warned people, 'Watch out, Tinoör, people from husband's village are coming.' That explained why Tinoör had to be guarded for some time.

While we sat on a bamboo sofa and drank coffee in Annie and Tenny's house, Tenny brought out his pride and joy: a stereophonic radio and cassette recorder. A flick of his wrist and we were flooded by electronic rock at maximum volume. Koert Jan threw up his hands and begged mercy. Annie was cross with Tenny. She had told him not to bother, we would only hate the sound. He was hoping to bring the machine back to the house but that was a prospect we didn't hesitate to veto.

'And was that the end of the story?' Koert Jan asked presently. 'Isn't there more to tell?'

'Yes.' But Tenny looked at Annie first for permission to go on. When she nodded his words came out rapidly. A short time after Alexander's death a blood relative tried to take revenge on a member of the *peracun*'s family. The family member in question drove a group taxi. One day a stranger took the seat directly behind the driver and when the vehicle began to climb the hill, the passenger pulled out a switchblade knife and tried to plunge it into the driver's neck. The Sangihe driver, however, just laughed. He had a charm sewn into his body that protected him. The knife couldn't even pierce his skin. 'True, Mr Koert, Mr Eric.' Then Tenny swore he had seen this same driver pour boiling water over his body without flinching.

Tenny's father was a relaxed man with a gut, a sweet round face, slow movements. Somehow I never got used to the idea we were roughly the same age. Practically every time we met he was lolling or slumped in a chair, cuffs of his trousers rolled to mid-calf, feet bare, the toenails yellow and cracked. Since Tenny had come to work for us, his father had no one else to drive his taxi and had to do it himself. This ate into his natural tranquillity. He much preferred work on the land. More recently Tenny's brother Mosby was acting as chauffeur even though he was too young to have a license. At police checkpoints to be allowed through he had to hand over sums of money.

Tenny's father was sleeping in the fields, except for Saturday night, standing watch over the paddy which was nearly ripe. Birds were the worst thieves, although groups of men had been known to descend by night and strip whole *sawah*s if the owner was unwary. Some farmers paid a *dukun* to protect their crops. The *dukun* would cast a spell, so that if a thief climbed one of the farmer's trees to steal, say, a papaya, he couldn't come down

29

again until the *dukun* personally undid his magic to release him. To be sure there were many imposters who claimed to be *dukun*s and their spells were worthless. Tenny's father relied instead on the immediate protection of his shotgun. At the same time he scared away birds by tugging at a string attached to a complicated network of wires hung with tattered strips of cloth.

Tenny much more closely resembled his mother. Her speaking voice was chronically hoarse and her manner abrupt, even crude, but she was essentially a warm, friendly person, eager to please. On our early visits she treated us to reminiscences about various Europeans who during the previous decade had put in an appearance in Tinoör. Surely we must know them. Our denials were only half-believed. We were also given a dog, the runt of a new litter, infested with more lice than I'd ever seen in my life, his stumpy tail off center. Still, the gift was a culinary sacrifice on the part of Tenny's family. The pup was black, the color most in demand for the supposed sweetness of its flesh.

Our early visits also brought to light that Tenny was the troublemaker in the family. As a boy he was always falling out of trees he never should have climbed in the first place. He had quit school at twelve, after being sent home for disciplinary reasons practically every day. Now a younger son, Kaspar, was about to enter the University of Manado to study economics. Kaspar's head had been shaved down to the skull as part of fraternity hazing. Tenny's other younger brother, Mosby, was leading his class in high school. He wanted to become a Garuda pilot. Tenny was proud without being jealous, an unusual combination in that corner of the world.

Only Anes, Tenny's older brother, the one who brought him to our house for his job interview, was not particularly beloved. As first-born he had buckled under too heavy a load of expectations. Years earlier, it seems, Anes had stolen a bale of dried cloves from his father and run off with the profit, by plane,

30

to Jakarta. Twelve months later his money was depleted, he was utterly alone in the Big City and suicidal. He broke a year of silence, cabling his parents for the fare to return to North Sulawesi by ship. His father met him at Bitung, the provincial port. Right there on the quay the boy was beaten senseless with a strap.

Tenny described these events while his father sat listening, nodding mild agreement, late afternoon sunlight on his forehead, the lower part of his face, smiling, in shadow. It was difficult to imagine the man capable of the brutality Tenny described. Since then Anes had atoned for his mis-step by marrying and giving his parents their first, and only grandchild. His wife, however, was not popular with Tenny's family. 'She's pretty,' Tenny's mother told us, 'but lazy.'

We hadn't been in Tenny's parents' house five minutes when his mother asked to see pictures of our wives. If she was surprised when we said we weren't married, she didn't show it. Instead she hinted we could do worse than take a local wife, temporarily. Didn't Indonesian officials posted to out of the way places 'marry' a woman in such circumstances?

When Tenny's father invited us to attend the ceremony to celebrate the upcoming rice harvest, a communal meal which would be cooked at a shelter erected at the *kebun* itself, Annie said she wasn't sure we could make the walk. 'Four hours,' she said, holding up four fingers gleefully, rounding her shoulders, making trudging motions with her legs. Tenny, too, judged us unfit for the strenuous journey. When the day arrived, however, the walk cost us far less pain and trouble than it did the two of them. It was unfair, they complained, our legs were longer. The walk led up and down through patches of dense forest. It took little more than two hours. Often below in the distance the sea was visible. How fine it was to leave the world of roads and traffic behind.

At the *kebun* about a hundred people had assembled in the lean-to that had been set up for the occasion. Poles were driven into the ground, lashed together with vines and roofed over with palm fronds. Four generations were represented. Tenny's father had bought the surrounding land for a good price and cleared it himself. It was unsuitable for cloves, but all right for rice and leafy vegetables. Before the thanksgiving meal we went on an orchid hunt in adjacent tropical woods. A few steps inside the edge of the undergrowth and the sun all but disappeared. In filigrees like glittering skeins of spider webs light penetrated the canopy of branches and foliage. Tenny's younger brothers and their friends accompanied us, whooping and racing. Birds startled from their cover flitted from sight with one rapid push of their bright wings. Orchids grew high up as parasites in the fork of branches of towering trees, white and purple clusters, delicate markings deep in the inside of their throats, roots dishevelled in the air. The boys scampered up vines, defied gravity, swinging possum-like out along branches to bring down the flowers we so admired. All of them carried bush knives and as we walked they wilfully, recklessly slashed around them, felling and scarring trees.

Tenny walked slowly by our side proud to show off his knowledge of plants, birds, insects. He also talked freely about his sex life. Just like that – one minute a mine of information about roots and leaves and nesting habits, the next, with no apparent transition, babbling in a confessional mode, but oh so casually. He told us he couldn't go to bed with Annie. It didn't work. He still made an effort sometimes, but even when he managed an erection, however hard he tried, no matter how long he kept at it, nothing ever came out. Tenny was afraid he had ruined his organ because he had started having sex too young, at twelve. At this age his older brother took Tenny along on visits to whores in Bitung. Tenny had gone back often. He'd screwed a lot of schoolgirls, too, but you had to pay them something anyhow and they weren't as friendly. Tenny felt sorry for Annie. It was his fault they couldn't have children, not hers, but she was the one people kept making fun of. Koert Jan promised he would try to help: he would take Tenny to consult a Dutch specialist, a gynecologist, a religious sister in charge of family planning at Gunung Maria, the Catholic hospital in Tomohon.

During our orchid search, Annie stayed behind to help prepare the meal. Special sticky rice was cooked. Paddy was first wrapped in broad leaves and inserted into lengths of bamboo which were stood on one end and leaned against a rack; then the bamboo was slowly rotated above hot coals. The meal was typical of Minahasa festivities: meat, dripping with fat, highly seasoned, dominated. A host won *gengsi* by serving more meat than guests could consume. Vegetables played no role. Heart attacks at feasts were not infrequent. These were popularly attributed to poison. There was never a shortage of stories to explain why someone had wanted to do away with the deceased.

On the *kebun*, gorged with *babi hutan* – wild swine – and countless gourds of *saguir* – sweet, unfermented palm wine – we felt at ease. Food was served on broad leaves, eaten with the hand. No distinctions were made for us.

'Here, try this.' Annie came to the table where we sat. She was holding half an open durian. She prised free two sticky globes of fruit and dropped them in our palm wine. At once the liquid began to fizz like Alka Seltzer. The result was irresistible, and intoxicating. The walk back, without doubt, would seem longer.

Here and there on tables under the lean-to there were straw baskets full of eggs. Yet no one ate, touched, or even seemed to notice them. Koert Jan, by gentle questioning, managed to learn these were offerings for ancestor spirits. Old rituals were derided, and observed.

Towards evening cool breezes swept up from the unseen sea. Elders began to speak nostalgically about Dutch rule. We held our breaths. In Manado no one ever spoke politics. The risk was too great. Yet here in a mood of celebration, among their

33

own, the Tinoör villagers gave vent to their true feelings. How they missed their former rulers. With what venom speaker after speaker denounced current corruption. Later in the months to come, back in Tomohon or in Manado we would occasionally see the same people silent and docile in the presence of the authorities. Now while the angry talk lasted, Tenny and Annie sat listening intently. Several times Tenny seemed to quiver with a desire to join in, but then Annie would lay a restraining hand on his shoulder or knee and he would subside.

The tests which Dr Voetberg, the gynecologist, carried out indicated that Tenny had a shortage of certain crucial male hormones. This doctor, a nun in her seventies, was dedicated to helping people who wanted to have children have them, and to preventing children from being born otherwise. 'The world is already crowded with unwanted people,' she said. 'Why make it worse?' The first time we met her, she had come to pay us a welcome call bringing a box of chocolate-covered cherries. 'Don't ask me how I get these things,' she said. 'People back home have a funny idea of what we miss, don't they?'

Dr Voetberg had unruly, thin red hair, restless blue eyes. And extraordinarily beautiful hands, the youngest part of her by far. We sat talking in the living room when suddenly a begonia blooming in the front garden caught her eye, a variety that flowers once, briefly and gloriously, in a year. Before we understood what was happening, Dr Voetberg rose and was out on the lawn snapping off the pale pink flowers one by one and popping them into her mouth. When she returned inside all the begonias had been stripped bare. She held out a cupped handful of petals. 'Sweet,' she said as she munched. 'You can use them to make jam.'

Tenny came home from his hospital examination giggling. 'Annie,' he announced in our hearing, 'that woman who ate the flowers touched my eggs. I have to eat these' – he showed a paper cone full of multi-colored capsules – 'and to fill this' – he

34

held up a small white paper cup – 'then she can tell us better what we have to do.'

Tenny's spontaneous, ingenuous openness never failed him. He and Annie were clearly best friends, a highly unusual state of affairs for married Indonesians. Whatever the state of their sex lives, they enjoyed each other's company very much. They invented games which they played together, told each other stories, slept in each other's arms.

A few days after Tenny's examination, we drove past two transvestites in mini-skirts walking along the side of the road. '*Panci*s,' Tenny said. He honked and waved when the boys jumped to one side. 'I could become a *panci*,' Tenny said. The boys had hair down to their shoulders, long, painted finger-nails. They wore lipstick and high-heel shoes.

*Panci*s seldom appeared alone. Often they wore cloying perfume and cultivated a kind of wiggle when they walked. Their voices were affected and effeminate. They did not engage in sex. People called them to their homes to give massages. *Panci*, which means pot or pan in Indonesian, is presumably a corruption of the English *pansy*.

Tenny took Dr Voetberg's pills faithfully. As for the small white paper cup, it sat on the window-ledge next to his bed where we could see it when we passed their room.

VI

Some months after Tenny and Annie came to live with us, Koert Jan and I had a quarrel. The cause? Not important. I seem to remember its having something to do with my weeding some of the orchids we brought back from Tinoör and Koert Jan in a fury telling me the weeds were as beautiful as the flowers and I shouldn't mess around with things I didn't know anything about. We shouted, that I know. I may have slammed a door or two. Work pressure had been building up. There was no one outside of each other to whom we could turn for understanding. The release of a short, sharp difference of opinion was at times necessary, and delicious.

The fight took place late in the afternoon. Dinner was on the table at the usual time. Koert Jan and I came out of our respective sulking places and sat in silence. Bowls passed back and forth, we began to eat. To our surprise Tenny and Annie came into the house. Annie had prepared dough – a mixture of flour and pounded soy beans – which she now put into the oven. During meals, Tenny and Annie always waited out back. When we were through we clinked a fork against a glass – Annie's idea – and Tenny would come in and clear. Depending on what we had left over, and what extras Annie had prepared in the back kitchen, they would then eat. The kitchen inside the house was a modern, open affair, only separated from the dining area and living room by a counter. That night while Koert Jan and I forced food down our throats, staring at our plates, longing for reconciliation but each damned if he'd make the first move, Tenny and Annie sat cross-legged on the green floor tiles in front of the oven. They whispered back and forth. Ostensibly, they were watching the bread rise and brown through the small window in the oven door. Really they were watching us. Tenny began to giggle. More than once Annie slapped his knee and said, 'Shhh!' and then giggled herself.

During the quarrel we had made a lot of noise. For Indonesians loss of temper, a display of anger, involves practically irretrievable loss of face. I don't know – I might even have cried. The orchids looked better without weeds. My eyes felt small. There was still a fist of anger in my heart, but the fingers were loosening.

'They don't know what to make of it, the poor kids,' I finally said, conscious of how my voice, sadder than I'd intended, floated out into the silence.

'Should they?' Koert Jan asked. His tone was still harsh but any answer was an acceptance of my overture. It was hard for

36

us to accept the intractable in our relation. Two people living together for long invariably batter their heads against the same stone wall. Patterns repeat. Roles solidify. After intervals of calm, something happens and – bam! Koert Jan and I, we have never learned to laugh at our irreconcilable differences, at the ways our characters rasp, but we have been able to keep recurring crises down to a raw minimum.

'I'm sorry. I'm not saying I was wrong, but I'm sorry. Do you want to try working after dinner?'

'If you'll act like a grown person. Jesus, if you can't even take criticism from me . . .'

Our *rapprochement* conversation went something like that.

'Try the fish, they're good.'

'They're too oily.'

'Why do you do it' – Koert Jan began to eat with appetite – 'when you know how it gets on my nerves?'

'I guess it's because I happen to have nerves, too.'

Suddenly Tenny was clapping his hands, hugging Annie. She was rocking back and forth, laughing.

'Mr Eric is the winner,' Tenny said to us, sliding forwards towards us across the tiles like some beggar.

'What?' Koert Jan put down his fork and frowned. Tenny pointed at me.

'Mr Eric wins because he gave in. He talked first. That's the hardest, to give in. Someone has to, or things only get worse.'

Before Koert Jan could sputter in his own defense, I asked Tenny if he and Annie ever had fights. Annie shrieked. 'All the time!' She was wearing a white cardigan, loosely crocheted. The sweater was bunched above her elbows. Her face tonight was an Asian version of Popeye's girlfriend Olive Oyl. 'He pulls my hair,' she told us, putting her fists into Tenny's hair while he twisted his head about. 'And I punch him.'

'When we make a lot of noise,' I went on, catching Koert Jan's eyes which were now smiling, 'that's a sign things are not so bad. In the West that's our way . . .' – it was difficult enough

37

to express what I wanted to say in any language, not to mention Bahasa Indonesia – 'of letting off steam. Yes? It doesn't really mean anything.' Koert Jan was pushing his fork around the table. He found my attempts at explaining ourselves to Indonesians futile and foolish. I hoped Tenny and Annie didn't understand his sardonic expression. If I didn't watch out, I'd be shouting in another minute. 'When we're silent – that's much worse.'

'How long have you and Mr Koert lived together?' Tenny asked.

'Ten years,' Koert Jan said.

'Good,' Tenny nodded contentedly. 'Then you won't split up, ever.'

'The bread,' Annie put a hand over her mouth. Koert Jan crossed to the oven.

'It's fine,' he said. 'Did you mix in the yeast this time?'

We had agreed Koert Jan would assume authority over Tenny and Annie. Having two of us to answer to, or rather to play off against each other, would make our domestic situation even trickier. That was fine by me. Only Koert Jan, by nature, often let discipline slide without realising it.

'Once in Tinoör we had two women who lived together and never married,' Tenny told us, lying back on the floor. 'Grandma Tall and Grandma Short. They went out to the fields every morning, Grandma Short riding on top of the cart and Grandma Tall walking beside. They fought in the Promesta, too.'

'They loved each other,' Annie said, 'very much.'

That night I think we were closest to the illusion of being a family that we ever reached. Even Koert Jan overcame his annoyance at Tenny's brashness. There was such a quality of sweetness on Tenny's face as he told his Grandma Tall and Grandma Short story, looking out of the corner of his eyes at Annie while he spoke. Annie sat watching him with admiration. That night all the dogs in Tomohon baying at the moon, the wind orchestral in the leaves of the banana trees – click, click, click – I fell asleep wishing there was some way to help Annie to a child. If I were the father . . .

VII

The first dark clouds on the domestic horizon were not Tenny's fault really. We were visiting the hill village of Masarang. Masarang is not far from busy Tondano town, the administrative center of the regency. There is, however, no road connection to speak of. Masarang was founded by Dutch Catholics. The cool climate agreed with them. They planted prosperous, sweeping coffee plantations there. During the war the Japanese invaders camped on the site, setting up headquarters in the church building. People still speak with awe about how silent the Japanese were among themselves. Masarang women were said to have given themselves freely to the soldiers, yet no trace of Japanese blood ever showed in the births which followed. At the time of our first visit, some eight hundred people lived in Masarang, all small farmers except for a few civil servants. Hardly any coffee trees remained. A few stunted specimens yielded berries that would shrivel before they were plucked. On the site of the former Catholic church, a water standpipe stood in the middle of an eternal pool of mud.

We made an appointment to go to Masarang with the doctor from the nearest district health center. She was a young woman who wore glasses. After completion of medical school in Surabaya she had been sent to do three years of service 'on the periphery' in North Sulawesi. Within a week of her arrival she married an auto importer, a business connection of her father's. He lived in Manado and they only saw each other intermittently.

Dr Nancy had full cheeks that shone like polished fruit, the beginning of wrinkles at the base of her plump neck, a small, round, receding chin. She was fairly bursting with ideas about how to promote rural development. She radiated enthusiasm, even dedication. When Dr Nancy learned we were about to brave the journey to Masarang with our Toyota, she asked if she might join us and bring key health staff to do a village-wide health survey. Although staff from the health center were supposed to visit Masarang to hold regular weekly clinics there, the arduous walk put nurses off. Something of a road – a stream bed of rocks and scree – did exist. By setting the engine on goat, a joke Tenny never grew tired of making, he managed to climb from rock to rock. It was a jolting, shattering ride. All the passengers held on to the roll-bar under the canvas roof to steady ourselves. Still hips and shoulders grated against each other, jaws snapped. Tenny inched along, biting his lower lip. He had a knack for selecting the right course. Branches swept the windshield and the sides of the vehicle, farmers on the way down to Tondano market and women with mounds of leafy vegetables in baskets on their heads jumped aside and smiled toothlessly as we caromed past, the stink of our exhaust trailing behind. The provincial government had been promising Masarang a proper paved road for years. We lurched from side to side. The staff with clipboards and questionnaires on their laps treated the occasion like an outing. Later Tenny told us he had been in mortal fear that the paint might be scratched. In all the time he worked for us his devotion to the machine never diminished. After every journey he inspected the Toyota inch by inch and groaned at the slightest blemish.

As we rose, mist lifted, burned off by the sun. The first sign that we were nearing the village itself was groups of small children, interrupting their play to stare and shout. Most were naked from the waist down. Shirt-tails trailing, they stood cheering at roadside, 'Golkar, Golkar, Golkar.' Golkar is the name of the government political party. The children ran along making a victory sign with their tiny fingers. Dr Nancy laughed at the chorus of voices. Elections were far off, but no stone was being left unturned.

Suddenly near the summit we passed a pool where boys were washing and currying squat, sturdy ponies. From this point a gentle grass track rose and after a few moments of smooth passage, eerie after the earlier jolting struggle, we found ourselves at the village head's compound.

He was there – playing badminton. We got down and watched him scurry around a badminton court scratched in the earth next to his house. A tattered net was stretched between a tree and one of the wood piles on which the house stood. At last the village head's opponent, the *hansip*, the local military policeman, leapt in the air and smashed the shuttlecock wide. The village head, in high spirits, trotted over to welcome us. His shirt was drenched with sweat and his brow and cheeks were streaming. He led our party up a flight of cement stairs to an enclosed porch where we sat on folding iron chairs painted in a series of different colors. Red, green, orange, blue – with rust as a common denominator. The house was a traditional one, wood bleached from exposure to the dead gray of ashes, inside walls decorated with calendars, plaster saints, plastic ivy and flowers. Daylight was visible through chinks in the floor. Most of the wood shutters along both walls were bolted against the coming heat of the day.

For the following few hours, we were held prisoner of the social occasion. It seemed to me that Koert Jan and I were far more restless than Dr Nancy, or any of her crew, to be out and about our work, even though we were likely to have far more chances than they to come back. She and her chosen handful of staff seemed satisfied by their having performed the remarkable feat of reaching the village at all.

We were given VIP treatment. A pair of freshly trapped wood rats were brought out for us to admire. We were urged to stroke the plump gray bodies, still warm, to exclaim at the length of the white tails before the creatures were whisked out of

41

sight to be skinned and roasted. The *hukum tua*, a slim man in his early thirties, had changed meanwhile into a western-style blue denim workshirt, holes painstakingly mended. He had thick, callused hands, an open, nervous smile, rather evasive, flecked eyes. He sat at a rickety table and made a show of countersigning our *surat jalan*, the official travel permit without which we were not allowed to set a single foot in any direction. Meanwhile the *hukum tua*'s wife solemnly brought us the visitor's book. It smelled of must. The binding was broken. We signed near the bottom of a water-stained page bearing a few faded signatures of various government representatives.

Then with a great deal of handshaking and nodding of heads we were introduced to village notables. They chatted to each other lickety-split in the language of Masarang. We sat. Dr Nancy wiped her glasses with the lower part of her white coat. Outside Tenny played badminton with one of the visiting male nurses. He played with great wild rushes of energy and frantic shouts of victory or disappointment.

Dr Nancy must have sent ahead advance notice of our intended visit. Notice, for example, that one of the items on her survey programme was to examine the condition of the village school, schoolyard and well. With exemplary Indonesian consideration, she hadn't wanted to risk arriving to find things looking less than their best. But of all the activities Dr Nancy was to undertake in the villages she visited, family planning had top priority. In Masarang, she had told us, she was eager to search for new 'acceptors', her enthusiasm whetted by a government bonus incentive system. Before this we had already worked in villages where a small wooden board was nailed to a pole in front of every home. A colored circle was painted on the board to indicate whether the woman of the house was practising birth control and, if so, what was her method of choice. A red circle, for example, signified an IUD, a green one an injection, blue symbolised condoms. Black revealed a non-acceptor. At the time it seemed whatever sign we

42

encountered out front, when the door opened to our knock, a pregnant woman greeted us in the doorway.

It was soon clear that although Dr Nancy had not been at her position for long she was an old hand at the statistics game. Before our meal, although she hadn't spoken with anyone from Masarang yet except for the few people seated on the porch, she filled in her report of the day's activities, in quadruplicate. This paperwork included notification to the Ministry of Health that she had located seventeen new family planning acceptors.

By any standards the meal set before us was elaborate. Koert Jan tried to plead that the wood rat served to him had too much red pepper and would burn a hole through his palate. This tactic merely delayed the moment of truth. The meat was carried out back, rinsed, and served again, austere and naked in its gamyness. We made our way through the meal mouthful by mouthful, just as earlier we had driven from rock to rock to reach the village.

As soon after our mid-morning banquet as we deemed decent, we asked to take a stroll to look around the village. The *hukum tua* started to look even more nervous than usual. However we suspected that he, like us, might be troubled by indigestion. Protocol apparently dictated that we drive. Motor vehicles were a true rarity in Masarang and the village head could not forgo turning our visit as much to his political advantage as he could. Tenny was summoned from the kitchen. He shooed away the small children that covered the Toyota like flies. He made a fanning gesture in front of his lips to show us his mouth was on fire from the peppery wood rat. Carefully he reversed out of the *hukum tua*'s compound and with the *hukum tua* striding in front we drove at zero kilometers an hour down a shallow, eroded ravine separating small, rather shabby village houses.

At the Masarang school we got out. It was closed for the simple reason that all the teachers had come to meet us. In front there was a long, narrow goldfish pond. This pond, a component of a community development project, was to provide a source of supplementary protein for the children. Koert Jan stooped, stirred the water with his hand but failed to turn up any sign of life. By now Tenny was mocking the backwardness of the village rather boisterously so Koert Jan told him to take the Toyota back to the *hukum tua*'s and wait for us there. We then politely informed the village head and Dr Nancy, who had developed the tic of consulting her wristwatch at ever shorter intervals, that it was our intention to visit a number of homes on the fringe of Masarang, or perhaps even to call on people living off on their *kebun*s some distance away.

A number of arguments were passionately advanced to discourage us from what appeared generally to be regarded as a fantastic course of action. It was hot, the paths were slippery, people might be asleep, dogs might bite, in anger people might attack us with knives. Besides, whatever we needed to know, the doctor or village head could tell us. Parrying resistance in a friendly way, we struck off with a single guide, a school teacher, and actually managed to spend a few productive hours. It was always exhilarating when we managed to break free from the nets of formality cast over us. During our walk we even learned the fate of the goldfish in the school pond. The teachers, our guide confided, took the mature carp – a good foot long – to the market in Tondano. With some of the profits they bought benches and desks for the school. And the rest of the profits? – we waited in vain to hear what happened to them.

Back at the *hukum tua*'s a large crowd had collected in the yard and in the house. 'Oh no,' Koert Jan sighed. We were in no mood for ceremony. No mood to play the honored guests. During our orientation walk around the outskirts of Masarang we had found appalling poverty. Even worse perhaps was the apathy. 'Buck up,' I tried to joke. 'They've probably saved us a bite of the tail.' Then I saw Tenny. He was seated on a side veranda, hunched forward, face ashen white, eyes desperate.

44

Koert Jan was already running. A child's cries came from inside, attenuated cries of fear and pain. Dr Nancy, subdued, came down the steps from the elevated porch and led us to one side. She removed her glasses before she spoke. Genuine concern made her face pretty. There had been an accident with the Toyota. A child had broken his leg, a compound fracture.

'But – ' Koert Jan whirled to locate Tenny, face red with anger. Dr Nancy laid a restraining hand on his arm.

'It wasn't your driver's fault. At the school children climbed on to the back of the car. He told them to get down. He drove away slowly, they ran after and jumped up again. He could see in his mirror they were there again, hanging on. So he stopped and yelled at them. In jumping off, one of the boys caught his leg and fell on to a stone. Your driver didn't realise anything had happened. He just returned here to wait, the way you told him.

'He was playing badminton with the *hukum tua* when the boy's father came into the yard, carrying the boy. He threw the boy down into the dirt – these people! The boy was bleeding and in pain, just lying at the driver's feet and the father said, "There, you can have him." So then the man took his bush knife and was going to attack. We were sitting up there and could see everything that took place' – Dr Nancy pointed to the porch, dense with interested faces. 'Your driver thought the man was mad. When the father started walking towards him, he had to defend himself with the badminton racket. He kept circling backwards and swinging the racket back and forth to keep them apart.

'Then the boy's mother who had seen the accident herself came running into the yard. She shouted to the father to stop, the driver wasn't at fault. It was the children who had been asking for trouble. The man listened with his head hanging. And then he started to beat his son. He used a belt. He picked the boy up with the point of the bone sticking out of the leg and just tossed him over his shoulder, like this. That one's the

45

father, him over there – with the long hair and the cloth cap.'
Distaste crept into Dr Nancy's voice.

I heard the boy's moan and caught sight of him on the
veranda near Tenny. The boy's leg lay in an impossible
position. There on the spot I fainted. When I revived,
surrounded by a concerned huddle of Indonesians, Koert Jan
was unable to resist a quick wink and a grin.

A plan was quickly made. In nearby Tondano was a
government hospital where treatment would be next to free but
we could not bring Sonny there. They were not equipped to set
a broken limb. Although there was an X-ray machine, they had
no one to run it. Instead with the Toyota we would have to
transport the boy back to Tomohon, to R.S. Bethesda, the
Protestant hospital. Yet to take him aboard for the rough
downhill ride was out of the question. Such a descent would be
excruciating and perhaps enlarge the break. Nurses fashioned a
stretcher out of bamboo and an old blanket. The boy's father
and three neighbors were to carry him to the foot of the hill
where we would wait and pick him up. Sonny's people, the
hukum tua let us know, were dirt and dirt poor. Much of the
father's wild reaction, his impulsive rage, derived from worry
about how to meet the expenses of the accident. Once Koert
Jan assured the man that whoever might be to blame we would
pay, everyone relaxed. Except Sonny.

At twelve, the boy was small for his age. He had fine features,
the dark, darting eyes of a bird. He lay with his head in his
mother's lap, Ruth, a stringy woman with frizzy hair. She sat
still. The only part of her that moved was her heart. You could
see it pounding through her dress. As soon as Sonny's father
came near, the boy whimpered louder and cringed. The man's
lip would curl back in an embarrassed smile.

Tenny trembled visibly as we approached him. When he
tried to excuse himself, the words caught in his throat. Koert
Jan simply put one arm around him and told Tenny not to be
afraid, *jangan takut*, we knew he hadn't done anything wrong.

46

That helped. Tenny insisted he could drive, and indeed he did so with full concentration. During the drive down no one spoke except for Dr Nancy. She bristled still against Sonny's father for his abuse of the child. She saw him as a perfect example of the kind of mentality that made life so difficult for anyone motivated to bring about meaningful change.

Just at the point where the rocky stream bed ended and a gravel road began, the patient was waiting. Here a number of health center staff dismounted and took their leave. Their homes were close by. Sonny was crying steadily now but not with much strength. His tiny eyes were full of hurt. We loaded him into the back of the Toyota. The others did. I tried to look without seeing. When I'm powerless to help, pain baffles me.

Sonny lay across his father's lap, both thin arms up around his father's neck. I forced myself to smile reassuringly at them but probably my face was past the point where it was capable of giving reassurance. As we sped to the hospital, I rolled the front window all the way down and let the air rush into my eyes, nose, mouth. On the way we dropped Dr Nancy back at her health center. She pointed out to us how conveniently the building stood next to a graveyard – and laughed. All the land between the graves was planted by health center staff with ripening corn. Bits of broken glass were cemented on to the tombs themselves to keep picnickers off.

Tenny pulled up in front of R.S. Bethesda, jumped down and opened the back of the Toyota. Together with Sonny's father he carried the boy, whimpering faintly now, inside. I went to follow but Koert Jan held me back. 'Wait,' he said.

A minute later we heard angry voices inside. We found Tenny heatedly arguing with three nurses in uniform who wanted him to take Sonny right back outside to the waiting room. Although Sonny's father was meekly prepared to obey, Tenny's anger was about to get the best of him.

'What's wrong, Tenny?' Koert Jan asked when we entered.

'No doctor,' he said.

As soon as the nurses saw us, their manner changed. According to the roster I learned that Dr Supprapto, a surgeon, should have been on duty. It was his custom, apparently, to sleep off the torpor of his midday meal at home.

'He has told us not to disturb him unless there's an emergency,' a nurse said.

'I'm sure he won't mind,' Koert Jan answered, 'just this once.'

A nurse sprinted off to the doctor's home, only a hundred yards along the road. Half an hour later, rubbing his eyes, Dr Supprapto arrived. He tried to be jovial. The effect was sinister. An X-ray was taken. Sonny's leg was set and put in a cast. The actual mixing and applying of the plaster fascinated him. Sonny also received medicine for anemia and worms. The whole time his father sat out in the waiting room, hat in hand. His dark, narrow face was ferine. The man had difficulty stringing the simplest phrases together. Speech seemed to exhaust him. He was abashed by his earlier behavior, ill at ease in town, in the hospital, in the company of white foreigners. This was, Ruth told us much later, the furthest her husband had ever traveled from Masarang. Tenny, displaying surprising sensitivity, sat next to the man and kept telling him everything would be all right.

'You don't want to kill me any more, *bapak*?' Tenny asked. The man smiled ruefully, shook his head no.

'It was lucky for that *hukum tua* that you came when you did,' Tenny went on. 'I was ahead 9 to 3 in the second game.'

Sonny and his father came back with us to our house. With his pain gone, the boy was excited, curious. He wanted to touch and to smell everything. His ordeal seemed forgotten, utterly. Sonny's father, however, shrank still further into himself. The more we tried to put him at ease, the more we discomforted him. We ate together and Sonny was delighted by spoon and fork and by the shadows they made on the living room wall. He wolfed down Annie's *saté* and a mountain of rice. The biggest

48

hit, however, was our pup, Tasty. Usually skittish with strangers, he tamely submitted to all the tortures Sonny could devise, wagging his off-center tail.

Annie, I must say, was behaving rather peculiarly the whole time. When we first returned, Tenny had gone directly to see her. We heard him rattle out his story breathlessly and then heard Annie raise her voice. Tenny came back, brow wrinkled, and asked Koert Jan to tell Annie exactly what had happened. She refused to accept his story. Koert Jan went.

After the meal Koert Jan asked Tenny if he could face the trip back to Masarang to bring Sonny and his father home. By now Tenny was his usual exuberant self. My first sight of him at the *hukum tua*'s, rigid, pale, eyes imploring, stayed imprinted in my mind. Tenny asked – in front of Sonny and his father – if Annie could come along to sit behind him. 'Otherwise maybe the old man will strangle or stab me.' Koert Jan asked Annie to keep Tenny company. On other occasions she had always been eager to ride out, escaping from the house, seeing places she had never laid eyes on before. Now she looked at Koert Jan, glared really, as if he were somehow insulting her.

'No,' she said, and crossed her arms. 'Whatever you say, that broken leg is Tenny's fault.'

'But – '

'But, but, but. He was driving, wasn't he?'

How Koert Jan found the stamina to make the trip with Tenny was beyond me. I knew I shouldn't let him go alone, despite his insistence, but my strength was gone. As soon as the others left, I went in to lie down for a minute. The last sounds I remember were Annie's washing the dishes out in the back kitchen, and her crying.

As Sonny's leg recovered, he learned to tear around Masarang on crutches. His parents kept him home from school because other boys could not resist running up to take a thwack at his cast with branches. Several times when we had to fetch him for

49

examinations at the hospital he came alone. After Tenny would drop Sonny at home, he was always sent back to us with lavish presents from the family's small garden. Baskets of avocados or oranges, crops that sold well. Finally Sonny's cast was sawed open. Tenny said the hollow halves looked like the pod of a durian. The boy's leg inside was white, spindly after weeks of enforced immobility, and wasted. When he first tried to walk on it, after a few quick, stiff steps, he fell down. Dr Supprapto was marvellous with the boy, explaining, very patiently, how Sonny would have to be careful for some time. The way the surgeon massaged the leg, he looked like he was playing a musical instrument.

When the nurse came to collect the parts of the cast, Sonny protested. In the first real burst of speech we'd ever heard from him, he said he wanted to take the pieces home with him.

'*Kotor*,' the nurse said and started to walk away, 'dirty.'

'No,' Sonny insisted, dark eyes flashing. 'No, no, no.'

In the end Dr Supprapto had the nurse put the pieces of the cast in a plastic bag for the boy.

'He's right, Mr Eric,' Tenny whispered to me as we left the hospital. 'You shouldn't leave things like that where the wrong people can get a hold of them.'

Annie asked to accompany us on our last return trip with Sonny to Masarang. She laughed practically the whole way up the road of rocks, holding her sides. No matter how often Tenny made the climb, it remained tricky and demanding.

Annie was wearing a kerchief knotted under her chin. She removed it when we stopped in front of Sonny's house. She had freshly washed and set her hair. With her she had some flat, round rice cakes to give. She wanted to be on hand to watch Sonny's mother welcome the boy back whole again. She also brought a camera to take a photo of Tenny together with Sonny's father, proof of reconciliation.

As usual when we had entered the village, from all sides children came screaming. Sonny's friends began to jump up on

50

the back of the Toyota. Tenny let out a great roar and banged his hand so hard against the outside of the car door that he made a dent.

'Not again, Mr Koert,' he said in earnest. 'You paid for one, that's enough.'

With his hair neatly trimmed, Sonny's father looked years younger. He had a special present for us. Pieces of smoked monkey. Two arms, two charred hands with the fingers curled, tiny, precise. The monkey's face, black with ash, features perfect, intact.

'Like Kojack,' Tenny had joked loading the basket in back.

'Like a baby,' Annie said.

We never knew what finally happened to the ghastly gift. Koert Jan simply made it known that he didn't want to see it again after we reached home.

En route once again to Tomohon, from the back seat Annie unleashed a tirade of rapidfire remarks at Tenny in the language of Tinoör. He didn't answer. Koert Jan asked what Annie was saying. Tenny, squirming in his seat, tried to catch her eye in the rearview mirror.

'Tell them,' Annie said in Bahasa Indonesia, 'go on.'

One of Tenny's most endearing smiles lit his face. 'She says' – we gathered speed, moving over level ground, the fields a dazzling green with paddy on both sides, hills hump-backed and blue rising in the distance – 'I'm lucky that old man didn't cut my head off.'

VIII

Real trouble began one Friday two weeks after Anneke joined our household. Koert Jan and I had begun traveling further and further afield, at times sleeping away from the house several nights in succession. Annie managed to cope with solitary days but didn't relish being left by herself at night. Who

51

could blame her? On occasion when we returned at the end of a workday, if we reached home after dark, Annie would already have drawn all the curtains and barricaded herself inside the house with the doors locked. Tasty had grown knee high. He had a fierce, shrill bark, but Annie's fantasies of rape and dismemberment, fed by lurid stories down through the years – not the least sensational of which were told with relish by her mother – drove her indoors. For a short while she used to visit the neighbors at nightfall to wait for us there, but their Assemblies of God ways quickly put her off. When it came to choosing between their family circle, prostrate before the throne of heaven, and passing the hours alone, she preferred to crawl under our bed and wait for us with the lights out.

Clearly if we wanted Annie to stay, we had to find her a companion. With the help of Hilda Kawatu from Manado we located Anneke. Anneke, nineteen, plump, and in a permanent, slightly-strained good humor, lived only a ten-minute walk from our house, along a back track that dipped through terraced *sawah* in an old river bed, then wound past a waterfall and series of graceful, feathery bamboo clumps, to emerge in the village of Kasuraten. Kasuraten itself was built right on to the lower slopes of the Lokun. Anneke's father drove a *bendi*, a two-wheel wooden horse cart, painted with flowers, tricked out with tassels, fringes and bells. He was an old broken man. The skin across his cheeks and forehead looked painfully taut. His breath reeked of tobacco. In Anneke's mother you could see where Anneke's smile and manner came from, all a trifle too ingratiating. For many years the woman had worked in the kitchen of the Protestant orphanage in Tomohon.

How our extraordinary friend Hilda learned Anneke was looking for work is typical of the grapevine mysteries that cropped up so often during our stay and to which we never found a satisfactory answer. After brief negotiations it was decided Anneke would work at our house by day and sleep at home. Whenever we would be off for some days, however,

Anneke would come and stay with Annie. Hilda was not so pleased with this arrangement and counseled us to search Anneke every day before she left or surely she would start smuggling things like coffee and sugar to her mother.

Annie at first seemed to act rather arrogantly towards Anneke. Hilda assured us that Annie was simply pulling rank and a thaw would follow. It did. With her outsize Cheshire cat grin, Anneke did everything Annie commanded. She scrubbed floors, windows, did the wash, burned the garbage. She was inexperienced, but willing to learn. Anneke knew little about cooking either, but in her best condescending manner, Annie began to teach her. From her first day with us, Anneke ate like there was no tomorrow.

Friday we returned to Tomohon, exhausted, unwashed, after a five-day excursion to Gorontalo. To reach this remote area we must have crossed fifty rickety bridges of saplings each of which sounded like it was going to collapse out from under us. At one point we had to ferry our Toyota across a swift, broad river on a float of dugout canoes lashed together and fitted with bamboo outriggers. Tenny was fearless. At one point the road had seemed to disappear completely. We had to snake along a goat path, then skid across broad mud flats until we found it again. 'The Trans-Sulawesi Highway,' Tenny giggled.

The further from the provincial capital we went, the more difficult the circumstances in which people lived, the friendlier they were, the more content. 'Expectations,' Koert Jan said. 'What you don't have, can't hurt you.' We had only scratched the surface, true, but even Tenny agreed that outside the Minahasa people at least weren't preoccupied by *gengsi*.

We finally pulled into our driveway about half an hour after sundown. In Tomohon we were living practically on the equator so that all year round at roughly the same time tropical nightfall slammed down with ever-startling speed. The light was shining above the front door. Tasty barked and whined with joy, nipping at the Toyota tires, Koert Jan calling to him to calm down. We heard Annie and Anneke laughing in the back kitchen. Even before Tenny killed the engine, I was on my way to the Pressmans' workshed at the rear of the property where Lauri slept.

Lauri was Dorothy and Morris Davidson's parrot, their surrogate child, really. She spoke five languages, all of them, except English, more fluently than Dorothy did. The Davidsons had raised her with tender loving care. When the time came for them to take six months' leave in the United States, they had turned to us to look after Lauri for them until they came back. We received elaborate instructions. About diet, bathing, nail care. The jocose theologian had boasted to us that he was the only living person who could get close to Laurie without her taking a vicious bite. He demonstrated how Lauri even took bits of banana from between his lips. Dorothy watched the spectacle with radiant pride, and a nervous laugh. 'I can't help it. I keep expecting to see blood spout from his mouth.' For some reason Lauri took a shine to me. She would hold my finger in one claw, let me stroke her back, even take banana from my lips. One day Koert Jan fetched me from behind my typewriter to hear Lauri calling Tasty in a perfect, edge-of-panic imitation of my voice.

'Lauri? Lauri?' I whistled on my way back to the workshed. 'Lauri?' What escaped my notice was that for once Lauri had failed to respond to the precise combination of squeak and rumble that our Toyota made when it turned into the drive. Usually she let fly with a burst of welcome squawks and hopped so hard on her perch that the wire frame rocked wildly through space.

'How's Lauri? Here we are again.' I entered the pitch-black shed talking in the sweet false bird voice so embarrassing to hear in another. One step, then another and the stench of death fell like a blanket over my face. I ran back down the gallery for a flashlight. The others, under Koert Jan's supervision, were unloading the car.

54

In the beam of the flashlight Lauri hung dead, head down. She dangled from the perch to which she had been bound since birth by a single bone ring around one foot. Her feathers – she was red, green and gold – were molting, ruffled. Her eyes stared, her breast was ripped open and her organs, in a black knot, spilled into the air. I guess I screamed.

Annie explained that the very day of our departure for Gorontalo, Anneke had gone to move Lauri to her daytime haunt out by the driveway and found her dead, hanging just the way I discovered her. Right away Annie had gone to her mother to ask advice. Apparently her mother told her that whatever Annie did the one thing she must *not* do was to bury Lauri or dispose of the body before our return. Otherwise we would think she had sold the bird and invented the story of its death. Thus the evidence of the girls' innocence had been left decaying in the shed. Koert Jan buried Lauri, still attached to her perch, under the sour-sop tree out back. I wrote the Davidsons a condolence letter. (Later we discovered a band of children from the Protestant theology school had been responsible for Lauri's death, wringing her neck when she had snapped at them. Presumably one of the rats who danced nightly in our attic raked open the corpse. What worried us most, however, was how the children had come on to the premises unnoticed.)

After dinner that same night I sat down in the study to do the accounts of our trip. Koert Jan told me it could wait but as long as there are odds and ends in need of tidying my compulsiveness doesn't let me sleep. When I checked in the locked cash drawer in our bedroom, I found fifty thousand rupiah missing.

'You miscounted,' was Koert Jan's initial response, although he should have known better. 'Let's go to sleep.' We kept money in an envelope and whenever one of us removed a sum for whatever purpose, we always wrote down the amount on the outside. Now the money left did not match the written total, nor my rough mental estimate about how much should be remaining.

'No, I'm sure.'

'Then *I* forgot. Come, it's late.' Koert Jan was annoyed. He feels, rightly, I am in general too money-conscious. I've always had to watch what I spend. 'Maybe it's just runaway inflation,' he joked. During the first year of our stay in Indonesia, the price of many basic commodities did indeed double. 'You'll figure it out in the morning. How much is fifty thousand rupiah?'

'Fifty thousand rupiah is fifty thousand rupiah.'

'So much?'

'Annie earns five thousand rupiah a month.'

Annie had her own household purse. She went to the market for us three times a week and kept an itemised list of all purchases. The first few times we went with her but she could bargain far more effectively without a white shadow. When she needed more money, she asked. Usually she came with the empty purse, turned it upside down, stamped her foot and laughed. Sometimes after marketing, even before unpacking her purchases, she would sit for hours racking her memory so her bookkeeping would balance to the last cent. Carrots, so much, rice, so much, smoked tuna, so much. A lot of erasing and moaning until it came out all right. Only once had disaster overtaken Annie. She had finished a heavy shopping expedition to the market and climbed into a horse cart to return home when she realised she had forgotten Kanari, a nut from Ambon which is one ingredient of the *saté* marinade which Koert Jan – and Tenny – were so partial to. She told the driver to wait and hurried back into the crowd to make her purchase. It couldn't have been more than a minute or two before she was back again, but the *bendi* was nowhere to be seen. The driver had seized his chance and driven off with all our food. In the melee, for Tomohon market days are thronged, it was impossible to trace the driver. Annie couldn't even remember clearly what the man had looked like. She took another horse cart home, clutching her Kanari. Koert Jan had heard her story and laughed good-naturedly. He filled the household purse again and sent Annie back for another round of shopping. Tenny made a good deal of fun out of Annie's folly.

Time and again, moreover, Annie would come to us with money we had left in the pockets of our trousers when putting them in the wash. Or we left money in view on a table or desk and never thought twice about it. Otherwise we would have felt like we were living in a state of siege.

The next day, Saturday, Anneke had a free day. We left early to work. Annie was alone at the house. When we came home, Tenny told Annie all about how we had been teaching women to weigh and to measure their babies. He took our tape measure and spent the evening playing measuring games with her.

Sunday Tenny and Annie received their salaries for the previous month. As usual on Sundays, when Anneke returned, they went off to Tinoör. Originally we had agreed to give them Sundays off because they had made such a point of wanting to go to church. A ruse. Really it was to socialise that they preferred Sundays free. It was unique to allow help so much time off, but it suited us. On Sundays villagers who worked outside Tinoör came home. All afternoon the streets were full of people walking in twos and threes, arms linked. We'd been guests at Tenny's house several times on Sunday and promenaded with him through the village, chatting and laughing. Music blared from radios and cassette recorders. Outdoors people played ping-pong and badminton. Local cock fights were arranged in make-shift cardboard arenas. People loved to gamble for stakes they couldn't afford. Annie didn't even like Tenny to stop and watch, fearing the next step was laying a bet.

Koert Jan and I enjoyed Sunday at home, reading and working in the garden, tired after our long work week. Anneke saw to our meals on her own. She had too heavy a hand with coconut oil, but she was beginning to catch on to simple dishes.

She was quiet and industrious practically the whole day. We couldn't help comparing her attempts to please with Annie's increasing sloth. Over time Annie was developing an allergy to housework.

Mondays Tenny knew he had to be back at the house by seven at the latest. By then we usually left for the field. This Monday it was past nine before he and Annie finally turned up. He had no apology to offer. Without as much as a word he went to fetch the special knife from Java we had bought him to use for cutting the lawn. Actually, after a few casual swipes at the ragged, long grass, he went to the workshed for a grinding stone and sat out back listlessly sharpening the sweeping knife blade. Bags under his eyes betrayed that he'd been partying in Tinoör until late.

Koert Jan, patience itself ordinarily, was furious. We had not planned to go out that morning early, but Tenny had no way to know that. We'd been warned by a number of sources, Indonesian and expatriate, to be on the lookout for the first signs of slackening discipline, and to take measures at once to correct it. Otherwise the rest would all be downhill.

'What time are you supposed to be here, Tenny?'

'Where?'

Unfortunately Koert Jan used the word for *there* instead of *here*. When Tenny, bewildered at first, finally understood, and sarcastically corrected him, it didn't improve Koert Jan's temper. The best Tenny could do to account for being so late, at any rate the best he bothered to do, was to say they'd had trouble getting transport. But we knew Tenny's father's taxi was always on the road bright and early. Usually Tenny and Annie rode back to Tomohon with it on the first uphill morning run.

Koert Jan apparently told Tenny he would overlook lateness this time but never again. And he added something to the effect that he expected Tenny to finish trimming the lawn by early afternoon, and not to neglect it again. All this time Annie just sat out in the back kitchen and made herself a cup of coffee. A pile of dishes lay in the sink. Anneke had prepared our breakfast. She was already busy with the wash. We knew by now that on Mondays Annie had even more trouble than usual getting going. And Monday after payday was the worst of all. She made no effort to hide her lack of enthusiasm at being back. Her face was sour, her shoulders slumped. Judging from past performances it would take most of the day for her to pull out of it. Even Tasty gave her a wide berth.

Half an hour later, maybe less, Tenny knocked on the back door. His eyes were moist. With a nervous stammer and a self-conscious, inappropriate grin he announced that he and Annie were quitting. They wanted a rest. Part of our agreement had been that Annie could stop work any time she felt like it, but she would always give us a month's notice. Tenny on the other hand to qualify for a cash bonus was supposed to last out the entire research period. True, from the very beginning we had a suspicion that at the first major clove harvest we would lose them, but that danger was still some months in the future.

'You're not satisfied with our work,' Tenny said, 'so we'd better stop.' As a rule Koert Jan is gentle to a fault in meting out criticism. I used to tease him that when he swatted flies they didn't feel it. Despite his annoyance that morning with Tenny and Annie, he certainly hadn't gone overboard. We were stupefied by such a display of super-sensitivity. It was so self-serving. Was Tenny's pride really wounded? In any event how offhand he was, with how few words he dismembered our domestic life. I thought of a child I'd seen on the rocks at Kinnilow idly torturing a captive frog, pulling the limbs to their limit until finally the skin, flesh, joints tore. The child had no meanness in its expression. Rather it blinked, mildly curious about the effects of the pressure it applied. Then, as the frog came apart in its hands, it tossed the body, twitching, down into the water among the swimmers below.

59

'Only if we just stop now,' Tenny grinned, looking down, 'the people here will say you sent us away because we were thieves.'

Through the gathering storm of our anger and chagrin, suspicion flashed.

'Check the money,' Koert Jan told me. We had more or less agreed to chalk Friday night's missing sum פים to our negligence. It was the most convenient fiction available. And we had left the key to the cash drawer in its place – under the lining paper of the drawer filled with socks right above. Just in case. Now a quick count showed that over the weekend thirty thousand rupiah more had disappeared.

The hurt in Koert Jan's eyes was painful for me to see. He called Annie and Tenny in and told them we would all go together to the police straightaway to investigate the matter of the stolen money. Anneke was hovering near the back screen door with a broom. I went to shoo her away and to escape from the scene inside. Koert Jan had shouted, Annie had shrieked and stamped.

'What's wrong, Mr Eric?' Anneke asked, brushing the long hair out of her eyes with the back of her hands, cocking her head to one side.

'Some money is missing. Do you know anything about it?'

'Money? No.' Then Anneke asked how much money.

'How much?' For some reason Anneke's question struck the back of my mind as strange. Perhaps it was also the way her eyes narrowed just ever so slightly?

'Thirty thousand rupiah,' I said.

Anneke shook her head. '*Saya tidak berani*, mister.' Oh, I wouldn't dare. Apron full of clothespins, she went to hang up the wash.

Annie came rushing outside, stormed into her and Tenny's room and then hurried back inside again, clutching her purse in two hands, sandals slapping against the cement walkway. Koert Jan, I gathered as I followed Annie inside, had accused Annie of taking the money. Annie had been alone in the house

all Saturday. Furthermore she knew the house well. Right away
Tenny had taken a distance from the affair. Once he had
impressed on us his own innocence by establishing his total lack
of opportunity, he seemed to watch the further proceedings
with curious, childlike impartiality.

'Here,' Annie sobbed, and took her savings and Tenny's
from her purse and threw them at Koert Jan and me. 'Take it,
all of it. What do I want with your money? I would die rather
than touch a cent of it.' She was in agony. '*Tuntut*,' she cried,
over and over. The word was beyond us. At first I thought it
meant heartbreak or shame. Slowly it became clear it meant to
search. Annie was telling us we had to look for the money until
we found it and never rest until we did. That was the way to
prove her innocence.

'Why should she take the money *now*?' Tenny asked clinically.
'All this time we could have taken anything. The camera, the
radio, binoculars.'

'Maybe she just found the key,' Koert Jan mumbled.

'What key?' Annie cried. Tenny's list left me dizzy realising
how he, and clearly Annie, knew the contents of all our cabinets
and closets.

Looking at Annie and Tenny – he was squatting and picking
up the money Annie had crumpled and thrown to the floor – I
felt how close we had become. Koert Jan was on the point of
tears. As soon as Annie had begun to speak in her grief and
outrage, I believed her, completely. Koert Jan, too, I'm sure.
There were lines in his face I hadn't noticed a few minutes
before. Suddenly a balance had shifted: we were no longer more
sinned against than sinning. To be the butt of a false accusation
is one thing. It is another to hurl a false charge in the face of a
loved one. The circumstantial evidence against Annie was so
overwhelming, true. We had been too hasty.

Koert Jan called Tenny and Annie into our bedroom. He
pointed at the cash drawer built into the wall below the mirror.
'If you didn't take the money, Annie – and, please,' Koert Jan

paused, 'please, forgive me – I believe you didn't – that can only mean Anneke did.'

'She's trouble,' Tenny nodded, patting his hair down as he eyed his reflection in the mirror. 'She told me no one else would cut your grass the way I do. And she makes fun of how little we've saved since we came here to work.'

Annie dried her eyes on her sleeve. Koert Jan gave her a Kleenex and she blew her nose. Then in a voice like a child's she told us what we had to do. 'Call Anneke here. Tell her about the stolen money. Say that if it isn't back in its place by six o'clock, you are going to a *dukun* to ask him to punish the thief by crippling him for life.' Annie flung one arm out and twisted it back, shoulders hunched and out of line, lips coiled.

Tenny, smoothing the money he had retrieved against his chest, nodded approval. 'I know one, too. *Om* Petrus, he can do it. After you find something missing, within three days you have to go to him and tell him exactly what is gone. Then he drinks a glass of water and in the bottom he sees your property and the face of the thief. Remember, Annie, how he found your mother's watch?'

'I'm sorry, Annie.' Koert Jan did his best to express his deep regret at having accused her the way he did.

'If Anneke has taken the money,' I said, 'that's a bad thing, but it would have been much worse – '

'I didn't take it!'

'Because we're like a family,' Tenny laughed.

'Yes,' I said, touched. 'And now that we've apologised, there's no question in our minds any more, none. We know Annie is innocent.'

'*Tuntut*. Find the money, you must, that's the only way.' Annie's voice rose again. 'Call her in here. Tell her about going to the *dukun*.'

Tenny and Annie went out and told Anneke we wanted to see her. She came into the bedroom drying her hands on the front of her dress. I almost couldn't bear to confront her smile. Her performance of confused innocence had been so convincing. Koert Jan pointed to the drawer and told her that someone had unlocked the drawer and stolen money. There wasn't the slightest perceptible change of expression on her face. Koert Jan went on to say that if the money wasn't back in its place by six o'clock we had decided to ask a *dukun* to punish the thief by crippling one of his arms for life.

Anneke tilted her head to one side, licked her bottom lip with the point of her tongue. Above our heads an avocado fell on to the tin roof explosively, making all of us jump.

'That money wasn't stolen, mister,' Anneke said softly, almost seductively. 'I found it.'

'You found it?'

'It was under the mattress.'

'Where is it now?'

After some thought, Anneke answered, 'I took it home to keep it safe for you.'

I didn't know where to look. Such a feeble lie. But clearly we were supposed to accept it without question.

Koert Jan, to my growing annoyance, was beginning to enjoy the situation. Through the incident he had learned, incontrovertibly, how strongly even the younger generation was still susceptible to magical beliefs.

'Go now,' Koert Jan told Anneke, 'bring it back.'

'That's the first money I ever heard of,' was Tenny's animated comment, 'that can climb down out of a drawer and walk across the floor to hide under a mattress.' He made walking gestures with two of his fingers turned downwards in the air. 'That's something I'd like to see.' Annie was very happy, swatting Tenny's arm with a dish towel. Vindication made her glow.

'If' – Koert Jan drew his breath, looked from Annie's face to Tenny's and back again – 'if you want to go – '

'No,' Tenny cut in, 'we'll stay.'

'You have to have someone to help,' Annie went on,

'otherwise you would have to stop your work. Even the neighbors' – Annie pointed with her small round chin towards the house where too much praying went on to suit her tastes – 'they say you are good people, trying to help us have children.'

Annie's invoking the neighbors made us realise we should try to keep news of the theft from spreading. Given the shrieking and carrying on already past, however, we were probably too late. Tenny dashed outdoors. When he came back a few seconds later he was carrying something behind his back, coyly. His smile took on a frozen quality as he looked back and forth from Koert Jan to me. My heart skipped a beat at the idea that some piece of lost property was about to be returned. 'What is it, Tenny?' My heart skipped two beats when Tenny held out his hand. Resting upright on his palm was Dr Voetberg's white paper cup.

'*Kosong*,' Tenny said. Empty. He turned the cup upside down and shook it 'No children.'

'That's not so bad,' Annie shrugged. 'Mr Koert he doesn't have any children either.' She was – there's no other word for it – magnificent.

About an hour after Anneke had shuffled out the drive, she returned. She left thirty thousand rupiah on the dining room table, pinning the worn bills with a fruit bowl. She didn't come to speak to us. She went out to continue hanging up the wash where she'd left off. Koert Jan watched her some minutes through the window. At last he called her in.

'Where's the rest, Anneke?'

'The rest?'

'You took more.' Anneke stared at the money on the table. She bit her nails.

'Another ten thousand, mister?' she said inquisitively.

'I see. You're keeping it safe for us, I suppose?'

'It was under the mattress.'

'Fifty thousand, Anneke.'

'Oh,' Anneke said, 'that's a lot of money.'

The three of us sat down for a grueling talk which yielded no profit. Anneke kept switching stories – as if she had forgotten the combination to a lock and hoped she just might get lucky. She would sit silent for long periods of time, running a finger along the edge of the table, or picking at wisps of straw at the corner of a placemat. Sometimes she looked to me like she was singing to herself. Koert Jan explained to her how serious a thing she had done. She was young. She should consider the consequences. We were both in awe of her audacity. The second theft could only have occurred during the five minutes on Sunday when she was alone in our bedroom making up the beds, the door wide open, Koert Jan and I in the study next door. After she had come to work for us, clearly she had wasted no time in a thorough search of the premises. Now she showed not the slightest regret that she had stolen.

'Where is the rest of the money, Anneke? What did you do with it?'

'There's only twenty thousand more.'

'No, Anneke.'

'I – I lost it?' We knew Tenny and Annie were listening at the screen door. We figured they were entitled. At times I would glance up and see Tenny, a palpable shadow through the fine wire mesh, covering his mouth with both hands but failing to muffle his laughter of disbelief. 'I was carrying it home in the dark and it fell.'

'I see. Anneke, you know what happens to thieves, don't you?'

'Yes.'

'What?

'I know.'

'Thieves have their heads shaved, right? And then they're marched through the streets beating a drum and wearing the evidence of their crime on a string around their neck. Is that what you want?'

'No, mister.'

The stigma of such an event was indelible. Once a girl was known to be a *pencuri*, she would have a hard time finding a husband. She would have to leave home.

Soon Anneke dropped her story about losing the money along the trail in the dark. Instead she said she had spent the money and couldn't give it back.

'What did you spend it on, Anneke?' Koert Jan's request met with resolute silence. 'Do you have a boyfriend?'

'No,' Anneke replied with a speed wholly out of character.

'If you won't tell us, we have no choice but to take you to the *hukum tua*. We don't want this to ruin your life, Anneke. Other people wouldn't even give you this chance. All we're asking is for you to tell us. Don't be afraid.'

Anneke's response wasn't so much hardened as that her behavior made us feel she was treading air in the middle of a dream. It was as if the world around her, her immediate surroundings, including us, didn't exist, didn't matter. She seemed drugged, dazed, distant. Back and forth along the edge of the table her finger traveled.

Without accomplishing anything, we talked on until dark. Koert Jan decided then that we would all go down to Manado where Hilda Kawatu and her husband could advise us what further steps to take. Hilda would feel responsible for having introduced Anneke into our house. She would probably be more successful at evoking the truth, too, than we were.

'What about dinner?' Annie asked.

'All right, we'll eat first,' Koert Jan told her. Anneke rose and set the table. She was practically jaunty. While we were eating Annie came in and closed the back door. 'Tenny almost hit her,' Annie whispered, eyes bulging. 'She said we were the ones who told on her. And she does have a boyfriend.'

The whole way down the mountain Tenny talked. Don't ask

66

me about what. Famous Minahasa thieves, I think. Anneke sat in back with Annie, to all appearances unconcerned. We had never made the trip at this late hour and were surprised by so many signs of life along the dark road. People were bathing with water from a bamboo aqueduct, their bare backs and buttocks glistening. Small groups with motorcycles and radios were chatting, jostling each other at lay-bys. They bristled with restlessness. Eating houses built out on stilts over the cliff side of the road were full of customers, brightly lit, appealing. Cars parked out front jutted hazardously on to the road. The moon was almost new. The vast sky was laced with stars and below us the crescent shoreline of Manado blazed with lights. Out in the bay the bulk of uninhabitable islands seemed closer to the mainland than I'd ever seen them, and menacing. A few fishing boats with pulsing lamps to lure their catch drifted near the horizon. Like different kinds of cloth, the black of the sea was distinct from the black of the sky.

At the Kawatus' the front gate was locked. Everything was dark and shuttered. The sound of our car and then our voices calling a greeting brought first barks, then light. Our arrival was welcomed warmly without any trace of surprise, without question. At first we sat in the front parlor and drank ice water sweetened with orange syrup. Annie and Anneke remained in the Toyota. Tenny clambered down and hurried out back to watch television with the children of the family and the servants who lay sprawled on a rug on the dining room floor. In his shorts Hilda's husband, a retired official in the Ministry of Health, a distinguished dentist, was a dead ringer for Buddha. As we sipped our drinks he told us about his fishing plans for the coming morning. He was going to try a new system to lure the fish to bite, one that used mirrors. Koert Jan himself finally had to explain the purpose of our visit without being asked. Hilda sat forward, visibly upset. As soon as Koert Jan finished speaking, she went out to the side garden and had Anneke summoned to her.

67

Through the windows and curtains and over the sound of an American gangster film on the television, we could hear Hilda rhythmically interrogate Anneke. Hilda never once raised her voice. Her cajoling was insistent, sing-song and forceful. Koert Jan abruptly told her husband how rotten we felt about having made a false accusation. He yawned so hard his eyes disappeared. Then he ran a palm across his smooth skull and gave us the benefit of his lifetime of experience. 'Never lose your heart to anything in Indonesia,' he said. 'The people here, they don't feel anything deeply, not anger, not fidelity, and they betray easily.'

'She has confessed,' Hilda came back to say. She was wiping her chin, and her neck with a scented handkerchief. 'Both times. All the money.' Hilda then packed an overnight case. She would accompany us back to Tomohon to spend the night in order to be there to visit Anneke's parents first thing in the morning.

'She won't tell me where the money is. She's a bad girl,' Hilda said in broken English during the trip back. 'Stupid girl, *adu.* "Take me to the *hukum tua*, to the police, to the governor." These people, what they lack is education.'

Dientje, Hilda's eight-year-old daughter, sat on her mother's lap. She came along to share her mother's bed. Sometimes when Hilda would visit us and none of the children wanted to come, she would insist that Annie sleep in her room. In her whole life Hilda had never slept in a room alone.

'Whose idea was it to threaten Anneke with the *dukun*?' Hilda asked. Neither Koert Jan nor I spoke. Even without English we were sure the girls in back could follow. 'Annie's?'

'Yes.'

'Very clever.'

We were roughly half-way up the mountainside to Tomohon when it began to rain hard. First one drop, then three, then a million. Soon rivers of silt boiled on both sides of the road, eerie in the refracted glare of the Toyota's dims. In such weather boulders could come crashing down on to the road silently, or rather unheard because of the roll and clap of thunder. Even at full force the windshield wipers didn't help at all. Tenny drove carefully, wiping the inside of the front window with the heel of one hand, eyes only inches from the glass, biting his lip. At one point we had to skirt a palm tree that had skidded off a bluff and lay across most of the paved road. Our outside wheels slipped for an instant on the soft shoulder of the road. Tenny was tense with excitement. He looked over at Koert Jan and took his eyes off the road for an instant.

'Watch out!' Anneke cried. A steamroller had been left, typically, in the middle of the road. There was no time to brake but Tenny did swerve and avoid collision. Nothing, providentially, was coming in the other direction. Annie shrieked oddly after the fact and buried her face in her hands. Tenny laughed. No one said thank you to Anneke.

The sky was clear again before we lay down to sleep. The wind was high. As days go Monday had been long and full of knots. The last sounds I remember were Anneke's knocking on Tenny and Annie's door and softly calling Annie's name. But the door didn't open.

By the time I was up in the morning, Anneke was gone. Koert Jan had caught a glimpse of her through the window, out back by the garbage pit, bent double, vomiting on to the grass. 'That explains it,' he told me. 'She needed money to pay for an abortion.'

We sat down to a lavish breakfast. Hilda Kawatu had made *nasi kuning*. The badly spoiled Dientje would eat nothing else! Outside in the driveway Tenny was washing the car for all he was worth. Sponge, bucket, suds, great sweeping strokes of his young arms.

While Hilda was preparing our food, Annie told her stories about Anneke which she had been keeping to herself. How Anneke was always chiding her and Tenny for not making the most of their opportunity working for us. Did they really think we would notice if little things were missing? Annie hadn't wanted to say anything before because she didn't like the way people were always telling stories. The Minahasa are fonder of nothing else. Gossip and lies are a favorite pastime. The disruption of marriages, the destruction of reputations. Consider this tidbit from the *Manado News*: 'Last Thursday during evening office hours an attractive, healthy-looking young woman went in to see Dr Pitoy. Although the waiting room was full, forty-five minutes passed before she came out again???' We never came to understand the motives behind such story-mongering, not beyond the day-to-day struggle for *gengsi*. People with nothing to be proud of in their own lives could at least snipe away at the pride of others. Annie was uncommonly discreet. We had sadly undervalued her moral sense.

Annie told Hilda how Anneke's boyfriend had urged Anneke to tell him what was in the house. She thought Anneke had probably given him the money so he would marry her. 'Saturday,' Annie said, 'Anneke received 18,000 rupiah from her savings club. She bought herself a dress and shoes. She didn't give anything to her parents.'

So much for the abortion theory. Instead of Koert Jan's being relieved, however, I honestly think he was disappointed at losing his last chance to attribute a motive to Anneke's theft that somehow might be pathetic enough to make her act seem forgivable.

Hilda was disturbed to find Anneke gone in the morning. She persuaded us to send Tenny with the Toyota to Anneke's home to search for her. He was just backing out the driveway when Anneke returned by herself on foot. When Hilda asked where she had been, she said quietly and with dignity that she had gone to her parents to tell them we were accusing her of being a thief. We didn't have time to worry what lies she might have made up. Hard on Anneke's heels her mother and father appeared, visibly distraught. Tasty was like a wild dog. He couldn't bark hard enough. Finally Tenny had to shut him in the workshed.

Hilda invited Anneke's parents inside to talk with us. We drank coffee and made conversation about this and that. The Indonesian way. Anneke helped Annie serve the coffee. For once Anneke wasn't smiling. Her father was trembling.

'I have my horse,' he said when we were talking about the few crops we were trying to grow in the garden out back, 'if you want fertiliser.'

Dientje kept clinging to her mother, half-climbing on to her lap. Hilda would slap her away but the next moment the child would be back again. Annie saw what was going on. She took Dientje by the hand to lead her outside. Dientje tried to tug free but Annie simply lifted her from the ground and carried her through the back door. The door slammed and then a full minute of silence must have followed.

Finally, in the softest voice we had ever heard her use, Hilda spoke. '*Bapak, Ibu*, your daughter has stolen money from these visitors to our country.'

'Proof?' her mother asked.

'On the table.' Koert Jan pointed, the thirty thousand rupiah were still there under the fruit bowl.

'She confessed to me,' Hilda added, 'everything.'

Anneke's father seethed with anger. Her mother said he had wanted to thrash Anneke and send her away. Now he struck a fist against his chest and talked emotionally about his shame. '*Maaf, maaf.*' Pardon, pardon. He was poor but there was no one who could say he was ever dishonorable. He would pay back the money, all of it. A lifetime of hardwork and deprivation showed in his face.

'*Bapak*' – speaking slowly and giving her words equal weight, Hilda kept her eyes down – 'despite what has happened, these gentlemen did not want to bother you. Nor do they want now to make a case out of it. But Anneke' – Hilda shook her head – 'is

71

uncoöperative. She won't tell what she did with the rest of the money.'

At that Anneke's father rose and went outside to talk with her. Her mother appeared to look out the window in another direction altogether, towards the Lokun, but clearly she was straining to hear. She held a handkerchief which she sat twisting into knots. The old man's gaunt face was bloodless when he returned. 'She's no child of mine,' he said.

With a display of petulance, Anneke's mother pushed her chair back and went to try her hand. Presently she entered the house again. 'Anneke used the money to buy earrings,' she said. 'Gold hoops.'

'Well,' Koert Jan spoke up, 'then she can sell them.' Gold was bought and sold at a great rate in Manado, by weight almost exclusively.

'No, they are antique earrings. Anneke bought them from a relative, an aunt who was visiting and has gone away again.' Anneke's mother inspired distrust. You felt in your marrow she had been in similar situations before, more than once, and nothing else mattered to her as much as muddling through, snatching her guilty daughter from disgrace. Perhaps she, too, as a younger woman, had slipped? Perhaps Anneke's silence was possible because she could count on her mother's complicity?

During our interview, we could hear Annie and Anneke laughing together out back. Tenny was on the lawn, blowing soap bubbles from detergent and water cupped in his palm. We all sat and watched, wishing if only life could be that easy.

The outcome of Hilda's mediation was an agreement that another thirty thousand rupiah would be repaid to us the following Monday. The rest, twenty thousand, Anneke would pay back gradually out of her salary. (Later in the day Anneke's mother brought the gold earrings to show us, folded in a handkerchief. At dinner Annie claimed these were the very ones the woman herself had been wearing earlier in the day.

72

Neither Koert Jan nor I could be sure. We kicked ourselves for not being more observant.) Anneke's father thanked us effusively for not contacting the authorities. There was still one more thing he had to ask of us. Not to send Anneke away. People would know then that the girl was a thief. Instead, he said, she should stay and work for us for nothing. Hilda, who was not at all happy with the request, suggested that indeed by allowing Anneke to stay we might help rehabilitate her. This suggestion, I must say, had originally been Koert Jan's and Hilda had opposed it vehemently. Now, however, under pressure of the moment, in the face of Anneke's distraught father, she advanced it as if it were her own.

The next week was singularly uncomfortable. We were mostly in the field. At home, however, it didn't escape us that Anneke was so cheerful. She never showed a trace of remorse. Tenny called her 'sporting', the way she carried on as if nothing at all had happened. The following Monday, the day designated for repayment, Anneke's mother arrived at the appointed time, but she brought only five thousand rupiah with her. Of course she didn't come without excuses. Koert Jan wasn't having any of it. He told her he wanted the entire sum now, at once, or he would report the case.

Quite apparently the woman had miscalculated, judging us to be sweeter and softer than we are. 'Yes, yes,' she agreed. 'I will go home and speak to my husband.' She left us, heading for the main road.

'Why isn't she taking the shortcut through the fields?' I asked. At that Koert Jan went after her with Tenny in the Toyota. Just as they reached the main road, they saw her stop a *bendi*, climb in and set off in the opposite direction from Kasuraten.

'If I thought she wouldn't notice me, I would have followed her,' Koert Jan told me later. Instead he had Tenny force the *bendi* to the side of the road and obliged Anneke's mother to board the Toyota. First they stopped back at our place. Then, together with Anneke and the few belongings she had with her, an extra skirt, a hairbrush, a prayer book, we drove to their home.

Anneke's father was asleep on the porch, his mouth open. At first when he woke he seemed relieved to have been called back from a grim dream to safety. Yet once he saw us he began to shake. Koert Jan briefly explained what had happened. Without a word the old man went behind a curtain inside and came back with a small black tin box. Methodically he counted out the full sum of his debt to us. When he was through, only a few coins remained in the box. His wife wept openly now. Anneke hung back. She was cool, indifferent to what she saw going on.

'Goodbye, mister,' she said to us as we left. 'Don't forget to come for the manure.'

When Annie and Tenny had returned that morning from their Sunday off in Tinoör, they had in fact let us know that their parents were unanimous that Anneke had to go. Annie and Tenny couldn't stay behind and work in the house with a thief. Anneke might poison them at any time. Or, as Hilda later said, Anneke might poison us.

'It was the boyfriend,' Annie said, 'that's where your money went, not earrings.'

'She wouldn't tell us anything,' Tenny added.

We didn't ask them if they had told their parents how at first we had suspected, and accused Annie.

'Mr Eric,' Tenny said, 'he was the most upset.'

'Yes,' agreed Annie, 'he couldn't eat.'

'But Mr Koert,' I told them, 'couldn't sleep.'

'"Eighty Thousand",' Tenny chuckled. 'That's what they're calling her already in Kasuraten.'

IX

Our family grew close-knit. Koert Jan cut Tenny's hair. Annie mended our clothes. Tasty had a litter, and we gave pups to Tenny's and Annie's families. We went together to the films in Tomohon. *Taxi Driver* was playing. The electricity was weak, so the image flickered and the sound was slurred. Indonesian sub-titles covered half the screen. The audience cracked groundnuts open, howled at antics they didn't understand. The violence notwithstanding, I felt homesick for a big city. Annie covered her eyes, buried her head rather than see bloodshed. Tenny would rap with his knuckles on her skull to sound the all clear. Later Tenny said he felt a bond with Robert de Niro. After all, both were drivers.

Our fitful attempts to replace Anneke and find someone to keep Annie company ended in vain. We were, I suppose, a bit leary of newcomers after our experience. Hilda did her best to come up with suitable candidates but more and more time passed without our acquiring another helper. Then Nora entered the picture. Nora was alert, intelligent and had impeccable references to vouch for her integrity. Since the age of three she had lived in the local Protestant orphanage.

We met Nora while she was helping to prepare an exhibition stand about the children's home for the *Sidung Raya*, the national convocation of Indonesian churches held once every four years on a different island. At Nora's age she should by rights have left the orphanage and be living with a foster family in preparation for setting up a household of her own. She was finishing the last year of high school. The school was only a quarter of a mile from our house but to reach it from the children's home she had to walk nearly an hour and a half each way – in dry weather.

From the beginning it was clear that part of Nora's motive for wanting to work for us was to get away from the current director of the children's home, a minister, himself an alumnus of the home. He beat children. He refused schooling to some. He mocked others. All his whims were justified by his being an orphan himself and therefore supposedly knowing better than anyone else what was good for the children in his charge. You couldn't help noticing *Domine* Tomengko. He drove through Tomohon on a motor scooter with a punctured exhaust pipe, wearing an electric-blue crash helmet, looking for ears to bend. He had no equal for buttonholing people in the street and haranguing them about the decline of morals and values. All he needed was to suspect that something might offer the children pleasure, Nora told us, and he would exert himself to the utmost to prevent its happening. If he learned there was a certain food the children liked more than others, he would strike the offending favorite from the menu.

Once the wives of foreigners in Tomohon initiated a toy workshop at the children's home. The sale of simple toys made by the children themselves would pay for outings to the sea or nearby sulphur springs. For years the project struggled at a loss made good out of these women's own pockets. At last the workshop began to earn its own way. Children came back from a first bus excursion to Bitung full of excitement, ready to work all the harder. *Domine* Tomengko stepped in and put a stop to the workshop then and there. 'Toys,' he sneered. 'Come, what do children here need with toys? Or charity for that matter.'

With an escort of giggling schoolmates, Nora herself came to visit us and to urge us to accept her in our home. Annie took to her instantly. She admired Nora's cleverness. When we approached the social committee of the children's home, composed of the wives of leading community members, they thought that Nora's moving in with us for a year would be a valuable step in the direction of her eventual deinstitutionalisation. While Nora was with us we, of course, would pay her school fees and, for the few hours a day of housework she would perform, a salary as well.

Everything seemed set but then Nora made a bad mistake.

She informed the director she was leaving, as if the matter had already been determined without deference to him or to his authority. 'Imagine,' he himself told us, blinking up through his rimless spectacles, 'a child who comes to her father one day and thanklessly announces that she is going away. Where is such a child's feeling? Something must be lacking in her upbringing, wouldn't you say?'

At first, however, Tomengko didn't dash our hopes. He asked us to display a little patience, to wait until after *Sidung Raya*. Nora was going to have her hands full delivering information to the public about the activities of the children's home.

'It doesn't bother you that she has that funny eye?' he asked. Nora had one wall-eye. 'After a time I'm afraid it can become annoying. A pity that.'

Preparations for *Sidung Raya* long under way grew even more hectic as the opening date approached. Police, army, religious groups – all donated labor. Civil servants in the entire province had, by decree, renounced ten per cent of their salaries for several months to meet the costs of the occasion. Plenary sessions would be held in a vast new assembly hall built so that no pillars inside would block the view of any delegate no matter how distant from the speaker's platform. The choicest materials, including marble for the entrance hall, were being used. Because Tomohon had no hotel facilities, housing for delegates – some two thousand five hundred were expected – was being requisitioned from local residents. Our spare room, for example, would hold two visitors for seven or eight nights – very much against our inclination.

President Suharto himself would come to open the *Sidung Raya* at a rally held in the municipal football stadium in Manado. A crucifix fifteen meters high had been erected for the occasion. It was made out of lightbulbs. When the president pounded down the opening gavel, the cross would flash on. The principal theme of the pending *Sidung Raya* was the role of the Church in a changing Indonesia. The 'sub-theme' was the Church's function in aiding the poor.

On the morning of Suharto's arrival, the sky above us swarmed with security helicopters. Tenny was entranced. Town bustled with visitors, many in splendid traditional dress. Delegates came too from Europe and the United States. The petrol pump, finished in the nick of time, broke down under heavy use so that profiteers with jerry-cans made a killing. Although eat, pray and discuss were the order of the day, the conference soon resembled an extravagant fun fair more than anything else. Regional dances in costume, Hammond electric organ recitals, barbecues, flagpole sitting.

On the third day, a venerable *dayak* poet from Kalimantan created a major sensation. At his turn to speak to a full assembly hall, the shriveled old man recited a new poem. Only slowly did his listeners fully appreciate the enormity of what they heard. Mincing no words, the poet denounced the colossal waste of *Sidung Raya*. His poem asked if they too didn't feel sick to their stomachs at the sight of a cross lighting up which cost ten million rupiah and whose sole purpose was *gengsi*. A blaze of shame, he called it.

The Panitia, the leadership committee of army officers, retired clergy, hospital administrators and the like, did not take kindly to the poet's complaint. When he folded the sheet from which he had read his verses and groped back to his seat, infirm with age, there was no applause.

After an evening's impassioned huddle, the Panitia, although admittedly none of their number was a poet, emerged with verses of their own. Their creation, in stammering rhyme, was scalding in its contempt for the *dayak*'s lack of vision. Once upon a time hadn't Christ Himself been anointed by Mary Magdalene who poured a cruse of precious oil over His head? Students who saw carped about extravagance. Why, let them sell the oil and distribute the proceeds to the poor! Christ silenced them with a rebuke: 'The poor are with you for all time, whereas I am with you but for a minute.' Well then, the composition of the Panitia closed on a note of triumph, the splendor of *Sidung Raya* was nothing less than a local re-enactment of biblical history.

Evenings during *Sidung Raya* we would wander uphill with Tenny and Annie to mix with the crowds thronging various stalls and refreshment tents. When we visited Nora at her stand, we never talked long – as if nervous someone might be spying on us. Odd, there was clearly nothing to keep us from freer contact, but somehow we thought it wasn't wise. Annie urged us again and again to find a way to help Nora.

Feelings were still running high about the *dayak*'s revolutionary poem when one evening we ran into the director of the children's home. He was in a lather. The *Sidung Raya*, he informed us, had exceeded its budget of five hundred million rupiah. Villages were donating choice suckling pigs by the hundred. Small fortunes in goldfish were being given away to feast the delegates. 'It is one sustained orgy of pride.' The dormitories of the children's home needed a new roof. Was that too much to ask? Should the children sleep in the rain? *Domine* Tomengko shifted his crash helmet into his left hand and slicked back his hair with his right. He made no effort to keep his voice down and seemed gratified if small groups stopped to listen. 'Maybe tomorrow the roof will collapse. The children will be crushed in their beds. They know it, the members of the Panitia, they do. And still they turn down my requests and say there are not enough funds. Hypocrites! If they had to sleep in those beds, then there'd be money on the table, and fast.'

Koert Jan thought that the man's taking us into his confidence was a good sign. He was relenting, and would allow Nora her freedom. From members of the social committee we had learned that Tomengko's harsh practices were common knowledge. Among themselves the women even spoke of him as 'disturbed'. Yet no one dared speak against him openly to the church leaders. Tenny helped us figure out why. The director raised chickens and pigs on the children's home grounds, with the labor of the children. He taught them farming, was how he put it. The produce, especially eggs, highly coveted, he distributed as *oleh-oleh* among church elders. It was not clear where the original capital came from, some overseas organisation.

After two weeks *Sidung Raya* ended with fireworks, song and a candlelight procession. Local life returned to normal. There was a great deal of litter and garbage about, that's all, but no one seemed to mind particularly, or to try to do anything about it. Inside the colossal assembly hall, until some other use could be thought of for the building, a dozen ping-pong tables were installed. With even two or three games going on at the same time, so sharp were the acoustics, it sounded, Tenny said, like Promesta. One morning not long after sun-up Nora came to our door in tears. It took Annie some time to comfort her enough so she could speak. 'Please,' Nora said, 'ask him one last time. Not that it will help,' and she fell to sobbing again.

That same day we arrived at the children's home, a cluster of four large, ramshackle wood houses enclosing a campus on three sides, at the close of the evening meal. Annie came, too, but as soon as we parked she disappeared into the 'baby house', the wing of the institution, overcrowded, where children up to the age of three were looked after. Here a midwife from Bali and her husband, a limb-fitter at the provincial hospital in Manado, did their best to look after twenty-four infants, several of them only a few months old. Tenny chose instead to stick close to our heels.

Despite the informality of our previous contacts, this time *Domine* Tomengko chose to receive us like official guests. Delegates to *Sidung Raya* had not paid any of the inspection tours to the children's home which had been scheduled. Instead they had gone by the chartered busload to island beaches and famous undersea gardens in the vicinity of Manado.

'Good evening,' the director bowed to us. 'So happy to see

you again.' He introduced us to his wife. She was a much older woman. Slightly taller than he, stoop-shouldered, alarmingly thin, with large, sad eyes.

'Pleased to meet you,' she said and shook our hands. 'I've heard such nice things about you from Mrs Batuna.'

'From whom?' I asked.

'Anneke's mother.'

Tomengko showed us around the place, pointing out all the disrepair, all the shortages and deficiencies. He worked himself into an unpleasant mood. Tenny was his echo. If Tomengko called the state of the kitchen disgraceful, Tenny agreed, 'Disgraceful.' If to show us how rotten a window-frame was, Tomengko poked a hole in it with his finger, Tenny poked a hole in it too. Koert Jan didn't help much either. He asked to see the pigs and chickens, the alleged base of Tomengko's power. Somehow Koert Jan was affable enough to get away with it, but just.

'I'm sorry, but they're sleeping,' Tomengko said.

'Maybe next time.'

Suddenly there was a flash of lightning and the blue sky swiftly darkened. Rain began to come down in big, heavy drops as we dashed back to the dining hall-recreation building. There we found the tables had been pushed aside, stacked on each other. Benches were arranged in rows divided by a central aisle. A curious kind of religious amateur hour was then staged for our edification. Among the very youngest of the children, soloists stepped forward to face the crowded room, to pray, to recite from the gospels.

Most of the audience paid no attention, swinging their legs, stifling yawns, holding hands or pinching each other. I kept my eyes on Tomengko. His lips moved silently in accompaniment to each successive performance. When a child forgot his lines, the director prompted him. The main act of the evening was a heart-rending song delivered by a mentally defective girl of eleven. She was fat and her clothes were too small. She screeched

81

rather than sang with full dramatic gestures and grimaces: 'Oh Mother, where are you, how can you have gone and left me so alone. I will search for you, forever, Mother. Will I find you there among the angels at God's side?' It was the first time in the evening the other children came to life, clapping, whistling, cheering. Tenny joined them.

Domine Tomengko continued the evening's programme by telling the story of his life. How he had grown up in the children's home, never knowing who his father was, discovering that his mother had been burned to death in a fire that swept the Manado nutmeg factory. How at the children's home he had learned discipline and the meaning of sacrifice and devotion. How he had the Lord to thank for everything. It was, to judge from the faces of the children, not the first time they had heard this account.

Tomengko's wife then sat behind a small harmonium to lead us all in a hymn. She played well, with her eyes closed. Tenny knew all the words. He sang out loud in a surprisingly sonorous voice.

Then it was our turn! Tomengko bowed towards us and asked for a contribution. I was still ransacking my mind for an excuse that wouldn't sound too thin and unsporting, when to my amazement, 'Yes,' I heard Koert Jan say, 'of course.' He walked over to the harmonium and Mrs Tomengko practically fell over trying to get out of his way.

'When I was a child,' Koert Jan told the room, 'there was a funny little song my mother used to sing to me. A "nursery rhyme". I always thought it was Indonesian, until I came here.' He placed his fingers spread on the keyboard and accompanied himself:

Im pompei pudernei pudernaska
impompei, impompa
im pompei pudernei pudernaska
im pompei en in pompa

While he kept playing he stood up and sat down several times, slapped the sides of the instrument and stuck his tongue out:

> *pudernesa,*
> *pudernaska,*
> *pudernesa,*
> *chira bum!*

The children squealed and hugged each other. I snuck a look at Tomengko who was fighting desperately not to crack a smile. Tenny stared at Koert Jan with his mouth open. Me, too.

'Please,' Tomengko said quietly, 'sing it again.'

The final event of the evening was a solemn prayer which *Domine* Tomengko delivered for the success of our work in Indonesia. He expressed his gratitude that we had come half-way around the world to help. 'The Lord works in mysterious ways,' he said, 'that strangers must do for us the things we should be doing for ourselves. Amen.'

'Amen,' the children said in unison.

And before we knew it, *Domine* Tomengko was walking us out to the car. We had caught no glimpse of Nora the whole visit. At times, we knew, she took refuge at the 'baby house' where she helped feed the children and prepare them for bed. It seemed clear Tomengko had staged the evening to prevent us from raising the issue we had come to discuss. At the last minute, however, when Tomengko stuck out his hand to say goodbye, Koert Jan rejected the director's scenario.

'Actually,' he began, 'we came to see you this evening with a request.'

'These visits are good for the children,' *Domine* Tomengko smiled without parting his lips, 'you must come more often.'

'We would like your consent for Nora to come to work for us. It would be a step for her towards self-sufficiency.'

'I'm sorry, who are we talking about now?'

'Nora.'

'Oh yes, Nora.'

'We understand that the subject has given you some distress. Nora was not diplomatic when she spoke to you. Perhaps it is our own fault and we should have come to you as soon as the social committee made the suggestion.' Koert Jan was at his best. Blond and beaming, charming, fair, firm. 'We're sorry but I hope you won't allow our mistake, or Nora's, to be a reason for preventing her – '

Again Tomengko stuck out his hand to say goodnight. 'If Nora likes to, she can. I have told her that.' His grin at our evident surprise had enough of a hint of the sinister to prepare us for what followed. 'It is her decision. After all, Nora is not exactly a little girl anymore, is she?'

'You've changed your mind then?'

'Not at all. I am only repeating to you what I told Nora. If she chooses to go, I tear up her record, that's all.' With both hands *Domine* Tomengko shredded invisible documents into little pieces and then blew them away. 'If she goes, she will not be taken back. Never.' Destruction of Nora's record, we well knew, would signify that the Church would not sponsor the further education which she had been promised. In a year we would be gone. Besides which, a trial period, especially for Nora to have a chance to see if she was happy with us, had been the social committee's recommendation. 'If you have the girl's best interests at heart, my friends, good. She can count then on your generosity, not ours.'

Domine Tomengko is one of the few people I've ever met unable to inject any human warmth into his face or voice. When he tried, the tone was painfully false. His heart had been stunned as a child, clearly, and he would never recover. It was impossible not to think back on all those lightbulbs in the giant cross, a mountain of broken glass the morning after.

Annie came running when Tenny, a bit too insistently, began honking the horn. The rain was falling steadily now, clouds

84

piling up in massive bales to blot out the moon. We could see almost a hundred faces pressed to the dining hall windows watching us as we swung around and started down the drive. Annie was chattering away at high speed about the babies. How beautiful they were, all of them.

At the gate Nora was hiding in the shrubbery with two girlfriends. She popped out to talk with us. One eye stared lifelessly to the side, the other was distraught. In a rapid whisper she confided something to Tenny and then melted away without even greeting us. I had learned to focus on her good eye, but tonight that wasn't possible for me.

We drove home. Tenny told us what Nora had said, laughing at places where we would never laugh, but by now we were almost accustomed to such symptoms of embarrassment.

'Nora says the director has threatened to report her to the Church board. Tonight when he saw you coming, he sent her out of the room and he made his threat.'

'Report her for what?' Koert Jan asked. It was raining so hard by now that we could hardly see anything on the road ahead.

'He says he knows the real reason she wants to work for you.' Tenny leaned forward, chest against the steering-wheel. Torrents of rain sent the glare of our headlamps back into our eyes. 'Sex.'

X

Hilda Kawatu invited us to the wedding of her brother Robert. Hong to his friends. He was a medical student. Yvonne, the lucky girl, came from a prominent old Minahasa family. She, too, was studying to become a doctor. Hilda was exasperated with them for marrying before completion of their degrees. Her own parents had not sent her to school past the elementary

85

level when all the special Chinese schools on Java, where Hilda was raised, were closed down by the Indonesian government.

'Robert went to school. He was a boy. But if he had a flat tire on his bicycle and my father wanted to go to the movies, Robert missed school until there was money again to pay for the repair.'

When Hilda had married she took Robert with her to North Sulawesi and paid for his education. Hong, affable and easy-going, was an unlikely Romeo in our eyes, but to listen to the stories, despite his lack of glamor, he was quite a successful ladies' man.

To prepare for the marriage feast Hilda asked to borrow Annie for a few days. This was a bit tricky since Annie was not overly fond of our friend. Hilda was too much of an old hand at managing servants. (All in all, although the number was constantly changing, there were some eighteen people in the Kawatu household – family, connections, servants; more than five kilos of rice a day were consumed.) Hilda praised Annie to us, true, praised her liberally, but she was openly critical of Annie's faults as well. At our place Annie had grown used to running her own show. What's more, Hilda was a government official's wife, ex-official, which conferred a lofty status – one she declared she found ridiculous herself but expected others to respect.

Still, Annie agreed. She looked forward to the chance of learning how to bake some of the cakes for which Hilda was justly famous throughout Manado, especially the glowing green and pink kinds served in boats of folded leaves and made from glutinous rice, brown sugar and raspberry sweetener. When the newest restaurant had opened in Manado, for example, the owner commissioned Hilda to deliver two thousand small cakes. From her earnings she had purchased a dazzling new Japanese gas stove. She never cooked with it – all Hilda's kitchen magic was accomplished on old-fashioned, single burner kerosene units – but as a showpiece the stove brought *gengsi*.

When we arrived in Manado the evening before the ceremony, Hilda's husband was out in his garden. We came in through the garage to find him crushing battery cells into the soil at the roots of his rose bushes, convinced these would then yield larger, lusher flowers. The groom, overweight, radiantly cheerful, was padding through the house in his undershorts, a thin gold chain around his thick neck. He was slightly drunk on a filthy home brew one of Hilda's nephews was at that very moment concocting in an old oil drum at the back of the premises.

'No, thank you.' We turned down the offer of a drink. Tenny leaned over the edge of the drum, sniffed deeply, rolled his eyes and slumped in a mock-faint to the floor.

Hilda, we learned, in preparation for the big day tomorrow, was having a massage – from an old woman who walked on her back. Annie was in with them, working on Hilda's hair. We collapsed in padded armchairs in the parlor. The chairs had wheels that squeaked and rasped on the floor tiles.

'Muggy Manado,' I said. Koert Jan didn't bother to agree, but put a hand on my knee.

It was more than an hour until we saw Hilda. 'Oh, bah,' she cried, emerging from the bedroom in her robe, hurrying towards us where we sat, holding her electric hair drier out in front of her at arm's length. 'It stinks.' Hilda's hair hung wet and limp, cleaving to her skull. She pushed the snout of the machine first under Koert Jan's nose, then mine. 'What do you smell?'

We smelled nothing surprising.

'A second ago' – Hilda sniffed at the chrome opening of the blower – 'it stank of dead fish.' Her voice swooped low. 'It's her.'

'Her?'

'Tineke.'

87

By now we had become close enough to Hilda for her to trust us with stories which previously she had suppressed out of fear we would find her ridiculous. She once sent us a message, for example, that the outboard motor of her husband's proa was broken and so we had to cancel a fishing expedition. We knew the Kawatus had a reserve motor. Deft questioning of the messenger by Koert Jan elicited the real truth. Hilda's husband had lost six teeth in a dream, a symbol of death all the more alarming because exactly six of us had been planning to go out together in the boat.

One guise in which spirits manifest themselves, Hilda, placing the hair drier on the table in front of us, explained, was through incongruous odors. Tineke was Robert's former girlfriend. Tineke – a photo album was produced – was very beautiful. She had, in fact, once been elected Miss North Sulawesi. Pale, with Caucasian features, long-limbed, she resembled in her photos a lean Sophia Loren, jittery. Tineke worked in the pharmacy of Gunang Wenang, the provincial hospital. Robert walked in one day in a white jacket and they fell in love at first sight. Then one fateful afternoon Tineke caught Robert sitting on the sofa in Hilda's house with his arm around another girl. Tineke shrieked and ran out the door. She headed straight for the pharmacy where she swallowed two containers of rat poison and died an ugly, very painful death.

Three days later, beautiful as ever but very calm, Tineke had appeared to Robert in a dream. She said she had acted wrongly and she was sorry. She should have given Robert a chance to explain and not let her emotions run away with her. She asked Robert to forgive her. She asked him to look after her old father. And in a final request she asked Robert to see that a tombstone was raised at her grave.

Hilda turned the page of the photo album and there stood Robert (now visible in the flesh in the depths of the kitchen drinking another toast among his friends) unveiling a large marble tombstone. The stone, a close-up showed, was inscribed: True Love Lasts Forever. The following pages had a number of other photos of Robert laying asters on the grave, or leaning against the headstone casually, smiling.

'Now' – Hilda picked up the hair drier and waved it through the air – 'Tineke has come back to give a sign she approves of Robert's getting married.'

Hilda's husband stood in the doorway. He listened to the familiar story impassively. One stubby finger marked the place in the Kung-Fu adventure he was reading. Tineke, he told us, was one of six romantic suicides committed in Manado the preceding year. All jilted women. An Indonesian love movie was not a success if by the end the sniffling of the women in the audience didn't drown out the sound track.

'Don't tell Yvonne,' Hilda cautioned us. She sniffed again at the hair drier. 'It might upset her.'

The wedding went without a hitch. No sudden strange fish odors, no possession. Actually it was a double ceremony. For Robert to marry in the church, he had to be baptised first. Hilda and her husband met Yvonne's parents for the first time at the church door. 'Von's father, a small secretive man in a rumpled suit, worked for Pertamina, the state oil company. He was rumored to have a secret fortune in a bank in Singapore. Up until the last minute no one had been sure he would condescend to attend the wedding. 'Von, he thought, deserved something far better than she was getting.

The bride herself typically wore a thick coat of make-up. True to her formal role she did not smile all day. A bride is supposed to be beautiful in a unique way on the day she marries. She presents a mask of perfection to the world. A *panci* had been hired to attend to Yvonne's hair and make-up. A few minutes before the ceremony began, Hilda managed to lure the *panci* outside the church and they disappeared together into the back of our Toyota. When she emerged, a few thousand rupiah poorer, she, too, had lips and eyes unlike any we'd ever seen her with before. Annie and she had done their best to imitate a magazine photo and create a hair style called the 'Lady Di Look'. I'm afraid even Hilda was aware the attempt had been misconceived.

Later Tenny asked us to feel his hair. It was stiff and sticky with scented spray. 'I didn't have to pay anything, Mr Koert,' he said, 'don't worry.'

We threw rice at the couple when they came out of the church. 'Annie's dress had more lace,' Tenny whispered too loud for comfort. 'It cost fifteen thousand rupiah to rent.'

The reception that afternoon was lavish. It was held downtown in the upstairs of a simple restaurant. The restaurant provided drinks. Relatives and guests brought the meal. When the wedding party arrived, there was a knife fight in progress in the muddy street below but the antagonists paused to admire the company on their way in. Upstairs Robert and Yvonne changed into *adat* costumes, special batik cloth in blues and browns. They sat in large peacock-back rattan chairs at the end of the long room whose walls were hung with twists of crepe paper and with artificial flowers. A number of tables pushed end to end stood in the center of the hall covered with a mouth-watering assortment of countless different dishes. Guests sat in folding iron chairs ranged along the walls. Spaced all around the room there were double glass doors, floor to ceiling, that opened out on to small balconies.

Shortly after we arrived a young woman came up to greet us. She was wearing a tight, high-collared dress of blue raw silk together with enormous diamond earrings and the largest diamond pendant I had ever seen. We spoke for some minutes about how we were enjoying our stay in Indonesia.

'Who was that?' Koert Jan asked – in character – when she walked away.

'That,' I told him, 'was Dr Nancy.'

The meal itself turned out to be a fiercely competitive sprint. Dozens and dozens of cameras, flashbulbs popping everywhere, gave the starting signal. Children, uncomfortable in dress clothes, began to chase each other under the table and to throw food down over the balconies into the street. I was still making a selection from the tempting array of dishes when the first grease-lined, empty plates began to clatter on to the removal trolley.

Even busy as she was, Hilda kept circling back to see we were all right. We had teased her into washing off the *panci*'s make-up. Undone by Manado damp, her Lady Di Look had curled back to its familiar shape. Now she was glowing, high on compliments for her cakes. She even managed to forget for an instant what a serious error Robert was making by marrying before he had a reliable income.

'Eat, eat,' Hilda urged us.

'Smell anything odd?' Koert Jan asked her, holding his plate, heaped with large shrimp from Ujung Pandang, under her nose. Hilda grew serious. She looked left and right to be sure no one was watching, then leaned forward and sniffed.

'Odd? No.' She sniffed again, pushing the shrimp about with her fingers. 'No, do you?'

'A second ago,' Koert Jan said, 'I could have sworn it smelled like an electric hair drier.'

'Koert Jan!' Hilda laughed so loud half the room turned to look. She covered her mouth with both hands and fled.

To be able to enjoy my meal without rushing I drifted out on to one of the little balconies. Here, together with potted plants not in the best of health, I found Hilda's husband. His hands on the railing, he stood watching the moon.

'Big day,' I ventured, mouth full. He nodded. Hilda's husband had always struck me as silly, idle, absent. A sweet man, well-intentioned, but, well, something of a charlatan. In the grasping culture of the Minahasa his snips and snaps of easy wisdom were like fish out of water. And I suppose I found his gentleness the most upsetting, disquieting of all. That night on the small balcony, however, while he smoked a cigarette between two straight fingers, his face expressionless, I had doubts about my ability to judge, to see. Perhaps he really understood more than all the rest of us put together.

'Almost full,' I said inadequately, 'the moon.'

'Are you enjoying yourself?'

I nodded, aware of my unhappiness. 'Hong and Yvonne' – there was a limit to the silence I could take while he stood there smiling at me – 'they seem very much in love.'

'Do you know the story of Buddha and the prostitute?' he asked.

'Yes,' I said, lying for some reason.

'It's one of my favorites.'

The highlight of the wedding reception was the cutting of the cake, a many-tiered white affair with monumental icing. Bride and groom fed each other a piece as a symbol of how they would cherish and care for one another. Then they fed their parents-in-law a piece as well – Hilda and her husband standing in for Robert's absent parents – symbolic of the fact that from now on the newlyweds would lead independent lives. We were hard put to believe what we were witnessing was an authentic Indonesian ritual.

'I thought they'd have a bigger cake,' Tenny said hoarsely from my elbow. We had left him waiting downstairs, guarding the car. He wasn't good, however, at being left out. Step by step he had crept upstairs to watch the party. Hong had spotted him peering through the railing and had put a plate in his hands. 'When Annie and me married, they couldn't fit the cake through the door. Look, Mr Eric,' he said, 'all Chinese.' There was an unpleasant note in his voice, rancorous. 'The only real Indonesians in the place are me and the bride.'

The Kawatus wanted us to spend another night in Manado, but we'd had enough of crowds and wanted to sleep. Whenever we were the Kawatus' guests, Hilda and her husband vacated their room, over our protests. The sheets on their gigantic bed were nylon which meant near suffocation for us in the oppressive climate. There was a rotating fan at bedside but if we left it on Koert Jan was guaranteed to wake up with a stiff neck. All the rest of the Kawatu household, eighteen strong, could sleep with ease in a room with lights burning, loud music playing, the floor trembling from an earthquake. Only Koert Jan and I, offered every possible comfort, couldn't sleep a wink.

By the time we started our drive home, Tenny's humor had vastly improved. As the Toyota climbed, the air turned fresh and the moon floated low ahead of us. Annie, exhausted from days of hard work, slumped asleep in back, pans full of left-over food from the wedding between her feet. Tenny grew more and more animated. He was full of a get-rich-quick scheme.

'Dr Nancy's husband, it's his idea. Smart, together wth the bride's father. Maybe you could get in on it, too, Mr Koert, Mr Eric.' We were so tired we could hardly pretend to listen. 'The way it works is Dr Nancy uses her friends in health to say that here and there there's been a report of a mad dog.

'People here think if you eat a mad dog you get mad yourself. So this report will make the price of dog drop to almost nothing. Then I go out in a van with lots of football jerseys and shoes and trade them for the dogs suddenly nobody wants.'

At this point from behind Annie cuffed the back of Tenny's head. 'Fine idea,' she mocked. 'Then they'll start calling you *RW*.'

Annie was up at dawn the next day to bake us the kinds of cakes she had helped Hilda prepare for the wedding. She tried and she tried. The consistency was all wrong. Miserable puddles of pink. Annie shed tears of frustration.

'She tricked me!' Annie blurted out. 'Oh! Oh! She wants to keep the recipe her secret.'

The following weekend Hilda and Dientje drove up to spend

a few days with us. To swim, gossip, to spin out Hilda's pet fantasy of a trip to Europe. When Hilda went into the guest room to put away her case, she gave a cry and staggered out. We hurried to see what was the matter. A ridge of white powder lay sprinkled in a circle on the floor all around her bed. Above the wash basin on the glass shelf there stood an empty container. Rat poison.

'*Mati*,' Hilda gasped. Death. 'It's the same one Tineke swallowed.'

Koert Jan called Annie in to explain.

'Droppings,' she said, 'on the floor. And see – ' she pulled the sheets on the bed loose and showed us toothmarks, small holes near the edge. Then she curled her lips back and gnashed her teeth. Hilda stood by and said nothing, but still her hands pressed against her heart. 'I found this' – Annie picked up the can of poison – 'there' – she pointed to the shed. No doubt it was a relic from Louise Pressman's sanitary epoch in the house.

'All right, Annie,' Koert Jan sighed. 'Clean it up.'

I don't think Annie's straight face really fooled anyone. It was Tenny in fact who swept the poison up, whistling, laughing to himself.

Late into the night we talked with Hilda. Dientje lay with her head on her mother's lap, her face so querulous by day untroubled in sleep. Hilda spoke more confidentially to us than ever before. She stroked Dientje's hair and told us she was frightened what racial tension might mean for the future of her children. There were riots in Jakarta, disturbances kept out of the papers.

'But surely no one wants trouble here,' Koert Jan argued. 'The civil war is still so fresh in memory.'

Hilda warned us not to be deceived by appearances, by the western-looking surface of things. 'A child can be starving,' she said, 'but put a shirt or dress on it and no one will suspect.' The well-fed Dientje stirred in her sleep, her dry lips coming apart briefly with a sticking sound. 'Here everyone might wear a smile,' Hilda looked up at us, 'but watch out.'

XI

The *cingkeh* harvest was now almost upon us. Further south in the province the crop was already ripe. Any day now Tenny and Annie would be gone. We felt it in our bones. The only uncertainty was how they would manage the break.

Formerly prosperity in North Sulawesi came from palm trees. There remain hundreds of copra-smoking huts, great mounds of discarded, fibrous husks. Yet today that the region is one of the richest in the whole archipelago of Indonesia is thanks not to coconuts, but to *cingkeh*. The government subsidises the price of cloves, the basic ingredient used in the manufacture of *kretek* cigarettes. Everyone smokes in Indonesia, from small children on up. At roadside *warong*s you can even buy cigarettes one at a time.

The clove industry, still relatively new in North Sulawesi, ten to fifteen years old in many places, has changed life totally and made the area, to put it mildly, a bizarre one for development co-operation. To flourish, clove trees need a cooler environment than the coast around Manado has to offer. Inland heights, the sharply pitched valleys between hills, are ideal. Here some double cropping occurs, with maize or fruit trees planted among clove saplings, but profits from *cingkeh* have been so overwhelming that farmers tend to be negligent about raising anything else.

Once every four years, approximately, there is a major clove harvest. Then *cingkeh* fever becomes epidemic. All else grinds to a halt. Towns empty out, everyone pouring into the fields to pick the crop. People sleep at the base of the trees. They eat there as well, cooking over small open fires or purchasing meals from mobile catering units. They stand guard with rifles.

People come from the mountains and from the Sangihe Talaud islands. Working long days they earn a small fortune, more than they can accumulate at other jobs in years. Old men and women grow nimble again and scale long bamboo ladders. Children scamper and crawl about the base of trunks scavenging for loose cloves that fall from the fingers of those at work above. As you drive along certain stretches of road, the whole forest seems to quiver, every tree yielding clusters of bright green *cingkeh* to quick acquisitive hands.

Cingkeh was the reason why when Koert Jan and I first arrived in Manado we had to rub our eyes. In the town shops, built in large concrete blocks with protective aluminum roll screens that came rattling down each evening at closing, everything was for sale – at a price. Colour television sets, the world's best brandy, Yves St Laurent clothes, Mercedes Benz sedans, gold, diamonds, you name it. Despite a glut of capital, there is no local industry or manufacturing so that everything has to be imported. Prices were high as a rule but, we were warned, during *cingkeh* harvests, they soared still further. To win *gengsi* fieldhands, paid on a piecework basis, would storm into the city and strew their cash about. 'Give me six of your most expensive shirts.' Or they would buy a crate of wine, a true luxury, only to uncork the bottles one by one outside and pour the contents into the street. In the end they would drag themselves home, no better off than when they left.

The real money-makers were landowners. In the recent past for very little outlay speculators were able to buy up sizeable tracts suitable for cultivation of cloves. Simple farmers, without future vision, were easily swayed to part with their holdings for fistfuls of ready cash. By the time of our coming, those new owners who had acquired land, paid to have it cleared and planted with clove seedlings, had become millionaires. Among them there were many Chinese, professionals and government officials who lived in Manado, a new order of absentee landlords.

Another money-making trick dear to those who already had money was to buy up a clove crop long before maturity. This practice, known as *ijohn*, is illegal – but it continues. A poor farmer in need of cash, for a wedding, say, or more likely to meet the costs of an illness or a burial in the family, sells so many potential bushels of cloves to a money-lender. This creditor is then entitled to collect what he is owed once the crop ripens. At the time of the deal, of course, the price is but a fraction of the market price once the harvest comes in, but that may be years away. A farmer embarking on an *ijohn* transaction seldom fools himself into thinking he has struck a good bargain, but at least he gains money in hand to meet urgent needs. And it feels like he has to do nothing to earn it – not even pick the cloves.

Vast fortunes have been run up in this manner. Throughout the province, however, hatred towards exploiters was brooding. Subtler tactics also generated wealth. During a bumper harvest, resourceful women, Hilda Kawatu among them, would sally out into the fields and, busy ten, twelve, fourteen hours a day, they would buy up small quantities of cloves from fieldhands, for one hundred, two hundred rupiah at a time. Although even petty theft was severely punished, the pickers would often risk lining their pockets. In fact an honest overseer was such a rare exception that legends sprang up about them! For small buyers who applied themselves vigorously, in a few weeks the negligible profit of countless individual transactions could accumulate into enviable gains.

We were even told how doctors in remote areas went on *tournee* only once every four years or so, during the *cingkeh* harvest. They let their patients pay them in cloves for whole batteries of useless injections – vitamins, liver, subtherapeutic doses of antibiotics. And they came back rich.

Once cloves are picked, they must be dried. On certain days we found ourselves driving through village after village where there was no longer a square inch of paved surface or dirt visible. All lay covered with *cingkeh* baking in the sun, turning brown, fragrant, shriveling as it gave up moisture. Sudden rain, always a threat, could retard the drying process, erode the quality and thus the value of the final product so that every evening the *cingkeh* was gathered in again, swept up, stored indoors.

At such times profit, always popular among the Minahasa, became a god.

On the outskirts of Tinoör, Tenny and Annie had their own land, a sweeping hillside planted with *cingkeh* trees that would soon be yielding a first crop. Along the Tomohon – Manado road, long ladders of bamboo began to appear, stacked in readiness. Money was on people's lips. Hardly a day passed without Tenny's boasting about how intelligently he was going to spend the fortune about to drop into his lap. He also began to hint, broadly, that he wanted a month off to pick his own cloves. We turned East-Indian deaf. He had 'not been with us long enough for such a leave.

For the first time we began to hear of a cousin who might drive for us while Tenny was away. 'You can trust him,' Tenny would say. 'He doesn't have any *cingkeh*.' At least this maneuver seemed to suggest that Tenny valued his post with us, not just the salary, but sharing our lives. He didn't want to shut the door behind him. As for Annie, she would be needed in Tinoör, too: to cook and supervise the vital drying operations.

For weeks, ever since our failure with Nora, Annie had been acting listless and bored. She had stopped cutting flowers to put in vases. She took less care of herself, too. Her skin seemed gray, she looked dowdy all the time. It was our impression Tenny was busy constantly trying to cheer her up. Annie's neglect of housework was, alas, no longer laughable. Great dunes of dust lay under our beds. Meals reached the table scorched and smoking. Colonies of insects fed themselves on a constant supply of crumbs in the dining room. The kitchen and toilet out back stank. Still we didn't say anything. Koert Jan thought that would only make things worse.

The final parting of ways was distinctly unpleasant and abrupt. Trouble, predictably, came on a Monday. The Monday, needless to say, after pay day. At the time we had in fact taken on another helper, Rose. Rose was only fourteen, excruciatingly shy and modest. And yet, the oldest of seven children from a poor, landless family, she was an experienced, resolute worker. The same height as Annie, Rose seemed taller. Her skin and hair .had luster, as did her dark eyes – when she wasn't squeezing them shut in embarrassment as she was practically all the time. When we spoke, Rose seldom answered. We had to guess her answer out loud and then she would nod if we guessed it correctly. When she spoke, we had to ask her two or three times to speak louder.

Tenny and Annie made good-natured fun of Rose's shyness. Tenny especially was adept at capturing her intonation and imitating the exact way she would turn her head away and bury her chin in her shoulder. He was a gifted mimic. Annie had at once pulled rank, apportioning to Rose an unfair share of disagreeable tasks which the girl performed ungrudgingly. By now, however, we recognised this behavior of Annie's as a kind of brief initiation period. Annie mothered Rose a good deal, too. It seemed to me that with Rose around Tenny turned into something of a show-off. Shirt off, a bit of strutting – that kind of thing, nothing blatant.

On the Monday in question Tenny and Annie returned late from their day off. Late again. We had slept poorly. Rats overhead, a strong wind, barking dogs. Moreover Annie had forgotten to tell us before she left that there was no more bread and our supply of home-made muesli was finished. Fuming, while we waited we drank tea and watched clouds bounce off the cone of the volcano.

Upon arrival Annie set to work with a diligence she hadn't demonstrated in months. Tenny on the other hand lolled around in the back kitchen. Our lawn was sadly overgrown, littered with pine cones which Tenny would first have to collect before he set about the hard work of cutting the grass. Tenny's eyes were full of sleep. He came into the house and without so much as a nod to us he began to rummage in the refrigerator. Finally slamming the door with one hip, carrying two dishes of left-overs from our Sunday supper, he went back out to the kitchen to warm himself a meal. We could hear him singing, '*Im pompei pudernei –*' No matter how often Koert Jan repeated the nonsense for him, or how slowly, no matter how hard Tenny tried, he never got it straight. His concentration only seemed to get in his way.

A few minutes later we saw Rose on the front lawn gathering pine cones. Koert Jan and I exchanged looks. Our previous experience had taught us caution in the handling of such a situation. We were, I suppose, feeling quirky and tired and more than a bit depressed as well, and we knew it. Our work had seemed to deteriorate recently into compiling a catalog of reasons why community development throughout the province was doomed to failure. Before our coming to Indonesia Koert Jan had warned me that we, and not those we came to help, were likely to be the ones who got the most out of our time there. Foolishly I clung to my do-good romanticism long enough for it to turn sour. By now the evidence was overwhelming that in the setting of North Sulawesi self-interest was little short of hysterical. There are definite limits to anyone's altruism, I suppose, and with our fat salaries and privileged backgrounds we could well afford a fling at selflessness; yet week after week, day in day out we failed to come across people genuinely interested in their neighbor's fate. People didn't seem to notice even what happened to others, no less care. Oh lip service to the principles of community was often eloquent, but absolutely hollow. You might say the lesson had been there for us to learn all along no further away than the tip of our nose. Reta. Tenny and Annie. Anneke. Nora. *Chira bum.*

Tenny and Annie had at least put themselves out to welcome us in their villages. *Gengsi* they acquired as a result was likely to have been a substantial consideration in their behavior, none the less, in many small ways they had been warm, friendly, attentive and forgiving. Koert Jan and I agreed, there was no point in our overdoing discipline. As long as things didn't fall apart. It was up to us, however, to see to it that Tenny and Annie didn't make Rose their slave.

Koert Jan came into the study while I was typing out an interview with a famous local *dukun*, a traditional healer. This healer had shown us a certain root. Cut it lengthwise and it had healing properties. Cut it sideways, it could kill. The piece we saw had markings to indicate it had been cut both ways.

'What have you been up to now?' Koert Jan asked.

'What do you mean?'

'What do I mean? I mean Tenny.'

'Tenny what?'

'Tenny's quitting.'

'Oh?' I took my hands off the keyboard and turned around.

'Yes, *oh*. He says you complained he was lazy.'

'He is, but I haven't spoken to him at all today. Maybe he can read minds, but you can't blame me for that, can you?'

'I'm glad you're amused.' Koert Jan left the room, but I hardly had time to find my place and start to type again before he was back.

'Ready for it? Now the story is that Annie heard the two of us talking about Tenny's being lazy. She told him.'

'That's crazy. Koert – '

'Rose backs her up.'

I laughed. 'Who are we to deny it then?'

What actually had happened, we worked out later, was that Annie, for some reason set on making every effort to do her work well, resented Tenny's settling in the kitchen to warm himself a meal without lifting a finger to do his work. So she teased him, after getting Rose to agree to the joke. But she, they,

101

hadn't counted on Tenny's overreacting the way he did. There had been tears, Koert Jan told me later, when Tenny, stung by my reputed insult, came to announce his departure.

'Mr Koert, you'll never find anyone to work for you like I did. Not anyone who can drive as good or take care of the car. You try, but you won't find anyone, not from around here, I can tell you.'

Koert Jan does not respond well to boasting. Still he kept himself in hand. Despite my laughter when I heard that Annie and Rose both were lying, I lost my temper. In Indonesia that is fatal. First I went to Rose on the lawn who was kneeling by a mound of pine cones. I asked if it was true she had heard me talking about Tenny. She closed her eyes, dug her chin into her shoulder, tried not to answer. Annie saw us together and with Tasty barking, jumping to snare the meat bone in her hand, she came out to join us. Her face was frog-like, crumpled in petulance.

'Rose, there is one thing more important with us than anything else,' I said. 'And that's honesty.'

'Ha,' was Annie's comment.

'Did you hear Mr Koert and me talking about Tenny? Did I say Tenny was lazy? Did either of us say it? Yes or no? Rose, yes or no?'

'No,' Rose said firmly, looking Annie in the eye. Annie kicked at the pile of pine cones. Tenny was outside, too, staring at Annie. For her there was no way back.

'I heard you,' she said to me, crossing her arms, not stamping. Her eyes seemed to plead for my complicity. 'Why doesn't he do his work?'

'Think, Annie,' I said. 'When you heard me, when I was talking to Mr Koert, what language were we using? Mr Koert and I, we never talk Bahasa Indonesia to each other when we're alone, do we? You know that? Dutch – where did you learn Dutch all of a sudden, Annie?'

Annie threw the bone in her hand at Tasty's head. She

pushed past Tenny and went back to their room. I followed. She had closed the door. When she refused to open it upon my asking, Tenny forced it open. Annie was packing her things. Their suitcase was open on the bed. She had stripped pictures from the wall. I saw the fine material we had given her months ago for a dress still carefully wrapped in protective tissue paper. The room they had made so friendly and liveable during the year was half-dismantled.

'If you're just looking for an excuse to go home, say so, Annie,' I persisted. 'If you want to stay, be big enough and admit the truth.' Annie didn't look up. She kept slinging things into the suitcase, muttering out loud unintelligibly. 'Why lie? I never said anything about Tenny's being lazy, did I?'

'Annie, answer.' Tenny put a hand roughly on her shoulder.

'Mr Koert accused me of stealing money that I never took,' Annie said. Perhaps we only got what we deserved. I hadn't figured Annie to nurse a grudge. A bad taste flooded my mouth and I felt afraid. Behind me Koert Jan exploded.

'You said when we apologised, that we could forget it ever happened.' In his anger Koert Jan kept his voice soft.

Annie stared at us, defiantly. 'I'm not a thief. That's what you called me.'

Was it a fair trade she was offering? To forgive Annie now for what we had so wrongly done to her months ago? But where would we go from here? How would the balance stand?

'And what about the money for petrol, Tenny – the time you drove Reta to the airport? The two times.' As soon as the words were out, I regretted them. We were all down on the same level now, scrambling, flailing, saying goodbye.

In less than half an hour they were gone. Koert Jan told Tenny we would drive them to Tinoör. Annie refused. A short scene with yelling took place between Rose and Annie before Annie went walking down the driveway for the last time, suitcase on her head, cardigan sweater bunched at the elbows, rubber thongs flapping on her feet. Annie accused Rose of

103

betrayal. Under the circumstances it was hardly feasible for Rose to have done otherwise. Or had Rose gone along with the joke only because, shrewdly, she had foreseen the outcome?

'You shouldn't have said that,' Koert Jan said to me later, 'really.'

'About the money for petrol?'

'Yes.'

'I know. I'm sorry.'

XII

Tenny we saw again before we left Indonesia, several times, but not Annie. He was driving his father's taxi again back and forth between Tomohon and Manado. At times we passed him on the road and he would always honk and wave, face split with a grin.

On the eve of our departure Tenny actually came to the house to visit us. A large crate stood under the roofed area of the driveway. Hilda Kawatu and Dientje were helping us to wrap our belongings in newspaper before loading them. At times Hilda gave such a loud sigh that Koert Jan or I presented her with another *oleh-oleh*. She always made a brief show of refusing in embarrassment. The roar of Tenny's motorcycle preceded him. He sped into the driveway dragging one heel setting up a shower of pebbles and sparks. His massive new machine had as many mirrors and reflectors as the eye of a fly has facets. The bike had been paid for out of the profits from his *cingkeh*.

Tenny was dressed in a flashy sportshirt, Hawaiian style. His hair had been curled with a permanent wave that didn't suit him. He came bringing a present for us: a small Christmas tree of clove sprigs, more than a foot high. Now bright green, properly dried, it could be preserved for years.

'Annie made it for you,' Tenny said. I don't know if that was the truth; if not, it was a considerate lie. He walked over to our

Toyota and frowned at nicks in the front bumper. 'Didn't I tell you, Mr Koert,' he said. Koert Jan himself had scraped the car taking a tight corner in Manado. Then Tenny stepped on to the lawn and whistled admiringly. The grass looked manicured. The driver who replaced Tenny was a diligent worker. Tenny walked over to the moon orchid arching up from the coconut husk nailed to the bark of a mango tree. The flower itself was languishing while a mass of weeds thrived at its base. Tenny looked at Koert Jan and pretended to pluck out some weeds. 'The woods are full, whenever you want to come.'

'Thank Annie for us,' I said. Tenny explained Annie was working at home. She ran a small restaurant where she served Reta's recipes. During the *cingkeh* harvest they had done good business. Now things were slow. Would we come to Tinoör for a visit?

'Of course,' we said, and I, at least, meant it.

Tenny looked ostentatiously at the digital watch on his wrist and said he had to go. After he turned his motorcycle around and mounted back into the saddle, there was an awkward moment of silence. It was as if he knew, despite our promise, we would not see each other again.

'Hey, how's Annie?' Rose called, leaning out of the back kitchen window, smiling at Tenny.

'Good,' Tenny replied. 'Annie's pregnant.'

When he saw the delight on our faces, he looked down and laughed. 'No,' he said, revving the engine, 'that can't happen.' He looked up at us and said in all earnestness, 'Who knows, maybe I'll have to take another wife.'

Beach Party at Yachtule

I

Our flight to Yemen bounced down in Sana close to midnight local time. The wheels had hardly touched the ground before my fellow passengers, a silent group until then, broke out cheering and clapping. What else did they expect? Besides which, we were six hours late. At customs my impatience must have showed. This was clearly a bad mistake. Otherwise I sincerely doubt whether the inspector would have taken such pains to memorise the labels in my underwear. By the time I passed through the barrier, a chalk X on my suitcase, my chest was full of angry bees.

Then it was my turn to feel like cheering and shouting. Koert Jan was there, waiting for me, just as I'd hoped.

'What kept you?'

'There was a corpse in Cairo late for its funeral here, but no flying papers.'

'Must go, can't go?'

'You've got it.'

The airport terminal in Sana has all the glamor of a rusty breadbox. It is in a state of perpetual repair, covered in wobbly bamboo scaffolding. Cables and sacks of cement turn the surrounding pavement into an obstacle course hard enough by day, doubly treacherous in the dark. Potholes, too. Note well:

107

the Yemeni take a dim view of visitors who fall in and break a leg.

'Steady on,' Koert Jan steered me past assorted hotel touts and glassy-eyed, slavering taxi drivers to his vehicle, a white Mitsubishi pick-up truck. He thumped his knuckles against the insignia painted on the door. Property of the Municipality of Taiz. 'Usually I have twenty sweepers in back,' he said, 'dancing.'

In the center of broad intersections as we approached the city, soldiers with helmets and machine-guns stood facing each other, smoking cigarettes. They barely bothered to follow us with their eyes.

'You look good,' Koert Jan said. His smile, my heart sank, was distant.

In 1982 when the vogue of primary health care was at its height, the Dutch put up a sprawling hospital complex on the outskirts of the city of Dhamar. This hospital was to serve as the nerve center for an outreach health programme. Even before recent earthquakes had brought Dhamar to the world's attention – for a few days – I was booked to visit North Yemen. My task: to have a look at how the outreach work was, or rather wasn't, getting along.

The earthquakes added a new dimension to my assignment. The first shocks, 5.8 on the Richter scale, had come by night. Dry-stone houses in hill villages collapsed on their occupants, or slithered off precipices, careening into the trembling darkness. (In Taiz, a hundred and twenty miles away, Koert Jan was thrown out of bed. He picked himself up off the floor, fought free of the sheets and ran out of the house, naked, only to find himself utterly alone, shivering in the cold night air.) Survivors straggled down to Dhamar, milling about government offices and mosques for help and support. The Swedes sent tents. The Americans tins of soya oil with a handshake on the front. The Dutch sent blankets, and me.

'The blankets are for sale in Sana,' Koert Jan lost no time telling me, 'on the black market.'

Through a maze of deserted streets we arrived at the Dar Al Hamd, a former sheikh's palace converted into a hotel. A towering mud-brick structure floating in a walled courtyard of cactus stubble and dust. Arabic neon letters flashed red at its crest. Under the moon, a full cusp, I could see turrets, windows and doors ringed in white. The Yemenis had the world's first skyscrapers, and painted them to look like clowns' faces.

We spent a short night in the Dar Al Hamd at great expense. Our room had a shower and bidet but no running water. Someone else's hair was sprinkled generously on the wrinkled sheets. No matter, the place had character. Besides I couldn't sleep. Too tired, I suppose. The bumpety plane journey had felt endless and now it seemed to continue while I stared for hours at the ceiling, white rinsed blue by shadows. Strange, how uneasy it had made me to be flying with a corpse aboard. All night long slow footsteps echoed up and down the stone stairs of the palace, and doors slammed. Through it all Koert Jan slept in a sliver of moonlight, his knees drawn up, one arm flung out over the edge of the bed, fingers curled. His fine lips were slightly parted. His expression was peaceful.

We left Sana, heading south for Dhamar, a three hours' drive, as the sun rose. Through loudspeakers wired to the gleaming towers of freshly plastered mosques, imams were calling the faithful to prayer. The faithful were nowhere to be seen. A few miles beyond the city we had our first military checkpoint. Koert Jan inched the Mitsubishi over a 'dead policeman', a mound of dirt obstructing the road as if a giant mole had burrowed beneath it. Then we eased forward between empty oil barrels flying state flags. On both sides soldiers' faces appeared in our open windows. By daylight I could see them better: in khaki uniform, with red berets at rakish tilt, they were really sleepy teenagers. Mine was chewing gum. Search and interrogation were reduced by our white faces to an exchange of handshakes, nods and smiles.

'Are there many of those?' I asked.

'Yes.'

'What're they looking for?'

'Weapons. And alcohol.'

In next to no time we reached open country and began climbing the first daunting mountain pass. The sun was low, and clouds had begun chasing each other overhead. The landscape was bleak, mostly black and purple. Koert Jan, who suffers from an acute fear of heights, kept pretty much to the middle of the road. A ribbon of new highway wound up the side of age-old rock, doubling back on itself, twisting in lazy loops like syrup dripping from a spoon. It was all very beautiful, on a grand scale, and treacherous. A cloudburst overtook us threading our way between sheer basalt crags. White lightning sizzled through the sky. Koert Jan hunched forward over the steering-wheel, gripping it so tightly that his knuckles showed white.

'Your glasses!' Rain drummed so hard on the roof that to make myself heard I had to shout. Koert Jan just shook his head. Twenty years ago, when he was a young officer in the Dutch army, the doctor had prescribed glasses. Koert Jan always had them with him, but never put them on, preferring to squint. The vanity of beautiful people, if not pushed to excess, is something I find touching.

The rain stopped as suddenly as it began. We pulled over at a cliffside café with a box-like front terrace. Here we sat some moments in silence watching the storm blow off down the valley. At last a woman wearing cloths of more different colors than I could count, polka dots, stripes, floral patterns draped and twisted together, came and took Koert Jan's order for tea. After she disappeared back into the dim interior of the café, crowded with tables, empty of customers, a tall, hawk-faced Arab in skirt and jacket ambled out to join us. Without ado he pulled out a folding iron chair so it rasped against the cement floor, and sat down on it backwards. The tongues of his shoes flapped. He wore no laces, no socks. He had tied his Arafat headcloth dashingly, legions of black spiders marching leg to leg. The loose end was drawn forward, under his jutting chin, and then draped back over his shoulder.

Almost directly behind the small restaurant was a clamorous waterfall, torrents of muddied water tumbling from a great height and rushing away through cement sluices imbedded under the road surface. Above in crumbling silhouette the remnants of a nineteenth-century Ottoman fort stood out on a jagged bluff. By rolling his eyes, baring his teeth and gesturing, our self-invited friend indicated that he'd like to take us for a climb up to the fort and show us the sights. He had a distracted, not unfriendly air about him, slightly feverish, as if we had awakened him from a nap he shouldn't have been taking. It wasn't *qat* either – his face wasn't deformed by a wad of leaves propped into one cheek.

Koert Jan had rested his hands on the table holding his wallet. The man tapped the ring on Koert Jan's finger – a family signet, black stone – and flung his chin up disdainfully. Then he called our attention to the ring he was wearing. It looked like a gold nugget. He wrestled it off and tossed it for our inspection – clank – on to the iron table top. The ring was a cunningly carved lion's head with diamonds for eyes. With deft finger work the man told us what he'd paid for it. Then suddenly he let his left forearm collapse on to the table and pulled back his sleeve to offer a gold wristwatch for our admiration.

'Swiss,' he said. 'Swissss.'

Once more fingers waggling, he told us the price. Once more we pursed our lips, made eyes, were suitably impressed.

Finally, as the climax to his display of worldly treasures, the man's right hand disappeared among the folds of his chemise and sash, groped behind the handle of his ceremonial curved dagger, and emerged with a pistol. He slapped it down in front of us: a US army Colt. Loaded, as he demonstrated, sliding a clip of ammunition out into his palm and then ramming it back into place. Just then, at the far edge of the road, beyond our Mitsubishi shimmering under its coat of raindrops, a flock of crows went screaming and plunging for unseen pickings dumped over the cliffside. One elbow propped on the table, the man took rapid aim at the whirling black forms, but he didn't shoot. Bullets, Koert Jan let me know later, were too valuable for such sport. They are still used for money in parts of Yemen.

Now it was our turn to be impressive, but we had nothing to show. I thought briefly of pulling out my traveller's checks, but decided no one would be amused.

Three cups of tea arrived, cloves floating on the milky surface. Delicious. Our companion hawked, spat and called for one of his daughters. She came tottering outside, four or five years old at the most, barefoot, dripping snot, wearing rags, a long diagonal scratch over one dark eye, hair in snarls. He handed her his prize Colt and told her to take it away inside. Before she turned to go, she smiled, and holding the gun with two hands, pudgy fingers curling around the trigger, she aimed it at us, first at Koert Jan, then me.

By reflex I slid off my chair and ducked under the table.

'So what's your secret?' I asked Koert Jan once we were under way again. A few weeks before the recent earthquakes, the new Dutch Minister for Development Co-operation had completed a first swing through the Middle East, including a week in Yemen. She had in fact never been out of Holland before – except to ski. With her initial budget coming up for defense in parliament, however, her advisers had urged her to go out and get her feet wet. She had come back disillusioned, vexed by much of what she had seen, but singing the praises of the Taiz Solid Waste Disposal Project. The discipline and team spirit Koert Jan had achieved were spoken of as unique. 'Why do you succeed, where others fail?'

'I only hire people with beautiful eyes.' He grinned. 'True!'

'I don't doubt it.'

'Last week, for example, Ali Achmed, one of our new inspectors – '

' – with beautiful eyes – '

' – brown with green specks – he came over to me and lifted his *futa*. He had on football shorts underneath. He asked for the afternoon off. There was training for a big game. All right, I told him, just this once. Then Ali whispered something in my ear. Mahyub saw – my counterpart, we have a lot of fun together – Mahyub saw and came over and wanted to know what Ali Achmed had said. So I whispered it in Mahyub's ear.'

Koert Jan fell silent.

'You're teasing,' I said.

'*Habibi*. That's all he said.'

'Which is?'

'I love you.'

Soon we found ourselves stymied in the poisonous exhaust of a convoy of dump trucks hauling rocks, inching upwards along the steep, twisting road, no room for a sane driver to try to pass. As long as I've known Koert Jan, Safety has been his middle name. Now to my horror he pushed the accelerator through the floor, gave a long blast on the horn and pulled out. He sped recklessly ahead, hugging the inside wall. We overtook three trucks and did a two-wheel screech around a blind corner. The road ahead was clear. '*Insh' allah*,' Koert Jan said, and patted my knee.

It took miles for my heart to slow to something like normal. Insects splattered against the windshield. Koert Jan turned on the windshield wiper. A given of our friendship has always been that Koert Jan doesn't ask me questions about myself, my life. If I complain, he gets annoyed and waves his hand through the air. 'If it's important, you'll tell me,' he says, 'won't you?' No matter how often I've made up my mind to punish him with silence, making secrets of my secrets, invariably I end up proving his point. Then he rubs it in, saying, 'Couldn't you wait until I asked?' But this trip I was empty. That was something I wouldn't tell him. I was only afraid he must already have seen it in my eyes.

'Did you like her?' I asked when the silence began to close in.

'The Minister?' Koert Jan turned off the windshield wiper. 'No.'

'No?'

'She was like you – asks all the wrong questions.'

'You made quite an impression on her.'

'Yes, well, they're hard up for a success in The Hague, aren't they? All those projects gone wrong. And after all, we gave her something to warm her Dutch heart – clean streets.' When Koert Jan laughs, he looks boyish. 'The Mayor of Taiz – you'll meet him – he's a real old fox. Or weasel. Connections *everywhere*. Simply amazing. Ever since I got here they've been predicting his fall, rubbing their hands, but every time the day of reckoning comes, before it's over his grip on things ends up tighter than ever. Well, when he heard the minister was *a woman*, he got the wind up and came charging over to see me. From the way the old man came through the door I could tell he had murder in his heart. Somehow he also knew she'd made a name for herself in Holland campaigning for abortion. That didn't help much either. "So – what else?" he wanted to know. "The Minister of yours, is she a Jew?"'

'I thought Arabs like to play beat around the bush?'

'Not this one. He's had two heart attacks and doesn't have the time.'

'What did you tell him?'

'The truth – I didn't know.'

'She is.'

'Anyway' – Koert Jan tapped his foot on the gas pedal as we headed downhill – 'I told him what I did know – that she was a vegetarian. He took it like more bad news.'

114

'How could you *not* know she was a Jew?'

'The next day he was back. He chased everyone else out of the office, shut the door and asked me what a vegetarian was. When I told him, his eyes lit up. He sat down, pulled out the Minister's schedule in Taiz and started changing it. When she arrived, dead on her feet, poor thing – I'll give her that – he took her straight away to see the new slaughter house. The whole time he was right there at her elbow to make sure she didn't miss a thing.'

Coming down out of the mountains to Dhamar I saw tent cities stretching out across the plain. Bright sheets of new corrugated iron, too, improvised shacks, dazzled in the morning sunlight. Elsewhere people, busy as ants, were rearranging the rubble of old houses to make new. Flat, wind-swept and treeless, I found Dhamar depressing at first sight, worse upon better acquaintance, a cinder in the eye of Arabia Felix.

Despite the early hour of our arrival at the hospital, the gates were jammed. People held on to the fence rails with both hands, pleading, shouting to be let in. Others sat on the ground with food and bedding, and dull hostile stares. Soldiers with automatic weapons slung over their shoulders kept order.

Inch by inch our truck glided through the crowd. Smoothly the gates opened in before us.

'What the –'

Before the soldiers could pull the gates shut behind us, the flatbed of the Mitsubishi was boarded. A whole family had climbed on, or been lifted on to the truck and rode with us into the hospital grounds. It was timed perfectly. The crowd outside screamed their support. After a conference where money undoubtedly changed hands, the soldiers allowed our passengers to stay. Two soldiers – children again – walked in front of us up the hospital drive. We followed through wasted flower beds up to the entrance of the wards. Aiming to mimic traditional styles, the architect had created a mud hen

115

surrounded by her chicks. The hospital resembled nothing so much as an American roadside motel. Here and there on the compound hot pools of volcanic mud had bubbled up, more gray than brown, and steaming. In places splits and cracks in the walls of the buildings were wide enough to see right through into the inside.

A nurse came to meet us. She wore starched white, except for what looked like jogging shoes on her feet. Hester, the head nurse, Dutch. Young, stout, shading her eyes from the morning glare with one hand. A man leaped down from the back of the truck, leaving the others. His eyebrows were at different levels which made it look like the two halves of his face didn't fit. He held out his arms and a child was passed down to him. A boy. The child, in great pain, was clutching one arm against his chest. Terror silenced his tears. The end of the arm was wrapped in a bloody cloth. Hester, clucking soothingly, pulled the cloth loose. Slowly, gently. When it was removed, a small whistle escaped her before she lifted the child and hurried away with it inside. The boy's arm had ended in a mass of bloody pulp.

The soldiers began now to herd the party that had brought the child back towards the front gates, brushing up against them and shoving with the stock of their weapons. The man with the staggered eyebrows, apparently the child's father, was strutting back and forth. He drew his *jambiah* and lifted it overhead and made a series of little leaps, birdlike, not ungraceful. He tilted his chin up and began to vomit words. His speech came out in a great, breathless rush. And all the while he continued his dance, feet swift, hips swerving, one hand slashing the air with wide passes of his dagger – all his loose garments swaying.

Koert Jan huddled with one of the soldiers and came back to report: 'The boy's a hero, that's what the father is saying. Praise Allah.'

Others had joined the dance now, they were shuffling in a

circle, each with a drawn knife, slow steps alternating with quick, faces tense with pride. The crowd outside the fence had begun to sing. Someone beat drums. In the openings of the hospital wards, the windows and doors, the new cracks as well, faces appeared.

'A hero?'

'He was playing in the house, the little boy. Found his father's shoes. Wanted to put them on, but his foot wouldn't go. There was something inside.' Koert Jan spoke softly, his eyes on the dance. 'So he reached into the shoe and pulled out a grenade.'

II

Three weeks later, as planned, I took a group taxi from Dhamar south to Taiz. A Mercedes, white, with green stripes running along both sides and down the middle of the roof and hood. The sleazy driver insisted that I sit next to him. He drove with one hand on my knee and kept up a virtually non-stop conversation, undeterred by my failure to respond with even as much as a grunt. He laughed, he scowled, he pinched my thigh.

Most of the way we teetered on the shoulder of sheer declivities. Medieval villages far below stood among contour terraces that glittered with captive rainwater. It was no trip for sightseeing, however. We tore into hairpin mountain curves like they were flat straightaways. How we avoided one large boulder that lay in the middle of the road, dislodged I guess by rain, I still don't know. If you ask me, we drove straight through it.

Altogether we were six passengers crammed into the hurtling taxi. The others, all Yemenis, slept. The inside of the Mercedes was upholstered in synthetic white fur, dashboard and steering-wheel included. Periodically I lifted the driver's hand from my leg and replaced it on the fluffy wheel. Or with a finger I turned his chin so instead of looking at me, his eyes for a moment would be on the road. Then he grew silent, and smiled furtively. Although the attention was meant to be friendly, I decided, and not sexual, I found myself getting excited – that and the discomfort it caused me didn't escape his notice.

It was late in the afternoon when we pulled into the Taiz taxi depot. Hundreds of identical cars, different coloured stripes for different regional services, were locked together like wasps in jam. As I stepped out of the cab, Koert Jan, once again, was waiting. 'Welcome to Taiz,' he hugged me. I tried to tip the driver but he wouldn't have it. His manner was positively aristocratic. 'They've never been a colony, you see,' was Koert Jan's comment as we walked to his Mitsubishi, 'and that makes a world of difference.'

First we stashed my things in the car. When Koert Jan didn't lock the doors I thought he must have just forgotten. 'Lock,' I reminded him.

He acted surprised. 'Here? Don't be silly. People leave the bank carrying money in see-through plastic bags.'

We set out at once for the heart of the Old City. To get there Koert Jan had to lead me through one of the only remaining barbicans in the original town wall. Inside the crooked market streets, uneven under foot, were crowded, bustling. To reach God's Own Terrace, Koert Jan's name for where we were going, we had to climb a steep flight of iron stairs loosely riveted to the outside wall of a building honeycombed at ground level with small shops. Across a narrow blind alley, on the facing wall, hundreds of used tea-bags hung at odd intervals from the rough cement. 'The dishwashers fling them out the kitchen window. You have to throw one just right to make it stick.' The wall made an odd shrine.

The waiters at God's Own Terrace, dressed like old men, couldn't have been much older than nine or ten. They swabbed the tables with large filthy rags, put on a look of self-importance

118

and then ruined it all by smiling at Koert Jan as if what they wanted most in the world was to climb on to his lap and cuddle.

We chose a table at the far corner of the terrace. Behind us loomed Jebel Sabar, sheer flanks gouged with wadis. The massive rock, so sharp in outline, somehow seemed to drift in the sky. Perhaps I was just groggy from the ride. Here and there, as I watched, lights flashed on in the windows of houses tucked along the lower slopes of the mountain high above. After Dhamar everything looked so green.

'Nice.'

Below us the streets of the souk swarmed with activity, fruits for sale, stringy meat hanging from glinting hooks, bolts of brightly patterned cloth, *qat* vendors sitting on the ground, women down from the mountains with gold bracelets, earrings, necklaces, piercing voices. The night sky closed in swiftly now. The clash of different kinds of light made the street scene more theatrical than real: electric bulbs, bare and pulsing, the softer glow of oil lamps, the flames of cooking fires, red tongues licking out from under vast iron frying-pans. Every movement cast multiple, rippling shadows. Shouts rose, chimes, the gnash of knives against whetstones. Vendors with loaves of bread stacked in wicker baskets came and went in a steady traffic. Packs of children chased each other, grabbing hold of shirt-tails, laughing, slipping in mud. The front stoops of beaneries in a row were clogged with customers mopping at their tin plates with chunks of bread. Beggars, immobile on the curb, sat cross-legged, chanting for alms. At the far corner were rival barber shops lit with flickering candles, encrusted with mirrors, points of light repeating in dark glass. Out front was a coin machine for men and boys to test their strength, a strange contraption of rubber and iron, painted in red and gold. One after another they stepped forward to try to force the handles of the machine to meet, faces puffed, groaning while spectators jeered.

'Yes,' I said, 'it's good be here.'

119

Koert Jan relaxed. He'd been waiting for me to admire his world. Everywhere the eye shifted it met with something to puzzle over, admire, question. The energy pulsed so. Iron filings captive in a magnetic field, dancing in place, shivering, ecstatic.

'What's that?' I pointed.

'A camel.'

Out from under the arched stone gate a large beast came lumbering slowly towards us. Under the switch of its grizzled driver, the camel, loaded with a dizzy heap of dry corn stalks, lurched down 26th September Street.

'Amazing!'

'The trouble with you is everything has to be so hyper-super.'

'The tongue – look!'

From the camel's mouth, the back corner, the tongue hung out, a swollen pink balloon, an enormous floppy baloney. Koert Jan was on his feet now next to me to watch the animal pass. Our shoulders touched.

'A she on heat. Can you see the tail?'

'No, it's too dark.'

'There, tied to her back leg. They have to do that, or it can kill her.'

'Kill her? How?'

'Tighten with such desire that it curls up under her belly and cuts right through her womb.'

During the ten days I had in Taiz to write up my field notes, Koert Jan and I saw much less of each other than I'd been counting on. He seemed nervous to me, edgy, closed. He was working incredibly hard. Despite how he disparaged outside praise, he was preoccupied with making a success of waste disposal. Koert Jan lived, breathed, talked garbage. Six days a week he was out of the house by 5.00 a.m. and didn't come back again until five in the afternoon. At dawn he would meet his brigade of sweepers by the market and send them out in special

120

crash unit teams to rid the city of its worst accumulations of waste. Two hundred and forty sweepers in all, half of them children twelve or thirteen. When cesspools backed up, which some did with the predictability of geysers, Koert Jan rode with the suction truck to the scene. For some reason most sewage crises seemed to happen in the middle of the night. He was tireless as well about visiting shops and hotels and small factories in Taiz, instructing, cajoling, dealing out fines.

Yet Koert Jan's stories at the day's end left me no doubt that he was happiest among the *achdam*, the lowest caste in Yemen, the despised blacks who before the era of DAF compactor trucks had traditionally swept the city and carted off its waste on donkeyback. Koert Jan had his favorites, too. He was always making fun of them, wrinkling his nose when they came near, sniffing. Then they would laugh and hug him with their bushy heads in the crook of his neck.

Until twenty years ago about forty thousand people lived in Taiz. The present total was pressing two hundred thousand. In a manner of speaking the city had gone to sleep one night in the Middle Ages to wake up in modern times. Speed of development brought many problems with it, but nothing to compare to the difficulties Koert Jan had to face which arose within the waste-disposal project itself. Bert, the chunky mechanic in charge of the garage and workshop, was a genius at coaxing dead engines back to life. The trouble was that he despised Arabs. And he made a virtue out of honesty. Bert almost always had a streak of grease on his face, a kind of war paint which entitled him, he apparently felt, to spout all kinds of filth. His idea of a joke was to throw a tire iron at you. He didn't always miss. Sober, he pretended to himself that he liked to be friendly. He was seldom altogether sober.

Malvina, Bert's wife, claimed Bert was only truly happy on his back. 'Snoring or under a car.'

'Poor thing,' Koert Jan told me after I'd had a chance to see for myself. 'She and Bert live behind the garage in a prefab

121

flown in from Delft. Trouble is the roof's too thin. It can't keep out the sun. So they have to leave their air-conditioners on all the time and the air-conditioners are too powerful for the house. They make the walls shake. Not only the walls either. Did you notice anything about Malvina?'

'She shakes.'

'No wonder really. She *never* leaves the house. Bert says he could learn to live with it, only Malvina and the house don't shake together.

'Bert, mind you, is child's play next to the Mayor.' The Mayor was the local figure with primary project responsibility. A wizened tyrant with a mysterious past as a waiter in Aden. 'He's made so many enemies consolidating his power over the years that now he's afraid to go out alone. Travels everywhere with a bodyguard from security – little better than a thug.'

I never saw the Mayor. 'There he goes – in the back seat,' Koert Jan would point to a car disappearing around a corner. 'Off after women.' Or, 'That's him, that's the Mayor,' he'd tug at my elbow just too late as a pack of featureless men in headcloths would sweep down the aisle ahead of us at the market. Koert Jan was renting the ground floor of the Mayor's house, but his landlord was never his host. The closest I came to this mysterious figure was to feel his footsteps travel back and forth over my face as I fell asleep.

Keeping the peace between the Mayor and the Mechanic left Koert Jan psychically black and blue. By the time of my arrival things had reached such a pitch that the Mayor had told project mechanics that the next time Bert insulted them, the next time he showed his teeth, they should slap him in the face and he would back them up. 'Since then they've all been trying to provoke him,' Koert Jan told me, 'but Bert has the cunning of an animal. Now that they're out to get his goat, he's gone all sweet on them. And he's discovered a way to get back at the Mayor.

'The Mayor hates beggars, pathologically: they don't look

122

good. Bad for a Moslem, very, you don't have to tell me – but once the old man latches on to an idea, that's it. And as far as he's concerned there is no place for beggars in a clean city. Once he made up his mind it didn't take him long to put most of the beggars in Taiz out of circulation. But there's one little fellow, Rachman, limbs all twisted, who's still very much with us. Has to crawl along with rubber straps on his hands and knees. So friendly and even-tempered. A smile for everyone. Afternoons Rachman sits on the corner at the foot of the hill that goes up to the post office. One of his younger brothers sells newspapers to people who go by in cars. Rachman is there to look after him. He's not a beggar, he says. People just come up and give him money. For the Mayor that's cutting it too fine. He told the security police to clean the corner. You should understand, I joke about the Mayor but he's a dangerous man. He has a lot of power and he uses it erratically. The prison is full of his whims.

'Now Bert – I don't think he ever noticed a beggar before, true, but as soon as he found out that Rachman had gotten under the Mayor's skin they became bosom buddies. Bert's always driving out of his way to give Rachman money, clothes. And for some reason this was one order of the Mayor's that security didn't carry out. Maybe Rachman has family on the force?

'No, instead of disappearing obligingly, Rachman turned up with a huge red and white umbrella with Coca-Cola written all over it. He sits now out of the sun. "Who does that cripple think he is" – the Mayor, believe it or not, is jealous – "sitting there with that umbrella like a prince?" And the next day Rachman had a blue and yellow umbrella from Pall Mall. And the day after that, one from Nivea, blue and white. Bert's behind it, I'm sure. The Mayor goes miles out of his way to avoid that corner. He's sent his bodyguard to threaten Rachman, but it seems Rachman doesn't scare easy. He may be a little simple-minded, I'm not sure.'

Koert Jan slowed down and looked at me. I was pushing tea-leaves and sugar around the bottom of my glass with a long spoon. 'I know what you're thinking,' Koert Jan laughed. 'We could use something like an earthquake around here.'

That evening walking home from God's Own Terrace I made my first direct reference to garbage. 'Ever notice that the dirtiest places in town are right where the containers stand?'

'Sure, but that goes to figure. Who takes the garbage out? Little kids. The containers those jokers chose are too high. A kid comes out with a bucket on his head and tries to pour it over the side. What happens? Most of it ends up falling all over him.' I laughed at the idea. 'Sometimes the kid even loses the bucket. It falls into the container. So, hup, the kid climbs in after it. He tramps around a bit, maybe does a little digging and climbs back out. Nice trap, isn't it!'

Towards the end of my first week in Taiz Koert Jan arranged for Elso and Saskia, Dutch physiotherapists working as volunteers at the large Chinese hospital – red – in Taiz, to take me to the top of Jebel Sabar. 'The view is incredible,' Koert Jan told me. Typically, he hadn't been up there yet himself. Elso and Saskia were making the trip up the mountain so that she could order a pair of black cloth trousers with coloured embroidery on the legs, a speciality of the mountain women.

At the end of their workday, at about two, Elso and Saskia picked me up at Koert Jan's house. I climbed into the back of their white Suzuki and settled on to a thin foam rubber pad. Together Elso and Saskia could pass for a fun-loving couple in a cigarette ad. Only she was shrewd, and that shrewdness showed in her face like some childhood skin disease. There was a slight gathering around her eyes and mouth. She wore her straight blonde hair short. Her voice was deep. Of all the foreigners in Taiz Koert Jan preferred her company the most. 'She fizzes,' he said.

Elso was handsome in a young, soulless way, robust, radiant

124

with health. His voice, on first hearing, was so improbable it made you want to laugh: twice as old, twice as pompous as it should be. Saskia said Elso had talked that way since he was a baby.

'How many Chinese doctors are there?' Saskia, I learned soon enough, always repeated questions before she answered them. 'Thirty. Fifteen men, fifteen women, fifteen marriages.'

'Friendly?'

'Are they friendly? Before they were let out of China they had to sign an oath not to learn another language. It limits their value as teachers.'

'They brought five ping-pong tables with them. These are set up in the hospital basement. An unending war goes on down there, around the clock. At the end of every month a huge crate arrives from China. It's full of ping-pong balls. Thousands.'

Saskia twisted around in her seat to look back at me. 'Comfortable?'

'Fine.'

'How do you know Koert Jan?'

As we jolted from tarmac on to the rutted rock and sand track that snaked up the side of the mountain, I nearly bumped my head. Koert Jan had warned me that one of the things Saskia did to fight against boredom, like jogging, was to make everybody's business her own.

'We've worked together.'

'Where?'

'Indonesia. Uganda. Lesotho. Turkey.'

'Work friends,' Saskia smiled. 'And you write him every day.'

Some like the tops of mountains best. I admit I'm often happiest half-way. Just beyond one of a series of villages that straddled the road going up Jebel Sabar, Elso pulled over to let Saskia take a photo down into the valley. Stupidly, I'd left my camera back at the house. We happened to stop directly above

125

a school where class was being held on the open roof. Pupils crowded on to rows of low, wood benches. Up front the teacher stood with a pointer tracing sentences on a green slate board covered with white squiggles. Behind stretched a sheer drop and way, way below, the sprawling modern city of Taiz, white and brown. Saskia clambered on to a low stone wall to get a better vantage. She crouched, pivoted, drew her breath in and was absolutely still.

'*Marhaba.*'

A whey-faced man, small, with compulsory moustache, tried to throw an arm around Elso's shoulder, but his arm didn't quite reach. Elso knew him. They parried phrases back and forth until Saskia came down from taking her picture. Then a rapid-fire conversation began. She was fluent in Arabic.

'This is Kassem' – we shook hands, his two to my one – 'a nurse at the hospital. He's been inviting us to visit his house for months.' Saskia pointed to a three-storey stone building about a hundred yards below us. To the right of the school, it was built out on to a shelf of rock, tapering slightly as it rose. 'That's it.'

'I've told him' – Elso spoke English now, slowly, presumably so Kassem could follow – 'we can't stay long.'

'Do you mind?'

'I'm delighted,' I said honestly. Jebel Sabar could keep. In Yemen now the better part of a month, I'd still not set foot in an Arab home.

Single file we followed Kassem down century-old stone steps worn into the mountain. I brought up the rear. From moment to moment we passed inches from the windows and doors of his fellow villagers. It was impossible not to look inside. Yet we weren't invading privacy so much as becoming part of it. It was less that we intruded than that we were absorbed. As we cut through pounded dirt yards, scattering chickens and children, Saskia, bless her, babbled amiably at every face that appeared, young and old. Kassem beamed.

126

'The rooftops are for women,' Saskia called back to me. 'See. Their world.' A row of giggling girls indeed bunched along the edge of one flat roof, studded for the rest with plants in tin cans and hung with laundry. Piles of millet were also set out on the roof to dry. These women weren't veiled, unlike the ravens of Taiz – shrouded in black down to wrists and ankles, the concealment ultimately suggestive and erotic. Here bright colours, clashing, and quantities of gold jewellery dominated – earrings, breastplates, bracelets, teeth. Hands and faces were marked with henna, too, deep red scrolls and swirls.

Contrary to first appearances the descent to Kassem's house was so steep I had to stop several times. As we zigzagged down the going was hard on my knees, the constant braking not to lose control. And yet Kassem told us that twice a day women fetched water from a spring half a mile higher up the mountainside, twenty liters at a go.

Inside we were ushered into the *mafrage*, the principal room of the house, reserved for entertaining guests. It was long and low, painted white. Small, square windows were cut out of the thick walls revealing glimpses of trees and terraced gardens and Taiz far below. On one window-ledge there was a Sony portable radio. At the far end of the room a Philips television set and video recorder glinted against the white wall. Linoleum designed to resemble ornate painted tiles covered the floor. There was no furniture, only dozens of cushions, no two alike, which lined the walls. High on the inner wall, displayed proudly, were diplomas in glass frames, a marriage license and family photos.

'Kassem's father?' I asked, indicating one of many portraits showing a dashing man in military uniform.

'No' – Saskia followed my eyes – 'that's the late, beloved President. You know about him, don't you?'

'Know what?'

'They found his body together with his brother's and the hacked-up corpses of two French prostitutes at the brother's farm outside Sana.'

'A stupid smear' – when Elso whispered his voice was louder than ever.

'How so?'

'Everybody knew he was gay.'

'Now the French prostitutes' families get a pension from the state.'

We were served tea with mint. Then Kassem's wife, blushing madly, carried in a deep bowl of liquid goat's cheese, mined with garlic and sprinkled with red paprika. Sisters followed with loaves of fresh-baked bread on round, silver trays.

'It's as if they knew we were coming,' I said.

'We're eating their dinner,' Saskia told me, 'but don't worry.'

As we chewed and swallowed – my first mouthfuls were cautious, but the food was delicious – the room filled. Girls, boys, women and babies. The whole neighborhood seemed to slip in shyly, to sit on the floor, gradually inching closer to us. Saskia ate heartily and talked for us all. Whatever she was saying people liked it. There was one child who caught my eye above all the rest – passed from embrace to embrace, coddled and cooed at, a permanent smile of contentment on its round face. The child was so beautiful to look at, so perfect, it was heartbreaking to think he would have to grow older.

Kassem squatted next to us but he wouldn't eat. He had put on a long rich white robe with white embroidery at the keyhole neck. Offering hospitality was the fulfilment of his ambition. After Saskia, the last of the eaters, pushed her plate away and laid her spoon across the opening of her tea glass, Kassem asked a question in a tone of voice new to the occasion. Gone the mild whine of cordiality, the rapid social simper. He spoke levelly, for the first time a man trying to do some work with his words. Saskia looked alarmed. Her eyes scanned the gathered faces. Kassem now spoke a short command and the child I'd singled out to admire was handed forward from the back of the room.

Such concentrated attention – all talk had stopped, all eyes turned – was too much for the poor child. To my horror and distress it began to howl. Elso leaned forward and reached out a large hand to caress the child's cheek. The gesture was strong and tender. The child stood for it but kept crying. Then Elso moved his hand slowly to the boy's shoulder: there were no arms, only deformed flippers.

'Thalidomide' – Saskia shook her head. Kassem hugged the child to him. 'You can still get it here, over the counter. Kassem wants to know if there's anything we can do.'

By the time we reached the end of the road, a good three-quarters of an hour after setting out again, my stomach was upside down.

'Radio station at the top.' Elso pointed to an aerial. 'Military.' Indeed two men with guns silhouetted against the vast sky peered down at us. 'This is as far as we can go.'

'The view's best from over there.' Saskia led us past a cistern – inner walls slick with a scummy green, surface bubbles disrupting the reflection of clouds – to a split in a rock formation that had tumbled from God knows where on to the edge of the mountain. The air was so thin that after only a few steps I had trouble breathing. I lay down and inched forward on my stomach, stone warm under my body, wind cold in my face.

All Taiz was reduced to a few spilled drops of milk in a saucer. If I held my thumb up a foot from my eyes it blotted out the city. In all directions, as far as the eye could see, there stretched pink and purple ridges, lumpy plateaux, lifeless massive gorges – wrinkles and creases in the earth's surface.

Elso nudged me in the ribs. Directly below our perch two eagles, brown, gray, and gold, glided on the wind. Staring down on their backs, we could see their vast shadows sweep across the scree slopes further down the mountain. One instant the eagles seemed to stand still, to hover in place. Then with the slightest movement of their wings, no more than a shudder – as if the eagles were yawning – they put on speed.

After a few false leads, Saskia located a woman prepared to tailor trousers for her. The woman came to the door of her stone house, face smeared with ochre. What I took at first for a cap on her head turned out to be a flat loaf of bread. During the negotiations, she would reach up and break off a mouthful at a time. Saskia had to work hard to persuade the woman that she was serious about wanting the trousers. I suspect the woman was enjoying the situation, having as good a time staring at us as we were staring at her. Saskia tried to say the woman should simply make another pair just like the ones the woman was wearing.

Finally Saskia had to pay in advance, an absurd sum that put Elso on edge. 'Try to get an evening dress for that in Amsterdam,' she said, counting out the money.

'Me?' Elso jested. 'No, thanks.'

Then Saskia and Elso led me off the road, down into a valley to a settlement with a sesame-seed mill several hundreds of years old. It was donkey-powered, a gnarled wood pestle larger than I am – a giant's club – revolving in a vast stone mortar. At invitation we climbed on to a roof and were served local coffee, brewed not from grounds but from the roasted husks of the bean. It was poured from a plaid thermos with great ceremony. First a few drops were used to rinse out our cups, and then, slowly, the cups were filled to the very brim. Elso displayed his good manners by making loud, smacking noises with his lips as he drank.

'Coffee, all coffee, comes from Yemen originally.' Elso had a habit of blinking when he explained things. 'In the beginning it caused quite a problem. The Imam wanted to forbid it.'

'Why?'

'It was a stimulant.'

'If that baby back there at Kassem's was a girl' – Saskia turned to me – 'they would have killed it long ago.'

When I told Koert Jan about the outing, I made a special

point of describing how spotless it was inside Kassem's house. How clean outside, too, as far as the surrounding wall. Beyond the wall, there was litter and garbage everywhere. I told him, too, about how loving the family had been to the thalidomide baby. How natural in handling it. How I hadn't noticed.

III

Late at night the bell rang and someone shook the iron gate to the garden. Through shattered fragments of sleep, I heard Koert Jan shuffle outside and slide the bolt back. Whoever it was sounded excited.

'Want to come?' Koert Jan shook me gently, face breathing in mine. 'The dump's on fire.'

We scrunched together in the narrow seat of Mahyub's Mitsubishi, the twin of Koert Jan's except for a battered front bumper and a gash down one side. Mahyub was short and curly-haired. In his plump face, weathered and lined, his eyes were full of mischief. Koert Jan was right when he called Mahyub's smile contagious.

'Third time this month,' Mahyub said. 'Bad winds.' He chewed on his moustache. 'Maybe the same fire?'

Subterranean fires at sanitary landfills, Koert Jan had told me, can acquire an almost explosive force by the time they surge to the surface. 'No rain, too bad.'

Mahyub ground the gears and we set off. We had the road, the city to ourselves. Here and there figures lay prostrate on the curb, or curled unconscious in shop doorways. Watchmen. Dogs skulked. One cut across the pavement ahead. Mahyub increased speed and swerved, trying to hit it. 'Wild,' Mahyub said, 'trouble.' When sweepers found the corpse of an animal, mostly a dog or goat, first they drenched it in kerosene, then after setting it on fire they stood back and watched until it burned itself out.

'Were you sleeping, Mahyub?'

'Studying, sir.' Mahyub had a passion for self-improvement. After the death of his first wife, a village woman who had given him three children, he had married a schoolteacher from Taiz. 'Excuse me,' he told Koert Jan, 'but village women smell bad.' Two afternoons a week Mahyub left the Waste Disposal Project early for English lessons. For me the English he spoke was unintelligible. Koert Jan understood it though, roughly the same way bats rely on radar to fly safely through the dark. Sometimes it would be a day or two before even Koert Jan could decipher some particular phrase. On school days Mahyub chewed *qat*. It helped him stay alert through the night, completing exercises in his workbook, copying out sentences about buttered scones and marmalade and the changing of the guard at Buckingham Palace.

'What is it, Mahyub? What's wrong?' Mahyub had stopped the car and pulled on the handbrake in the middle of the road. He pointed to the row of shops on our right, all veiled with retractable aluminum shutters. It took a minute for my eyes, heavy still with sleep, to adjust to the gloom. Where Mahyub was pointing, the pavement seemed to tremble. A localised earthquake. Then I saw what trembled was a man, lying there on the ground, apparently asleep. From head to foot he quivered. His hands, his feet, his body shook and shook. Was he in the grip of some violent nightmare, the quarry in a chase, less and less room to maneuver in?

Mahyub got out of the car, leaving the door wide open. He scooped a handful of dirt from the road and tossed it towards the supine figure. The dirt, a clod, hit near the man's face, sprayed him with small particles. An old man, gaunt, he sat up startled.

What I'd taken for a ragged blanket pulled over him were the clothes on his back. He heaved himself upright, rose to his feet unsteadily. No – there was nothing unsteady about him really. It was the shaking, the bodily tremors that gave that

132

impression. The man's thin arms snaked in the air, fingers curved, trembling. His head fluttered like a leaf. All of him – he was like a tuning fork giving a pitch to God.

'St Vitus's dance' – Koert Jan squeezed my arm.

Now the man stepped down off the curb, lurching. He waved to Mahyub, the lifted arm a blur in the air. We watched him walk away, pulling at his rags. His locomotion was made eerie by the violent waste energy of his vibrations.

'He never stops' – Mahyub got back into the car, grinning broadly. 'Night and day.'

'You should have left him alone!' My words came out, I'm afraid, more harshly than I'd intended. Mahyub's brow wrinkled.

'He asks me himself. Whenever I find him sleeping always to wake him up.'

'Otherwise the dogs' – Koert Jan braced himself with a hand against the dashboard as we jolted on – 'would eat him.'

The dump was some five miles south of the city center, not far from the City of Light, the provincial leprosarium. The leprosarium, a village of small buildings behind a low wall, glowed white as we passed it. The place was staffed entirely by nuns from India. The Sisters of Mercy, disciples of Mother Theresa.

'If we had those sisters to clean the streets,' Mahyub said, 'you could eat off the ground. No arms, no legs, it doesn't matter – they make those patients keep the place in order.'

By the time Mahyub veered on to the access road to the dump, rutted and scarred with the imprint of compactor truck tires, I was wide awake. Soon we could see the fire-fighters dashing about. There was hardly any gleam coming from the earth. The worst appeared to be over, a good thing, too, for in the event of a serious blaze twelve hours of continuous effort might be just the beginning. Men went running about with buckets of sand. Laughing, calling out, stumbling. Flakes of ash drifted by in the air. People broke out in fits of coughing. There were hundreds of birds, too – hundreds and hundreds. Pelicans. They looked on like an audience that didn't want to get caught in a rush at the cloakroom. Occasionally a few would take off, flap their huge white wings and cruise over the dump for a better view. I think they were hunting rats and snakes. Pelicans by starlight, drifting through smoke – it was splendid and dismal.

When Mahyub honked at the barrier, no one came. He had to get down and lift the striped wood himself.

'Where's the watchman?' Koert Jan was indignant. 'Can you tell me that?' Troubles often started when unauthorised vehicles brought loads to the dump at night and to destroy evidence that might be traced back to them, set the waste on fire. To prevent this from happening was up to the watchman; actually permitting it was his main source of income.

We climbed out of the Mitsubishi. Mahyub stuck his arm back in through the driver's window and leaned on the horn. On and on and on. It so tore the night I wanted to make him stop. The pelicans began a mournful cawing. At last a lanky youth stumbled out of the darkness into the headlights. He was doing his best to run, but his *futa* kept slipping down off his hips, tripping him.

'Sir' – the watchman stood breathless in front of Koert Jan, panting. While he spoke, he slapped at the front of his *futa* with the back of his hands, as if beating out sparks, or brushing off crumbs. His nervous gesture called our attention to wet stains.

'Where were you?' Koert Jan asked.

'Fire, sir.' The boy didn't meet his eyes.

'Fire!' Mahyub laughed. He got into his truck, backed it up several yards and then swung it around to shine the headlights out in the direction from which the watchman had just come running. There, coat luminous in the distance, browsing among the garbage – I took a step forward to look over Koert Jan's shoulder – stood a donkey.

*

134

'The Koran says no to cows, sheep, goats. These are animals that give milk humans drink,' Mahyub explained to us on our way back to Taiz. 'And another thing about a donkey is, the donkey is so obliging.'

'What was it, Mahyub,' Koert Jan asked, 'a male or female donkey?' Mahyub laughed until tears came to his eyes.

'Exception or the rule?' I asked.

Koert Jan only answered me later. The sky was by then runny with light. We were back home, sipping Yemen coffee. He was about to leave for work. 'There was another boy who did it with donkeys, but the Mayor had it in for him. Security took pictures. Now he's in prison for six months.'

From what Koert Jan told me, the incurably good-natured Mahyub knew the quiddities of many figures at large. For example, one day at the souk he pointed out a sixteen-year-old boy selling dates. Small eyes, craggy nose, thick lips, a seedling beard, kinky bush of hair. Semitic to the hilt. Clouds of flies would settle on the mounds of dates, the boy would reach under the stand and pull out a can of insecticide. Psssst! Hundreds of corpses.

Mahyub called the boy over. Together with Koert Jan they stepped into the nearby shade of a gold merchant's awning. Mahyub took a ten-rial note out of his wallet. The boy accepted with a smile, turned his back, dropped his *futa* and lifted the tails of his shirt.

'You are seeing the most beautiful backside in Taiz,' Mahyub told Koert Jan.

'You can look, but not touch,' Koert Jan explained to me. 'Arms and legs are different. They're public domain. You can stroke them. Not so the buttocks. Touch them and you're making a claim. Touch them and you're saying, that's mine.'

Another time Koert Jan and Mahyub were driving through the city together when Mahyub singled out one of the sweepers, an old woman, as 'special'. Special how? Koert Jan had taken the bait. Mahyub stopped the car, got out and walked over to the woman who was bent over sweeping the gutter. He greeted her. She stood to face him.

'Then Mahyub reached up and took the baseball cap he was wearing and threw it across the road. Immediately the woman, who had no hat, made the same gesture – even crossing to pick up her non-existent hat and put it back on top of her head the way Mahyub had his. He kept looking back at me to make sure I was taking it all in. Then he reached down and pulled the hem of his *futa* above his knees. At once the woman seized her skirts and pulled them back over her thighs. She wasn't wearing anything underneath. The other sweepers stood around cheering. Mahyub patted the woman's shoulder. She patted his. He came and got back into the car and she crouched down and went on with her sweeping.

'Cruel? Why cruel?'

Of all the absurdities Mahyub brought to Koert Jan's notice, in the end it was the Copycat who haunted me most, the woman who had to act out whatever you did in front of her. How does something like that happen to the human spirit? We are all like her, I suppose, to some degree. Koert Jan said she was one of his best workers. In a fairy tale, I kept thinking, there would be some special gesture, a magical action that, forcing her to copy it, would free her from bondage forever.

IV

At the end of our expedition up Jebel Sabar, Elso and Saskia had invited Koert Jan and me to go windsurfing with them the following 'weekend' at the Red Sea. (Friday was everybody's day off.) Koert Jan had accepted but his enthusiasm knew bounds. During the few intervening days our small party grew. People Elso and Saskia knew rang up from the Dutch embassy in Sana and were asked to join. They arrived early, bringing unannounced friends.

136

After dinner Wednesday night we went to meet the arrivals. The plan was to drive down together Thursday afternoon and camp out on the seacoast, returning late Friday. The Sana group were staying with Elso and Saskia whose house was built into the top of a rough knoll near the center of Taiz. The site was surrounded, as in so many places throughout the city, by unfinished houses with rusty iron rods jutting out of floors and walls. Below there were small foundries where work went on well into the night. Across a sharp bend in the wadi, moreover, was a shanty town where *achdam* lived in old car wrecks and sheds patched together from crates and cardboard cartons and sheets of plastic.

Itself, Elso and Saskia's house, was of concrete with iron grillework across the windows. Bits of colored glass were imbedded in the façade. The effect was garish. As we approached from below, reggae music spilled through the open windows into the night. Koert Jan, I should add, is allergic to popular music.

Elso met us at the door with a formal Arabic greeting. He was wearing swimming trunks with the strings hanging out, and a hooded red sweatshirt open down the front. The corridor he led us along was lined with a roadmap of Yemen and various mid-East travel posters. In the *mafrage* mattresses and pillows had been thrown down on the floor in imitation of a Yemeni interior. Artefacts were strewn about as well. Alabaster lamps, daggers, silver breastplates tacked to the side of a bookcase, a water pipe. 'Yes,' Saskia laughed, following my eyes, 'we're very acquisitive.' Then she crossed the room and turned off the tape recorder which looked like the cockpit of a small airplane, blinking lights and all.

'Hello, I'm Hans. This is Ulrike. Jacqueline. Jonathan. Soave, chilled? Courtesy of the embassy cellar.'

Expatriates together, white faces. Koert Jan sank back into a cushion and suddenly I saw how tired he was, and how determined not to let it show.

Hans, number two man on the two-man embassy staff, was a thin-hipped chatterbox that night, a master of ceremonies. He overdid his pawing of Ulrike, his Austrian girlfriend. His sidelong glances of admiration for Koert Jan were more authentic. With her pointy chin, stick body and shrill voice, however cuddly Ulrike came on, she was not going to blind the world to Hans's sexual preferences. Tall Jonathan, all deference to Ulrike, could have crawled out of a blurred print of *Woodstock*. His checked shirt and eyeglasses both managed to look slept in. There was a Boston twang to his speech. He made a lot of comments to himself. Everyone seemed to have something to hide, unsuccessfully. With Jonathan it was baldness. The long strands of black hair that he draped across his crown called attention to what they were intended to conceal.

Jonathan had come to Yemen on a Rockefeller Fellowship to save paper, to study with Ulrike, one of the world's foremost paper savers. She was busy – and would be for years to come – rescuing an endangered collection of pre-Arabic parchments. No one had deciphered them yet. No one had made even an educated guess about their contents. First things first. Doubtless the effort and expense to save them from disintegration would be worth it.

'The printed word's never been more in danger,' Jonathan assured us. 'On library shelves all over the world books are being eaten away by acid rain. If we don't do something, and presently, we might as well kiss them goodbye.'

The large girl who hung on Jonathan's every word was Jacqueline, an embassy secretary. Her complexion was an unfortunate even pink disconcertingly close to the tint of her frock. With her Cleopatra haircut and forearms and calves exposed, she reclined uncomfortably for all the world like a supremely kitsch piggy-bank. Indeed, when she laughed it was as if something loose rattled inside her. Personally I've never been able to get used to kisses from strangers upon introduction, but as the evening wore on I no longer blamed Jacqueline for seizing her chances.

'Anyone who wants to come is more than welcome' – Jacqueline spread her arms to the room at one point. She was taking Hans to the Taiz Museum early the next day, the late Imam's palace. 'They've left it exactly the way it was the day he died from the wounds inflicted on him by his assassins.'

'Martyrs,' Koert Jan corrected. 'That's how the Yemenis see it.'

'Everything's covered with dust, inches thick,' Jacqueline went on. 'The guide is a deaf mute. He has keys to all the rooms. He lets you in and follows you about acting things out. Swords. Binoculars. He acts them out, grunting.' Jacqueline rose to her knees and imitated the guide. In front of her mouth the air filled with spray. She squeezed her eyes shut, her lips writhed, her fingers wriggled like worms. 'Priceless things mixed in with junk. They say all the real jewelry – gold, pearls, diamonds – got stolen long ago and what's left in the cases is paste. His soap, his toilet paper. It's all there. The morphine he used against pain when the chest wounds wouldn't heal. The bloody shirt. There's a cinema, too. A room with a projector and a screen where the Imam used to watch movies with a few friends when films were still banned to the public.'

'What Jacqui really wants to show me' – Hans seemed to give us all the benefit of his profile at one time – 'is the world's largest bra.'

'It's there,' Jacqueline squealed. 'Belonged to one of his wives.'

'The world's largest bra *in captivity*,' Hans said, 'that's what she's promised. And I won't settle for less.'

'Don't forget the eagles,' Koert Jan added.

'The what?' Saskia sat scrubbing antique silver earrings she had just purchased. She used a toothbrush dipped in cleansing powder, then dunked them in a plastic basin full of water.

'Eagles. Out back, in a cage. There are three. You have to go through the army offices and pass the baboons.'

'A tautology,' Jonathan mumbled.

'Their cage has rusted open, but nobody notices. Not even the eagles. They just sit there molting, covered in their own shit.'

'How big did you say?' Hans had lowered his head on to Ulrike's lap. Jacqueline carved enormous arcs in the air around her own melon-sized breasts. We all laughed and found we had nothing to say.

'We'll bring a cake,' Koert Jan pledged.

'You're not going to drink?' Elso asked. 'I'm collecting from the rest.'

'I don't mind chipping in.' I reached for my wallet.

'That's silly if you're not going to drink,' Saskia said. 'Don't forget to bring socks.'

'Socks!' Ulrike shrieked. She might have been a Playboy bunny shrunk in a pressure cooker. 'Oh God.'

'Sand-flies,' Saskia shrugged.

'I'll be eaten alive.' Ulrike seemed pleased. 'I'm always the first one they go for. Zzzzz. Zzzzz.'

'Maybe we'll be lucky' – Elso grinned – 'and there won't be so many jellyfish this time.'

'Oh God.' Ulrike's eyes goggled with revulsion.

'Do they go for you first, too?' Koert Jan asked.

As we walked downhill from Elso and Saskia's, loud reggae followed us through the open windows. I looked back once over my shoulder. Jacqueline was leaning out, waving goodbye. We were up to our ankles in garbage, tin cans, plastic and paper. Thanks to Koert Jan the main road was clean, but woe to the unwary who turned off it. Here there were loose stones, too, which made it difficult to walk without feeling your way. Still, under the vaulted night sky children raced about playing tag, wrestling each other to the ground, hugging and kissing their closest friends. On the mountain-side in front of us, electric lights high up sparkled like constellations.

'Good group,' Koert Jan said. His flat intonation left me guessing, as so often, at the level of his intended irony.

For the beach party at Yachtule, Wardah, Koert Jan's half-caste Ethiopian help, baked the promised cake. She used a Magi-mixer that came with the house. It had attachments to put on the attachments. For the rent Koert Jan paid, he might have had a large flat in the heart of Paris, London, or even New York. Or rather for the rent which his employer, indirectly the Dutch tax payer, was paying.

'Elso and Saskia pay double for theirs,' he told me defensively.

'I thought we were supposed to be helping the poorest of the poor.'

Koert Jan laughed. 'We have to live somewhere while we do.'

When Koert Jan and I had worked together in East Africa, we lived in a round mud and thatch hut. Hard dirt floor, vaulted roof, bats nesting in the straw. We'd never been happier. Now Koert Jan had a bathtub with hot-water heater, a freezer, a stove with oven and rotisserie, and air-conditioners. ('I need them to sleep.' 'You? You *hate* air-conditioners.' 'True. Only after my first night here, the Mayor asked if I was happy. Yes, I said. Then I did something stupid. I didn't know the man yet. I told him dogs had kept me awake. The next day he had fifty dogs poisoned. So now I sleep with the air-conditioner on to drown out the barking.')

The sound of Wardah busy with the Magi-mixer did not make my task any easier. My eyes were open but I wasn't awake. That morning Koert Jan had left the house at his usual inhuman hour. Some time later, dutifully I'd dragged myself up. The report about Dhamar was proving slow, hard work. And my time was running out.

To escape the whir of the electric beaters, I took my cup of instant coffee out on to the back balcony. There from a deckchair

141

above a garden of scraggly hibiscus I watched the morning light change on Jebel Sabar.

The cracks in the hospital buildings were the least of it. These could be filled in. No, it was pressing my tact to find an acceptable way to describe how, in the wake of the earthquake, relief teams from various and sundry Arab states had refused to speak to each other, much less work together. Their fierce bickering, nurses assured me, had filled the corridors while patients, unattended, lay dying.

Most earthquake victims were long gone now, either back to their villages to dig out and begin anew, or into one of several mass graves outside Dhamar. Disease? Nobody seemed to have heard of disease. Most cases admitted to hospital were the victims of gun wounds, or car accidents, or overeating. My visits to distant settlements, up cliffsides and across streams, left me cold at the idea of village health committees. Another fashionable drawing-board indulgence. More United Nations chic. With all I had seen and heard, I was having a devil of a time trying to peck out passable sentences on my bouncy portable. And the aroma of cake in the oven paralysed my ability to think still further.

When the morning reached that point at which the heat begins to make a fist, Wardah came out to clean the balcony. She was black as night, slender, quick. Large, doleful eyes dominated her pretty face. Head to toe her presence was aggressively sexual. 'Rose', for so Wardah translates from the Arabic, was wearing tight white slacks, silver slippers, a flimsy white blouse. She had a twisted ribbon, red and gold, around her forehead, running through what Koert Jan called her wild, gypsy hair. When she dressed like that, he flatly refused to go with her to the market. Because Wardah wouldn't wear a veil, security had arrested her as a 'streetwalker' more than once. She shrugged these episodes off lightly, but they were a great humiliation to her father, a foreign worker in Saudi Arabia. Wardah's younger sisters all wore veils. She was too independent.

142

'Good morning. Smells delicious,' I said when Wardah came outside with a mop and bucket. One hand on her hip, she took her time looking me up and down. Finally she decided not to ask me to move but to clean around me. Wardah's idea of cleaning was to douse the tile floors liberally with Dettol, as expensive in Taiz as good wine in the West. But she never dusted. She didn't see the point. 'It's sand,' she would say. 'Sand comes back.'

Wardah had picked up her English looking after the children of a US marine for a year in Sana. Every day she brought a small cassette recorder to work with her and sang along with the Arab melodies that warbled from the machine's throat. She never played it loud, though. Sometimes I would walk into a room I thought was empty and find her sitting on the floor, back against the wall, head forward between her knees, singing.

'Steve come,' Wardah grinned at me, jamming her mop into the bucket and sloshing it around. Steve was her roly-poly Australian boyfriend, an ungainly geologist. He flew into Taiz from Sana for occasional weekend romps. These visits taxed Wardah's considerable resourcefulness at lying to her old mother, and to Koert Jan. Invariably she rose to the occasion brilliantly. Illnesses, accidents, job interviews. For that matter Koert Jan and I were playing a rather odd game with pillows and pajamas every morning, rumpling sheets to convince Wardah that we slept in separate rooms. I'm sure we never deceived her for a minute, and she didn't care. Wardah told Koert Jan that she knew Steve would leave her, he was more interested in his rocks, but it was fun while it lasted. 'And it's good for my English.' Recently Wardah had begun making efforts to expand her relations with Koert Jan. At dinner one night, with Koert Jan sitting right there, she told me that he was too nervous. 'What he needs, you know, is a girlfriend.'

'It's the tomato sauce,' Koert Jan said, 'that's what I really mind. Everything with tomato sauce.'

'Tell her you don't like it.'

'I have. But when I tell her the tomato sauce is coming out of my ears, suddenly she loses her English.' Koert Jan sighed. 'The thing is, it's hard to find help.'

'It's what?'

'Before Wardah I had Ting-a-ling. A Vietnamese boy. He couldn't even open a can of tomato sauce. He wasn't in the house two days when he showed up with his face all bloody and bruised and told me his father had beat him for selling his body to men. Then he stuck out his hip.'

'What did you do?'

'He made it easy for me – he started to steal things.'

'Did he want to get his hands cut off?' Koert Jan didn't answer me. 'How did you come by Wardah?'

'The Mayor.'

Koert Jan only got back to the house late in the morning. He was driving a Toyota canvas-top borrowed for the trip from the project workshop. To reach the Red Sea we had to cross the sands of the Tihama and would need four-wheel drive.

'Sorry. The Mayor was planning to raid Rachman and I had to talk him out of it. He's got an air mattress on that corner now, too – Rachman has – I'm not sure who gave it to him, Mahyub or Bert, but the Mayor's heart can't take much more.'

While Koert Jan bathed himself and shaved, I went back and forth loading the car. For a one-day expedition we were taking an amazing amount with us. First Law of Vacation Dynamics: the shorter the journey, the more gets packed. Two large jerry-cans of water were the last things I crammed in. The others were supposed to supply water, but experience has taught me that in the desert too much water is never enough. Departure was delayed another ten minutes when Koert Jan couldn't find the mosquito lotion. Our frantic search ended when Wardah saw it clutched in his right hand.

We were ripe for a holiday.

*

144

Just as the others were deciding to leave without us, we pulled up at Elso and Saskia's.

'How you doing?' Hester and Pim had arrived – with a second surfplank – from Dhamar. Pim, also a trained nurse, had come to Yemen with the status of 'partner' because there was no job vacancy for him. The hospital director had been strict, not to say rigid, about not allowing Pim to work, not even as a volunteer. The earthquake had given Pim a chance to show what he could do. All reports agreed he had pushed himself hard, his kindness and generosity outstanding. Once the emergency subsided, however, the hospital director made it his business to remind Pim that the hospital wards were off limits.

During my talks with the director the man had been preoccupied by one thought and one thought only: would the Minister of Development on her return to The Hague 'remember her promise' to build a swimming pool for the Dutch community in Dhamar? Would I include a gentle reminder in my report? I knew the man was about to be recalled in any event. He and his wife, in their late fifties, had a habit of wandering around their house naked which had come to the attention of the security police. The couple sat down to dinner naked, played Scrabble naked, put on pajamas to sleep. Pim was rumoured to have taken photos of them through the window and to have passed these on to security.

Counting Hester and Pim's steel-gray Toyota Land Cruiser, we were four vehicles in all. 'The more the merrier,' Jacqueline crowed. Maybe. I was annoyed, I admit, at having living reminders of Dhamar along unexpectedly. I hope it didn't show. Koert Jan immortalised the chaos of our departure with my ancient Yashica, holding it belly-button high, peering down into the viewfinder. The fine thing about the relic was how you sighted on an image exactly the same size as what would appear on the negative.

Hans was driving a fawn-colored Land Rover with embassy plates. By daylight, with his clipped moustache, styled hair and super-erect, slim posture he seemed the prototype of a KLM steward. Only his teeth weren't very good. Elso and Saskia had packed their little white Suzuki to the bursting point. They both were dressed completely in white, too, except that Elso wore a leather belt with a buckle made out of his initials in gold. It was agreed that for the first hundred kilometers or so, paved last year by a hoard of visiting Koreans, everyone was on his own. We would rendezvous at the 26 km signpost along the road to Moccha.

As we left Taiz, Koert Jan talked non-stop about garbage collection. How much the project had accomplished on the outskirts of the city. 'See,' he kept saying. No, I didn't see. I had nothing to compare things to. (Only when we reached Hagda, the next village, where nothing had been done, could I form some idea of the difference between 'before' and 'after'.) 'In one week we haul eighty wrecks,' Koert Jan boasted. 'Thirty-five tons of garbage a day. Up there, see, that's the army base.' Along the bluff as we drove past the muzzles of a line of anti-aircraft guns stuck out from under green canvas wrapping. 'It used to be you couldn't see the hillside. There were millions of flies – like in the Bible. The General wanted us to spray the kitchen three times a day with a high concentration of DDT. I was tempted. In the end my conscience won out and I had him put his men to work cleaning up the place instead.'

'Still looks pretty bad to me.'

'That? That's nothing.' We turned a bend and left the army camp behind. 'Maintenance is a problem though, naturally. And we can't fine the army.'

We were driving through farmland now, chunky pale soil churned up into furrows. Young trees, hardly any old ones. Olive groves with snaky branches, shimmering leaves.

'They just don't see it,' Koert Jan explained, 'literally. They look right through it.'

Here and there a plastic mineral water bottle glistened like

146

precious metal along the roadside. Better not to see it, I thought, than see only it.

'Twenty years ago nothing in Taiz came in a package. The city was self-sufficient, as good as. They brought in fruit, oranges mostly, from Aden – in crates. That's all. If you owed someone, if you wanted to do someone a special favor, you gave him an orange. There's a story that the Mayor's wife even got him out of prison once by bribing the jailor with oranges.

'Now? Try to find anything that isn't wrapped. Wrapped twice. Everything from Pampers to cigarettes. They're even packing *qat* in plastic now instead of keeping it fresh in leaves. Taiz has its very own plastic factory. Carrier bags with polka dots. Modern measles.'

It wasn't easy, a few times I began to rejoice prematurely, but I finally managed to change the subject. And as we began to descend towards the Red Sea coast, Koert Jan began to sing. He has a tenor voice of fine quality. In fact he only passed up a musical career because he thought 'the life' was too competitive.

'How happy, happy, happy we are,' Koert Jan sang, 'to be together again.'

'Switch into fourth,' I sang. To improvise arias was an old pastime of ours.

The sky was enormous. We were surrounded by odd clumps of hills, spiny mountain ridges peculiarly flat, bleached of depth by the glaring midday haze.

'Loaves of bread. Gum drops.'

'Camels guzzling before they gulp.'

We passed a roadside firewood farm. Bundles of wriggling, severed roots, Some were arranged tepee fashion. Wood in Yemen fetches high cash prices. The land has been largely denuded of trees.

'Pipe organs,' Koert Jan sang out, pointing to rock formations near the summit of a bluff. The intermeshed stone fangs made the hillside seem to smile.

'The oranges come from Jordan now,' Koert Jan suddenly

said, sadly. 'Sent by that hypocrite Hussein to his Palestinian brothers. But they don't want oranges. They want money. So they sell the things to the government, and the government markets them at a profit.'

Along the way we made only one stop, at a combination petrol station–small store near the T-crossing where we would head west towards Moccha. Here Koert Jan bought a dozen bottles of pop, lurid red and orange. The pop came from a fridge. The fridge was not plugged in. Typically the boy who lugged the bottles to the back of the Toyota looked sixty-five. He had long hair, the clothes of an adult, too large for him and too tattered for self-respect. The skin of his face was taut, his expression deadly serious. It was anybody's guess how many hours a day he stood in the small tin shack next to the petrol pump and shook a whisk at flies. Crates of empty bottles rose up on all sides of the counter behind which he sat, installed in the splendor of his petty commercial authority.

In the shade of a side terrace half a dozen men already lounged on string beds of colored plastic. The chomping of *qat* had commenced. Everyone had his own pile of leaves. One toothless old man sat with a small plastic Moulinex parsley mill. He pushed several sprigs of fresh *qat* into the mill at a time and cranked the handle. Then he took the shredded bits that came out, oozing juices, and propped them into his cheek. A water pipe with glowing coals stood in the middle of the gravel bed of the terrace. The mouthpiece, attached to a long striped hose, was passed from hand to hand.

'Oh Jesus,' I said as I closed the back doors of the Toyota. 'Guess what? We forgot the cake.'

'We?'

'I put it in a special box. Then in the last minute rush – '

' – we forgot it.'

Hester and Pim sped past us en route to the 26 km signpost. They appeared to take a wrong turn. Koert Jan assured me, no, they were off to visit the smugglers. Yemen is dry, officially. Dispersed throughout the desert near Moccha, however, there are clusters of look-alike farms that provide Scotch, gin, beer, wine – by the case. A few palms, a few low stone buildings built in haste, palisades of millet stalks that crackle in the sea breeze. Here you drive up into a compound and wait. Soon three or four bright-eyed youths come to take your order. They ask a ridiculous price. You shift into reverse, begin to back away. They change their tune. The charade is part of the fun. The boys go out to dig up your order. With bottles and crates loaded, draped with a blanket, you sight by the sun and tear off through the desert where dirt tracks criss-cross each other endlessly. It's a game that fools no one.

Most of the contraband evidently comes from Djibouti. Everyone agrees some of the revenue, 'indirect taxes', ends up with government officials if not with the government. The most notorious local smuggler, a certain One-arm, was thrown into prison, fined and released at regular intervals, the rhythm apparently as regular as the phases of the moon. Rumour had it that One-arm had a television in his cell, color, that his cell door was never locked, and that five times a day he strolled across Moccha with the police captain to visit the mosque.

In his possession Koert Jan had a letter from the governor of the province entitling him, as a foreign consultant, to have a specified, limited supply of alcoholic beverages. This permit, and Koert Jan's indifference to alcohol, were instrumental to his staying in the Mayor's good graces. On occasions when Koert Jan made runs for the Mayor, however, the smuggling was just beginning when he reached home. Back in Taiz he had to find a way to sneak the booty in upstairs without the Mayor's wife catching on. It wasn't that she had religious objections. Drinking was supposed to be fatal for the Mayor's heart.

At the 26 km signpost we were the last to tip off the tarmac and draw up on the sand. The others cheered. 'Hi ho,' Elso called and we were off. Our caravan across the desert sent up clouds of dust. Each car had to keep its distance from the one in front. We followed a track of sorts – with washboard ruts that jarred the bones unless you could reach a speed where the corrugations melted into an illusory smooth surface. Packing in haste, I hadn't anticipated such a bumpy ride. Everything, dishes, folding beds, thermos, jerry-cans, went crashing about in back.

'Good thing we forgot the cake,' I tried, clutching one of the roll-bars overhead. 'It never would have survived the trip.'

'Good thing.'

Deserts have always appealed to me. The emptier the better. I stop thinking. At least I stop being aware of thinking, but all the same my mind feels charged to its limits. The vastness terrifies and comforts me at once. The desert is pure contradiction of ego, and yet, by imposing that perception on an observer, it is the self's reaffirmation. Nowhere else is individual effort so stark – since childhood I have been deeply attached to the image of life as the flight of a butterfly across the Sahara. Night and day, nonstop. Nowhere else, surrounded by non-life, by mere matter, spilled, abundant, our noses rubbed in natural indifference to human survival, do we feel so painfully the ironic persistence of an inner voice, the desire to deny our enduring isolation from each other, to interpret, to understand, to comment.

Far off to the east, as we pitched along trying not to lose sight of Hans & Co., there were hump-backed prehistoric mountain ridges, reddish and purple, cloud topped. Dwarf acacias and mixed varieties of sagebrush and tumbleweed stretched in all directions. Some low plants had silver tassels that scintillated in the glare of the Tihama sun. A fine green-gold moss grew in patches, seared in places to yellow. This desert was not all sand though, there was flint and gravel and volcanic rock. We drove for half an hour without seeing a soul. From time to time we sighted a solitary camel nibbling at branches or standing in scrawny shade. Large improbable beasts, I found them, of a good humour apparently unparalleled in the animal kingdom.

'You know why marauders prefer she-camels?' Koert Jan

150

shook his head at my question. 'Because they keep silent when you mount them. Lawrence, T.E., tells of a she-camel who had just foaled. The foal died. A canny camel trainer skinned the corpse, rolled it up and stuck it in his saddle bag. On the next march the mother, usually dependable, balked. To make her go on, Lawrence was ready to beat her. There was a war on. The trainer was there like a shot. He unrolled the dead foal's skin under the mother's nose. She took a good whiff and off she went again. Until the mother had enough of mourning, the trick had to be repeated four or five times.'

'I wish they'd stop,' Koert Jan said. We were skirting a nomad encampment. Huts of straw, goatherds, dark children racing about, scratching in the dust with sticks.

'The sight of so much poverty feels like a luxury,' I said. 'It ain't Taiz.'

In answer Koert Jan pointed to a flimsy dwelling. From the roof, at a tilt, rose a TV antenna, silver bright. A few minutes later we saw a sand dune ahead of us. One. A single, solitary, monumentally sculptured dune, guaranteed to moisten the palms of even the most jaded topographer. And it was walking. A constant wind displaced surface grains of sand which never seemed to snarl or entangle but hovered and then settled in place so that the form of the whole was recreated in a new location. It took hours, perhaps days, for the dune to shift as much as a foot forwards, but it was in no hurry. The motion, the drift felt not only perceptible, but irresistible. Like some infinitely slow yawn. The top of the dune had a spine with scalloped swirl. All on the near side of this stunning curve was pale and dazzled. Glimpses of the far side revealed a deeper brown. On its stroll the dune had already advanced half-way across our auto track. To avoid running it down, Koert Jan had to swerve.

'We should have color film,' he said. 'Too bad.'

Just past a diminutive mosque with two domes and one crumbling wall, the others veered seawards. In our attempt to follow, the Toyota sank into a patch of soft sand. Our wheels spun without purchase. Koert Jan hit the horn. Elso alertly circled back in the Suzuki. He had to show Koert Jan how to put our vehicle into four-wheel drive. Hans swung back as well. Jacqueline bounded down from the Land Rover, pointed at the forlorn mosque and laughed. Hans walked to a point in the desert, extended one arm shoulder high out to his side, cupped the hand and turned it palm downward. Jacqueline snapped a photo.

'Rembrandt's Jewish Bride,' Hans informed us. To the camera his hand appeared to cup the dome-breast of the disintegrating shrine. 'Sad to say we failed to find the world's largest bra this morning' – there were red threads like underwater weeds in the whites of his eyes – 'but don't think the deaf mute didn't act it out.'

The domes were indeed magical, as in many settings in Yemen. The curve so proudly man-made, mathematical. A white boast on pinnacles, in valleys, on plateaux, or here, deep in the desert. Implanted, restful.

For another twenty minutes we carried on, always westward, but never directly. Twisting and winding, we reached Yachtule. The village was picturesque – but under such a coating of filth and waste it took an act of the imagination to see its beauty. '*Et tu*, Yachtule,' Koert Jan muttered. Elso and Saskia led us down streets with high clay walls on either side, across a central square with a covered well, past scaffolding hung with gory goat pelts. At the edge of the desert a group of children were playing ping-pong on a rickety table, using home-made paddles, square in shape. They did their best to bat a dented ball back and forth. Our arrival distracted them.

'*Sura, sura*,' they swooped down on us calling. *Sura* is Arabic for photograph. Tourists with Polaroids had reached the Tihama. The miracle had made a deep impression. Satisfaction in sixty seconds. People longed to press a piece of paper to their hearts while, from a pale blur, the surface grew darker and darker until finally there it was, a sharp image of themselves.

And in the middle of nowhere: a tree hung with plastic bags of every conceivable color. Koert Jan stopped when I insisted to let me take a photograph. Wicked, permanent confetti.

When Elso in the lead sighted the sea, he sounded a series of shorts blasts on his horn. We had to negotiate our way slowly through a deeply rutted wadi, the ground littered with felled palms. When finally we emerged from a clump of trees on to the narrow strip of shimmering, gently banked coastal beach, it was like crawling through a leafy keyhole.

'The good life,' Koert Jan grinned. For ten minutes we drove north, our left wheels churning through frothy surf, right wheels, elevated, gouging a track in firm sand. All in all it had been a beautiful drive, but it was a pleasure to reach Elso and Saskia's campsite, kill the engine, and step out.

V

We pitched our camp at the central bulge of a semi-circular bay. A barrier reef stretched across the mouth of the bay out near the horizon. The sea beyond was cerulean, closer to shore a pale emerald. It took half a minute for me to slip into swim-trunks and plunge into the water.

'Oof.' The Red Sea was warm, almost bath temperature, with a strong salt taste. I suppose charging into the ocean I always expect to splash down into the cold North Sea of my childhood. Years in the tropics, swimming in soup, never seem to erase happy, early memories of gasping for breath on account of the chill, limbs tingling. At Yachtule all the way out to the reef the water was hardly more than knee high. After a narrow band of sharp shell fragments near the shore, the bottom turned to smooth sand. There was a strong wind which whipped the water into froth. Exposed to the air, your body was colder than crouched down in the water.

As soon as I toweled off, I tried to make myself useful. Sort of. My helplessness is something of a standing joke. The one thing I can do is change a flat tire but then I'm careless as hell about checking whether there's a working jack in the car. How to suck snake bites, give mouth-to-mouth resuscitation, rig up crystal radios – forget it. So far my luck has held, I've not been put to the test.

'All I can add to your efficiency,' I used to tease Koert Jan, 'is my admiration.' I may be wrong but I always thought he liked me in the role of the bungler – as long as I didn't milk it too hard.

Elso found the pit where last time they had sunk the cooking primus. Doggie-style, he dug away the capsized sand. Pim reparked our Toyota parallel to his, some twenty yards away, facing the sea. From carrier rack to carrier rack he stretched a length of sturdy blue plastic cable. Between the vehicles the girls set out our stretcher beds, side by side. A few reed mats and sleeping-bags broke the pattern. Then Jacqueline and Ulrike hung mosquito nets from the blue cable, round affairs, some with green netting, most with white, a few with attractive embroidery at the top, like Arab headcloths. I drew Koert Jan's folding bed and mine, their canvas sagging, into the line next to our Toyota.

Pim, assisted by Hans and Jonathan, both endearingly clumsy, excavated a broad, shallow cavity in moist sand for a campfire. Everyone scattered to collect wood, palm branches or planks tossed up by the sea.

'We'll be too close to the fire,' I pointed out to Koert Jan, 'downwind.'

'The smoke will keep off the mosquitoes.'

'True, but we won't be able to breathe.'

With all the mosquito nets in place, whipped into motion by the sea breeze, it looked like a row of veiled dancers were swaying between our parked cars. Backing out ankle deep in the gentle, lapping waves, I took a photo of the ghostly chorus line.

'Really a good picture' – Jacqueline splashed to my side. 'Mind if I take one, too?'

'I can't believe it,' Jonathan kept saying. He stood up on the beach spit polishing his glasses with the tail of his checked shirt. 'The Red Sea. I'm really at the Red Sea.'

Rigging of the surfplanks took next to no time. The boys were brisk in their movements, the procedure in their hands, not their heads. The bright sails with inserts of transparent plastic, bold white numbers and symbols, conjured up competition – and privilege. Late afternoons the wind along the coast could suddenly turn harsh. Special storm sails smaller than ordinary sails were needed. Saskia was the first to mount. Trim in a clinging silver bikini, her blonde helmet cut gleaming, she rode one plank towards the horizon, crouched, arms fully extended. The board skimmed across small waves at high speed. Pim, with a red tank suit showing under more modest madras boxer trunks, rode the other. He was a stunt man and could flip the sail and walk around the mast with nonchalance.

Pim was deeply tanned, with a hard, lean body except for a protruding belly, as if he'd swallowed a melon. Every male in Yemen had a moustache – as if prescribed by the Koran, compensation for removal of pubic hair. Pim was growing a moustache too, tending it, shaping it and talking about it. 'Sex makes it grow faster,' Pim said, 'that's a fact.' Hester shrugged. Almost every time Pim spoke, Hester shrugged.

We non-surfers splashed and frolicked – all except for Ulrike that is who seemed intent on posing for a peninsula version of September Morn, wading out to mid-calf, dunking her frail body without getting her head wet, without cracking a smile, cupping handfuls of water to pour demurely on to her shoulders, back and breasts. Her swimming-suit looked like a few hastily licked postage stamps. Her body was clenched. The kind of woman who early in life too easily resigns herself to being found unpleasant, she was slowly shrivelling, not from age or exposure, but unconsummated anger. Then she screamed.

There *were* jellyfish. Large gelatinous, extravagant freaks of nature. Washed ashore, helpless, they held their gleam long. The dome of the body sensual, the tangled tentacles like the guts of the dead dogs whose rigid carcasses littered Yemen's roads – but purified, transparent. Ulrike appointed herself jellyfish undertakeress. She seized the large pointed spade Pim had brought and tipping the stranded jellyfish on to the iron blade, the ribbons of muscle in her upper arms taut under the weight, she shuffled off among the surrounding palms to found a burial ground. It was an emblem, it was – the sight of the scrawny, sexually high-strung Austrian staggering with that blob of life delicately balanced on the tip of her shovel – an emblem for development co-operation.

Ulrike's foray flushed a lurking jeepload of Yemenis. When our entourage arrived, a family had apparently been napping and dallying in the deep shade of the neighboring palms. Women with bare arms but veils down to the ground. Children in what looked like miniature wedding gowns. Men with sleek faces, lumpy bodies, no hard lines. Now as they reversed out of the grove, they stared hard at all of us through car windows rolled all the way up.

'Voyeurs,' Jonathan said. His stabs at humor all seemed to be made with a blunt instrument. Again he was breathing on his glasses, in preparation to polishing them. Watching him, I wondered how an American undercover agent could ever infiltrate any foreign group – the peculiarly American combination of arrogance and innocence was practically iridescent. Without glasses, Jonathan's head was a papaya about to fall. Behind his lenses, however, the eyes became impish, alive. He wore baggy California swim trunks, a rainbow of bright colors. His torso was peppered with freckles. There was a thin Christmas tree of fine hair on his chest.

'Coming?' Koert Jan could never settle in a new place

without reconnoitering. I felt a jolt of love at the sight of him in his black shorts, the smooth body of a boy. Pictures of Koert Jan as a young man were dazzling, but I wasn't trying to flatter him when I said he looked soulless to me back then, distant and cool, and his face has only acquired character with age.

'Take these?' I asked, handing him a *futa* and draping one over my own shoulder.

'Good idea.'

In the direction Koert Jan was striking out, south – towards a sand spit that marked the farthest reaches of the lower arc of the sickle-shaped bay – there were signs of habitation. Fishing boats up on the sand, wisps of smoke a short distance inland. In Islam the male body from the waist to knee is *aruda*, sexually provocative – that is why we thought to take clothes with us in case we should run into people.

The pleasure of a walk with Koert Jan is that he is comfortable with silence. He doesn't expect you to keep up a running patter of conversation. What's more, he sees everything worth seeing, so by watching the movement of his eyes you can learn a great deal. Not more than half a kilometer from our campsite we came upon a group of fishermen removing the net from their boat to pile it in folds on the shore. The boat was brightly painted, and peeling. We stopped to watch.

They were enacting a fable, surely. The net was maybe three meters wide, but hours and hours long. Two men by the side of the boat, still half in the water, kept shrugging new folds of netting loose which three men higher up on the beach would haul steadily, hand over hand, towards them. The fishermen near the boat were old, grizzled. Those at the receiving end of the net were boys, loose-limbed, lambent. To remove the entire net from the boat to shore in this fashion would clearly take all the time available until they had to load the net again for the next fishing voyage. Ah, the men were captive in a magical conspiracy to protect the lives of fish.

Dogs sat, chin on their forepaws in the sand, watching the men work. We smiled, the men kept at their task, never missing a beat. The dogs lifted their heads, sand trailing in their chin whiskers, tails beginning to thump. Back among the trees we saw rafts of wood the color of bone and a cluster of flimsy reed houses with large clay and copper vessels on wooden racks. Children, half- or undressed, ran about getting in each other's way, pushing each other down. Women ducked in and out of arched doorways. They wore bright wraps and in their arms they carried winnowing baskets heaped with cones of grain. Bare, weathered faces were startling after the enforced modesty of Taiz. The absence of jewelry was striking, too. It was a scene too disordered to be idyllic, too minimal. But at least it belonged to where it took place.

We walked on. It was my favorite time of day. The memory of heat still comforting, but colors stampeding back into the world on the heels of the departing sun. Where the glare of light had punished the eye, shadows created life, drew vision into adventures of imagining.

'Do they mate?' I asked Koert Jan. When his eyebrows went up, I pointed to jellyfish coughed up on to the beach by the now rapidly receding tide. 'They don't hatch from eggs, do they? I can't picture them oozing out of a shell. You'd think they'd stick together – if they fuck. God, I'll bet a jellyfish foetus is grotesque. Or splendid. Maybe they recapitulate backwards? Maybe all the details are finished and perfect and as time passes everything goes blurry and vague? What do you think?'

As we approached the spit we could see large numbers of birds hovering over the packed sand, large numbers, too, standing on thin legs, wings neatly folded. Most were white, some had dark markings on the crest of the skull. To our left was an extensive, dense palm grove. Date palms. Most of the trunks strained towards the sea with a curvature of the spine. And as we walked we became aware that the grove was full of men. Dark-skinned, huddled in small groups around wood fires. Some were cocooned in clothes, sleeping full-out on the sand.

'Fishermen?' I asked Koert Jan, more statement than question.

He was bearing down, however, on an extraordinary sight ahead. Beyond our bay, on the far side of the tawny, undulant spit, was a second bay, backed inland by a series of glistening salt flats. On the shore, on the far side of the palm grove, four black men huddled in the water. One to the left stood stabbing and hacking at some captive creature in their midst. His bloody knife flashed up – and then leaning forward he put all his weight and strength into a downward thrust, twisting the blade, gouging at whatever it was that lay at his feet. We kept our pace. Soon the puzzle yielded meaning. One of the other men turned away from the group and came half-walking, half-running in our direction, legs scissoring through rags. And in his hands, held together, cupped out in front of him, a knot of gore, entrails dripping and beribboned, almost trailing in the sand.

On the hard shelf of coast still wet from the retreating sea we made out two giant sea turtles on their backs. One had been decapitated. The head, severed neatly, stood sentinel in the sand next to the body, erect on the stump of its neck, beak like some unforgiving judge's, the eyes large and flooded with bubbling blood. Red stood out in that landscape.

The second turtle was still alive. The pulse in its yellow throat throbbed hypnotically and the pale flippers moved, wriggled slightly as the beast lay there staring up at the sky crushed under the unnatural weight of its own organs. The turtle's sex was revealed – and utterly confusing. The decapitated beast was a female. The male organ, however, when withdrawn, left an opening for all the world like a vagina.

In such situations, as at the scene of accidents, Koert Jan presses too close for my comfort. He doesn't intrude with advice or offers of help, no, but he makes himself present, available. He

159

honors requests when they come. As we reached the scene, the man wielding the knife was kneeling in water and scouring the insides of the shell of a third sea turtle, scraping out every last shred. He was so dark that the whites of his eyes and teeth were startling. Even the palms of his hands, his gums were black. I fancied that when he finally saw us – for so intense was his concentration that before he was aware of our standing there, we were merely a few feet away, Koert Jan close enough to reach out and touch – I fancied for an instant that before the man gained control of himself his hand with the knife had pulled back and made an instinctive, murderous move towards us.

When stared at, especially if there is no mistaking the hostility of a stare, my strategy of choice is always to pretend to be oblivious. Fear provokes aggression. Down the beach, at the first sight of the fishermen with the net, we had wrapped our *futas* around us. Now shading our eyes we turned to gaze at the sea with fixed smiles. How we gazed, at the birds, the jellyfish, the men, the sea turtles, the pools of blood and viscera.

'Good catch.' It is Koert Jan's conviction that where he is at a loss to speak the local language he can establish good will by conversing in Dutch, calmly and naturally, as if everyone in hearing can understand him perfectly. 'Fresh turtle, nothing quite like it.'

The black man rinsed his knife in the sea. He wore a checked *futa*, his cotton undervest bloodied and torn. Standing erect he snarled and snapped at the men with him, all a lighter brown. They were slack somehow, almost absent-minded, simple when compared to his fierce purposefulness. In response to his command they splashed towards the still-living sea turtle. One man to a flipper they crouched to drag the creature higher on to the sand. Gulls, screeching, hovered near our heads, diving at skeins of blood in the warm sea water.

'Aaiieee.' Three men dropped the turtle which had begun to struggle in their grasp and mightily strain its flippers. Only the

160

dark leader, knife in mouth, kept his grip. With disdain he waved the knife in the air and scolded the men who went scampering back some yards before stopping to stare shame-facedly at the helpless turtle, rocking on its shell. They inched back together, laid hold of the flippers once more and dragged the beast, gouging a runnel in the sand, up towards the palm grove. They did it, but they didn't like it. And their leader shortened their lives for sure when he suddenly let go of the flipper in his grasp and, squealing, did a mincing dance in imitation of the others. This whole time the head in the sand, straight up, the red eyes, seemed to be making an appointment to meet me in my dreams.

'Men without women,' I remarked during our walk back to the campsite. 'Fish all week, home for the weekend?'

'Tomorrow's Friday, Holmes.'

'Hard row to hoe.'

'Stick to the sex life of jellyfish, you're better at it.'

I took Koert Jan's hand. He shook me away.

'Come on.' I undid my *futa* and slung it over my shoulder. 'Men here walk hand-in-hand all the time, and you like that.'

When we passed the five fishermen hauling in their net, they were still at it. Where the dogs had sprawled, there were impressions in the sand. The animals were off now, stalking.

VI

Back at camp I wanted to have a go at windsurfing. Elso discouraged me. 'The wind's too strong for a beginner.' He was right, but I am proud and stubborn. I didn't even mind falling on my face, time after time after time. Because the undertow was far stronger than I'd realised, however, when at long last I tired of playing silent comedy to nobody's amusement but my own, before regaining the campsite I had to tug the surfplank and sail behind me for the better part of an hour.

The sun was sinking fast. There was a flurry of dinner activity. Drinking had begun. A fire was burning and people were sitting around it in folding chairs. Hester and Pim had removed the back seat from their Land Cruiser. It made a handy divan on the sand – Hans, Ulrike and Jonathan sat there giggling in disrespect at the sunset. As I trudged ashore Koert Jan came to meet me and tossed me a towel. As I buried my face in it, my eyes stung with salt, a cheer went up.

'Jan Willem!' A small jeep came careening towards us along the beach. It had a canvas top, rolled back, and the driver was standing so his head came up over the windshield. 'Jan Willem, you're crazy,' Saskia clapped her hands. The jeep jerked to a halt. Jan Willem, a beanpole with a shock of blond hair rising straight up from his forehead, sprang down and ran whooping fully-dressed into the sea.

'We stopped for you' – Elso ran into the surf bringing Jan Willem a beer – 'but they said you were working.' Jan Willem, from a small, fundamentalist farming community in East Holland, was a peace corps volunteer too. He was in Yemen to teach farmers about wind-powered irrigation.

'Very funny.' Jan Willem was notorious for taking his assignment seriously. The equipment he had to work with was hopeless. It was said he held his bulldozer together with rubber bands. Because most of his time off he chose to go on solitary hikes, backpacking in the mountains, making watercolor sketches of the birds and wildlife he saw, gossip made him out to be odd.

For the outing both Saskia and Hester had made huge pots of chili – with plenty of tomato sauce. Saskia was opening cans of pineapple and tilting them – plop – into the chili. Hester, the red nail-polish on her toes cracking, squatted next to the cooking fire, stirring the beans. Smoke made her eyes water. The front hood of our Toyota was turned into a serving table. For the bread Jacqueline brought as her contribution, small imitation French loaves, she apologised to us all. 'They were out of the native stuff, sorry.'

Saskia handed out forks and spoons and did a number about how she expected to get every last piece back, washed, before anyone left the beach. Light had drained from the sky and she was still wearing only her bikini. Patterns of salt and fine hair glistened on her shins. Elso poked through the food and called aloud every time he found something new. 'We've got olives soaked in lemon juice. And that's goat cheese. We've got baby corn on the cob.' Ulrike tossed a sack of oranges into the collection. To uncork a monster bottle of wine cost Hans every last ounce of strength he had.

The meal never happened. There was more than enough to eat, but somehow our beach party did not become a social occasion. People helped themselves. No one waited to begin. There was an edge of greed to how most of us ate, as if afraid there wouldn't be enough if we shared fairly. The first few beer cans went flying through the air and fell in the campfire. Off to one side Koert Jan and I sucked at bottles of warm soda pop. He announced that I had forgotten the cake. No one seemed to listen.

Rummaging around in the back of the Toyota I found our calf-high plaid socks. The sand-flies weren't bad though, not yet. The strong breeze was also keeping the mosquito count down.

'So, how was Dhamar?' Jacqueline cornered me neatly.

'Still shaken.'

With little encouragement Jacqueline then told me her life story, such as it was. Today marked the end of her first year in the Yemen Arab Republic. Before that she'd 'done' two years in Vienna. 'Oh the music was everything they say it is. Unfortunately, so was the pastry. Vienna was a consolation prize, you see. My first assignment was Iran.'

'Uh-huh.' Back by the fire my chili would be getting cold.

'Teheran was no picnic, I can tell you. We lived *in* the embassy right through the revolution.'

'Did you like Iran?' On the edge of a fit of giggles, I slipped my hands and forearms into the plaid socks.

'It was all right. The people weren't bad. A little bit fanatic.'

How often had Jacqueline had this same conversation, word for word? Then, still fighting laughter, I saw how even as she spoke, she cringed slightly – as if expecting ridicule for her opinions. No doubt she came from a large family. A middle child. 'The Shah really had something. He was about the most handsome man I ever laid eyes on.'

Jacqueline herself was like a developing country: determined to make the most of a few resources, proud, ultimately dependent on foreign aid.

'How do you like Yemen?' I asked.

'The problem is I never get to meet anyone. The people who come to the embassy aren't exactly the people, if you know what I mean.'

Out of the dark Koert Jan floated up to the rescue. Earlier in the week he had received an engraved embassy invitation to attend a party for the Queen's Birthday. The event would be celebrated at the Sheba Hotel in Sana, chandeliers, punchbowl fountain, polished marble floors. Men were to wear suits, women evening dresses. In terms so circumspect and polite even Koert Jan seemed impressed by his diplomacy he asked Jacqueline if she didn't, perhaps, find the clothing restrictions more than a trifle bizarre.

She washed down a mouthful of chili with wine and shook her head no. 'What we want, of course,' she put a hand self-consciously on Koert Jan's arm, 'is to discourage people from turning up in jeans and sneakers.'

'I don't own a suit,' Koert Jan said.

'Whatever *you* wear,' Hans joined us, 'will be fine.'

'We get a clothing allowance, you see' – Jacqueline smiled merrily at me as I pulled the socks off my hands – 'for just such occasions.'

There was no moon. The stars were like powdered sugar. Pim set to work to ignite a kerosene lamp. One of those pump jobs.

I live in mortal terror of such lamps, expecting them to explode at any moment. No sooner had he stood the thing on the hood of the Toyota than it was surrounded by flying, creeping, crawling mini-life. The mantle glowed white – the kind of pulsing light that, for me, means desperation.

'You through with that?' Hester took the fork out of my hand. She wore a black, one-piece swim-suit, wool, that clung to her chunkiness. A gold crucifix twinkled at her throat. Her blonde hair was pulled back into a tight knot that seemed to change the shape of her eyes. Hester's voice, naturally husky, was growing huskier by the swallow. All in all she called to mind an actress I'd once watched do a hatchet job on Hedda Gabler.

At the earliest possible moment I excused myself and withdrew to go to bed. The damn Petromax was shining right in my eyes. I clawed my way back out from under my mosquito net and lowered the lamp on to the sand in front of the Toyota. Back on my stretcher I realised sleep was not going to come easy. The air was damp, the mosquito net seemed to interfere with my breathing and cramp my freedom. I drew up my knees and folded my hands on my chest and tried not to listen to the chatter around the campfire. At the same time I didn't miss a word of it, relishing disdain. Koert Jan said nothing. He soon came to bed. I felt a friendly pat on the knee. We turned on our sides, facing each other the way prisoners might who live for the moment when, from opposite sides of a stone wall, they tap out the secrets of their hearts.

Without being able to see, I knew exactly the small smile he would be wearing.

Hours of torture followed. The drinking went on. Bad jokes erupted. Shrieks, more insults. The steady hiss and throb of the kerosene lamp worked on my nerves. Every time the fire died down far enough so that through closed lids the dancing light no longer bothered me, Saskia flung on new wood. As foreseen, Koert Jan's bed and mine were in the worst of all possible

165

places. A few times, after a great burst of laughter, Elso would say, 'Shhh, people are trying to sleep.' He spoke in a loud, drunken voice. No one paid him the slightest attention.

There was constant motion under Koert Jan's mosquito net, a shifting, a restless search for a position he could hold. He needed his sleep, I knew, badly. He didn't like my worrying on his behalf, never has, but the habit was intact. The more the party swilled, the emptier they were revealed – like trick barrels into which untold gallons of oil are pumped only to ring the more hollow when their sides are thumped. Pim made a great thing out of his need to pee. He said he was too tired to move so the others should shut their eyes or fetch their cameras. Elso was crawling about with a spoon scraping crusts of chili off unwashed plates, complaining of hunger. 'Hey' – he stood and hurled sticks at scavenging dogs – 'the competition.'

We might have been anywhere, our gathering – except near Yachtule at the edge of the Red Sea under the star-spangled skies of Arabia Felix. It was another form of pollution, I felt, hugging my jeans rolled into a pillow. This raucousness would damage the air, rip and shred and bruise the peace and quiet that had hung here protectively for thousands of years. What were a few stray bits of wind-blown plastic to compare to this? Separate voices parodied themselves. How I would give anything to sleep in the palm grove off to the south among the exhausted fishermen. Could they hear us? Did our voices carry that far?

Suddenly there was applause and shouting. As I sat up I almost tipped my cot, catching my face in the webbing of the mosquito net so I had to beat my nose and lips free. At the far end of the row of stretchers, Hester had climbed into the Land Cruiser and switched on the bright headlights. In the parallel beams that fell flat on the sea, I could just catch a glimpse of the bare backs of two men hiking out from surfplanks speeding true ahead into the inky distance. Now there was no horizon. Low stars drowned in black water, that was all. A curtain hung at the end of the world.

Long after the others fell back into their chairs for more chit-chat and guzzling, I sat and stared at the point where I had seen Elso and Pim swallowed by the darkness. There were hazards to night surfing. Fishing nets, boats, floating debris – invisible until too late. From the surfers' vantage there would be the eyes, round, glaring, of the Land Cruiser to return to, the red glow of the campfire and the tiny, white blur of the kerosene lamp. They were out there walking on water, free, wind sheathing face and body, balanced, arms, legs taut, enough alcohol in their blood to feel chaste and invulnerable. I could taste the fountain of laughter in their throats.

Hans and Ulrike, perhaps moved, too, began a mimic striptease. Jacqueline crooned low, Jan Willem made an empty beer can moan, Jonathan played spoons, back to back. From the shadows I watched the dance. I was thirsty but the water from our jerry-cans was so disgustingly warm I had to spit it out. With a series of short, shrill cries, tongue trilling, Ulrike began to bump against Hans. His gopher smile appeared fragile. Hans wore a tiny bathing-suit with the merest hint of a bulge. He held his arms out from his sides. Firelight twined around his smooth body. He licked his upper lip with a kind of distracted feline pleasure as he slowly turned in place, barely lifting his feet, shuffling them in the sand. Ulrike by way of contrast, cavorted. She kept running her fingers through her hair, complaining out loud how sticky and tangled it was. 'Socks,' she howled, 'I forgot to bring socks.'

In a moment of sympathy for her, a rush, I suspected she would rather be anywhere in the world than where she was. Her giggling was part panting, part tears. What she hoped for, clearly, was to be tipped on to an iron shovel, carried into the dark and fucked inside out, upside down and backwards. She needed irrigation.

Jan Willem collapsed on to the sand, rolling over and over until his head, the thatch of fine hair, almost lay in the fire.

'What's with him?' Hester asked.

'He's homesick,' Saskia said.

When Elso and Pim rejoined the party, dripping wet from their midnight surf, a can of beer in both hands, they began to flex their muscles in the firelight. Biceps. Thighs. The way they met each other's eyes, they were more than playing. Jonathan staggered forward and imitated their poses.

'You should've told me,' he was snickering so hard he could hardly speak, 'I would've packed some, too.'

'Some what?'

'Muscles.'

Then Jacqueline yawned her way into the center of attention. She announced that she was ready for her beauty sleep. 'Will anyone carry me?' she broke into a clatter of self-pitying laughter. In her robe and gown and slippers she would have been a credit to the embassy at the Queen's Birthday gala.

'Finally,' I whispered through gritted teeth.

'Don't bank on it,' Koert Jan shot back an answer.

'Oh my God,' Pim called out, 'Jacqui's praying!'

'Shhh, there are people sleeping,' Elso blared.

'Okay, you guys, I'm missing three forks.' Saskia beat the forks she did have against the empty chili pot. Dogs howled.

'Don't panic' – Hans was still coming down from his little dance – 'you'll find them in the morning, dear.'

'Morning, nothing. What's that in your bathing suit?'

'Not three forks, I can assure you.'

'Everybody all right?' Pim called. 'Christ, now Jacqui's brushing her fucking teeth. Inspection.' He seized the Petromax and swinging it at his side he began to stalk back and forth along the row of beds and mosquito nets, his military manner all too natural and convincing. By now Ulrike, horizontal on her mat, was seismic with tittering. She was sleeping next to

Jonathan, her fellow paper saver, not Hans. They wrestled over a thin, striped sheet.

'An inch. Just give an inch.'

'Then,' Jonathan gasped, 'you'll want a mile.'

'Shhh!' I went.

'Shhh?' Ulrike echoed, convulsed with new laughter. 'Shhh? What's that?'

'Take that thing out of my eyes!' I growled at Pim. He put the Petromax back down near the fire. I was a pot boiling, the lid tipping back and forth.

'There are limits,' I said for Koert Jan's ears. A few minutes of silence followed. 'Finally,' I repeated and nestled lower in my cot.

Not everyone was ready for sleep, however. Pim had merely gone to fetch his nail clipper. He returned to his chair by the fire. Elso had come back from rinsing plates in the surf. With audible grunts he was heaving the rest of the firewood on to the blaze. He seemed to reach right into the flames without feeling the heat. His display of excess energy left me wondering why Saskia had retired to curl up in her sleeping-bag alone.

To this day I could swear Pim had a hundred fingers, each with a nail that he clipped with a sound that troubled the night worse than thunder. An irregular metronome. I lay there waiting for the next clip, cursing it in advance, impatient at delays. Worse followed. Pim and Elso started talking politics.

'Permanent erection,' Pim said. 'Those kids, can you blame them? First of all they can't even get near a woman. Then the Imam promises them six lays a day in Paradise. Fighting for Allah. Dying for Allah. They tie themselves together and walk the mine fields in front of the soldiers. I'll bet their pricks are stiff when they blow their heads off.'

VII

'Coming?' Koert Jan tugged at my mosquito net. 'This will go on for hours.'

I climbed into my jeans. They felt tight and damp. I had to poke around the back of the Toyota for my sandals. And the flashlight.

We walked between Pim and Elso and the roaring campfire. Instead of drinking a can of beer, Pim was slowly pouring it down his chest.

The tide was turning. There was a stretch of packed sand that sloped gently some three meters wide between the tongue of the waves at full reach and the first growth of shoreline palms and shrubs, a black ribbon for us to walk on.

'Wait,' I said to Koert Jan who was moving ahead of me. I fumbled with the flashlight switch. The beam flashed on and I aimed it in front of us. The sand was alive. Paved with shellfish, thousands, all scuttling. A mottled mosaic. The beach writhed, conches of various size and a dizzying assortment of crabs all dancing, zigzagging across the wet sand. My circle of light inspired frenzy. Yet there were too many creatures for them all to dig for shelter. Even as we walked we crunched down on crab backs. It was a horror film setting. I clutched at Koert Jan's arm. Whoever fell, swarms of tiny crabs would cover his poor body instantly, seize the flesh, shred it with their pincers. Any attempt to scream would be drowned by crabs invading the throat, severing the tongue cleanly at the root. On and on, as we advanced, the profusion of hidden life revealed continued, a carpet down to the edge of the sea. Did this agitation, such effluence take place every night? Or was it the absence of the moon that summoned them to forage, mate, bask in the cool dark, safe from enemy birds?

'It's like staring through a microscope at a cell,' Koert Jan said. I spun back and flashed the light behind us on the sand. The countless phalanxes had not disappeared. They were weaving and feinting still, spotted backs, stripes, blurred pastels polished by sea water. There was no trace of our footsteps.

Koert Jan pointed to a fallen palm further up the beach. We

went there to sit, facing the sea. Elso and Pim's voices were indistinct and muffled now. Fortunately the sky was immense. We sat close, content. Koert Jan took my hand, played absent-mindedly with the fingers.

'Is it our age?' I asked.

'My mother' – whenever Koert Jan was about to draw a sharp moral distinction, he invariably invoked his mother, a vigorous woman of eighty-eight – 'can forgive just about anything people say as long as there's some trace of wit.' Koert Jan's mother, the widow of a minister now for more than forty years, was straight-laced but her severity admitted joy. 'Some spark, however faint.'

We sat close. Intimacy can be an intimidating, lonely thing when solidified by an awareness of isolation.

'They need to let off steam.' I leaned my head on Koert Jan's shoulder.

'You call that steam?' Often in the past when, disillusioned, I had turned on people, Koert Jan took me to task for my high expectations. His philosophy, he was fond of reminding me, was to expect nothing from anyone. On those rare occasions experience proved him wrong, he could be delighted.

'That Pim and Hester,' Koert Jan sighed, 'they wrote an article for the Dutch volunteer bulletin. Did you see it? About how filthy the hospital was when they arrived. How nobody cared. How it takes an Arab six months to fix a leaky faucet. It should never have been printed.'

'It's not us then, it's them?'

'Poor suffering heroes – that's what they made themselves out to be.' For a time Koert Jan fell silent. He slipped one of his hands into my back pocket. 'At least you've seen the Red Sea.'

'Where do you suppose the name comes from?'

'From sea turtles, with the head chopped off.'

'Koert Jan, do you think our lives will just go on like this?'

'Like how?'

'Knocking around from country to country, experts in this

and that.' Hurting more, getting less and less done – only I didn't say that.

Koert Jan laughed, nodded.

'What I'm asking really, I guess, is what you're willing to settle for?'

'You know,' Koert Jan said, 'that The Hague receives reports in quadruplicate about the exact weight of garbage we collect every day. When the totals went up so sharply in February, we had a telegram asking why. I sent a telegram back. One word. Rain. Wet garbage, like wet coal, wet rice.'

'Wet ambition?'

'Are you sorry you came?'

'I've been wanting to windsurf for years.'

'No, I mean to see me.'

A shooting star seemed to unzip a seam in heaven. Wind off the sea set palm fronds clacking.

'For what it's worth, I'll tell you a story I heard in Dhamar.' I lay my head back on Koert Jan's lap, my body balanced along the rough bark of the fallen palm. I loved his face upside down, the jut of his chin, his nostrils. 'The day after the earthquake, the Chargé d'Affaires came to the hospital. Helicopters were air-lifting casualties from the mountains. Emergency cases were pouring in. The halls were packed with people, many dying. There was such a mob at the gates the soldiers kept firing shots into the air. Even so they could hardly keep them back.

'The Chargé d'Affaires drove down for the day from Sana with his wife and kids. She, apparently, was looking very smart. The nurses described her dress to me. Crisp, stylish – yellow with red flowers. She went drifting about with a hostess smile, bravery and concern on display. She had her two little boys with her, holding on to their hands. One of them had a teddy bear. But then suddenly something went haywire. Her face fell, her body began to twitch. Just then Hester came along with a dead child in her arms, skull crushed. Not the first of the day.

172

She was returning the child to its mother crouched down in some corner. The Chargé d'Affaires' wife started tugging on Hester's arm. She – '

'I've heard this story, of course.' Koert Jan's voice was not unkind. 'It's made the rounds. She wanted the key to the staff toilet, right? One of the little boys had to go.'

'Ugly story, isn't it?' I waited but Koert Jan simply brushed the hair back off my forehead.

'It's an ugly story,' he finally said, 'because people enjoy telling it so much. Such an easy target.' Again his fingers through my hair. 'Probably in that dress, looking fresh, clean, she did more good than harm. For her to come at all probably took a lot of courage.'

'Where were you?' I asked. When news of the earthquake first reached Amsterdam, to find out if Koert Jan was all right, I sent him a cable. Then I wrote a letter describing how I imagined him ditching the comedy of garbage collection for more serious matters. A letter I had not sent.

'I was in Taiz.'

'You didn't go to help?'

'No. You heard what I told Jacqueline – I don't even own a nice, crisp dress.'

'What'd you do? Carry on with your crash program?'

'That's right. Thanks for making me feel guilty.'

Koert Jan shifted his legs so I had to sit up.

'To these people Dhamar is like the other side of the moon, you know that? Yemen is hardly a country. The government has some control in three provinces, that's all. The rest is still run by the sheikhs. Sana pays them money to stay out of their hair. Loyalty money, taxes in reverse. An earthquake in Dhamar is no skin off the nose of people in Taiz. Allah disposes. Are you scared?'

'Why?'

'Because you're a Jew?'

'Most of the time I forget. True!'

173

'You wrote me you were afraid to come.'

'On the visa application I did what you said.'

'Remind me.'

'Under religion I wrote Unit-Aryan.'

Koert Jan took the flashlight and shined it in my face. 'Anne Frank,' he said. So years ago on a houseboat in Amsterdam I had appeared to him during a mescaline trip. 'This city is full of little Anne Franks. In the pool last week a boy swam up to me and made a thumbs up sign. "Hitler," he said. "Hitler good. Should have finished what he started." They show films here with Hitler as the hero.'

'You let him climb on your shoulders, no doubt, and dive off.'

Koert Jan shone the flashlight straight up. How far does light go before it starts to fall?

'Khoumeni will have the bomb, KJ, inside two years. The story broke just before I left. Our friends the Germans are helping him. They're picking up where the Shah and the CIA left off.'

'Israel will pre-empt, don't worry.' As a rule Koert Jan was, to put it mildly, unforgiving towards Zion. The worst of all possible sins in his eyes was for the victim to become the victimiser.

'The Christian bomb. The Communist bomb. The Moslem bomb.'

'Don't look at me, someone has to keep the streets clean.'

'Is that what you said to the Minister?' In The Hague they were still talking about how late one afternoon when the Minister had appealed to Koert Jan to let her see 'real problems', he had arranged, with the connivance of the Mayor, to take her to the annex of the prison where they kept the insane. A hundred human beings, manacled into a small and stinking courtyard. And at the gate a hyena paced back and forth, one with filed teeth, its mangy fur gone sunset pink.

Koert Jan closed his eyes and smiled. 'I told the Minister we would be starting to beautify the city soon with trees. The

Mayor was trusting me completely to decide where to plant them.'

'I'll bet she was pleased.'

'You see – you see, if I try to do anything but what I'm here for – if I look around a corner, peek behind a curtain, if I lift a single finger – well, you know what happened in Indonesia.'

'I know.'

'They've bought me, you see. That's the bottom line. That's how the Yemeni look at it. The Arabs buy experts, they don't welcome them.'

'Can you blame them?' I pointed back to our campfire. But my earlier anger was gone and I was, I suspected, doing our party an injustice.

Pim was still up drinking, alone, when we returned to camp. We walked past him but he didn't see us – so intently was he staring at the sky. There was a beautiful look on his face, not sadness, not resignation, although something of both were visible. He was undefended, that was it. Both his hands were plunged inside his double bathing trunks, resting on his sex while his toes slowly pawed the sand.

Under my mosquito net there were easily as many insects as outside. Yet I sank into sleep the way a key fits a lock.

VIII

First light woke me from dreams that didn't impress me as worth the trouble to remember. Koert Jan's cot was empty, his mosquito net tied in a knot from the blue cable. Elso and Pim were down at the water's edge, mounting their surfboards. They looked none the worse for the night's late carousal. How was it possible? The flesh hung loose and heavy on my bones.

For early morning there was an unusually brisk wind. Saskia hunkered by the cooking pit, boiling tea water. The primus hissed. A new sprinkling of jellyfish gleamed slack on the sand. Ulrike was still sleeping with her mouth open, back-to-back with Jonathan, who clutched his glasses in one hand sunk between his thighs. The sheet was twisted down around their ankles. They, too, looked washed ashore, stranded.

Wading out, I shivered. The sea had cooled overnight. Well, Gurdjieff swore by daily cold showers: they lengthened life. Recklessly I threw myself into the water.

'Morning.'

I surfaced near Elso. 'Sleep well?' he asked.

I chose to ignore the remark. 'How about a lesson?' I said.

With great care, falteringly, Elso went on to explain certain basic principles of surfing to me – which he himself only partially understood. Struggling to haul the sail upright out of the water I somehow could never keep the board pointing properly into the wind. 'Choppy,' Elso commiserated with me. The few times I managed to get the sail into position, I clutched at the horizontal bar too eagerly. Knees flexed, my heart inflated with anticipation. Any second the swift glide would begin! Invariably I tumbled into the water with the sail falling on top of me. Down, down, down. Elso loyally kept blaming the wind. For an hour I persevered, ignoring the renewed evidence of my ineptitude. At times a gust of wind would wrench the mast clear out of its socket. Then I would have to ram it back in place, plugging a gap with a tattered rubber sandal.

'Had enough?' Hester swam out to have a go. In the pale morning light her face was like a shell sea-washed until it lost all its markings. Hester dragged herself awkwardly up on to the surfboard, first flopping on her belly, then rising on to hands and knees.

'Ever done it before?' I stood back and watched.

'Once or twice.'

I was about to give advice, to rehash Elso's instructions. Before I could begin, however, she was away. Neither graceful nor strong, she made the feat look like child's play.

The late sleepers were crawling awake as I sloshed, dispirited, ashore. Jacqueline dazzled us with a new bathing suit. The exposed parts of her body were spotted with red welts. Her eyes were crusted with sleep. As for Hans, someone appeared to have let the air out of him while he slept. Everything now was fine, too fine. Fingers, arms, nose. He fought a yawn, self-conscious about his bad teeth.

Ulrike sat thrashing her hair. 'Such stu-pid hair,' she kept saying in rhythm to her angry brush, 'it ties itself in knots.'

'I saw you out there.' Koert Jan was back from his wanderings. 'You almost had it.'

We shared some flat round millet bread, coarse and filling, and gulped some acid tea. The bread had been wrapped in a sheet of newspaper. Without thinking, I started to read it.

'Hey, this is Indonesian.'

'Malaysian.' Koert Jan smiled.

'How'd it get here?'

'There's no paper in Yemen. So they import shiploads of old newspapers from Malaysia.' Koert Jan pointed to the date at the top of the page. The paper was from four years ago.

'Hey, Jan Willem,' Saskia called out, 'look alive.' Jan Willem had spread a thin foam rubber pad on the roof of his canvas-top jeep and slept up there, his gawky frame scrunched into a question mark. I took a nice photo of him lifting his head, blinking at the sun.

'Still missing two spoons, shit,' Saskia announced.

'Hans?' Koert Jan's voice rose.

'Not guilty,' he said hoarsely.

Hester and Pim surfed back and forth, back and forth across the horizon.

'Jesus' – Ulrike started to beat her first jellyfish of the day, swinging the shovel with two hands like a hammer. On to her welts, Jacqueline was rubbing a white ointment with an overpowering odor of cloves. 'We weren't the only ones to have a party,' she said.

At that moment we heard the roar of an engine and our heads turned. Down the coast a motorcycle broke through the tree line on to the beach. At the water's edge the machine went into a skid but somehow the driver, lost to view for an awful instant, righted himself and now came racing straight towards us, spraying a wake of sand.

'Bert!' Jan Willem called. Bert it was, indeed, in a heavy black leather jacket with a thousand diagonal zippers. His crash helmet was black, too.

'Two hours' – Bert consulted his wristwatch – 'and eighteen minutes.'

'If you hurry,' Jan Willem said, 'you can make it back before Malvina misses you.'

'Christ, Bert, don't you ever take her anywhere?' Saskia shook her head. 'No wonder she has days when she thinks she's still in Tanzania.'

Bert dug a water bottle from his saddlebag, tossed back his head and chug-a-lugged. 'My wife's too good for you people,' Bert grinned, wiping his mouth with the back of his hand. 'Besides she had a busy night.'

'Yeah,' Jan Willem said, 'those late games of solitaire can really take it out of you.'

'Don't tell me' – Elso tore at the peel of an orange with his teeth – 'she forgot to cheat?'

'Coming?' Koert Jan asked me. This time we struck out due north along the coast.

'Get any sleep?'

'No,' he smiled. 'But you did.'

We walked in companionable silence without meeting anyone. The landscape was less habitable still than the other half of the bay. Marshland with stagnant, slimy pools. Trees with roots thrusting up like arthritic joints through the opalescent sea. In places we had to wade far out to keep making progress, careful to avoid stepping on the sharp stubble of

178

sprouting reeds. The sun, early as it was, blazed. It was as if somewhere behind us a child was playing with a magnifying glass, focusing its rays. I could feel the back of my neck, shoulders and knee hollows burn. Birds skimmed the inland waterholes. Dragonflies glinted. We passed ramshackle blinds for hunters, reed shelters for fishermen. Offshore poles jutted in formation, marking the fixed loops of submerged fishing traps.

'I went back,' Koert Jan said simply.

'The fishermen?'

'Yes, only they're not.'

Suddenly three small boys came racing, scrambling over the sand towards the water. They saw us at the same time we saw them. They stopped in their tracks, shouted and ran to hide. They stuck with us along the coast, peering out from behind undergrowth or palm trunks, chattering, laughing, not daring to come closer. At last we sighted a settlement ahead. At the outskirts was a large herd of goats, wearing bells. The boys went whooping off towards a line of women in bright clothes walking the ridges between blinding white salt pans, sagging baskets balanced on their heads.

We turned back. 'Who are they then?' I stood still a moment, knee-deep in the water. You could see so far in every direction.

'Ethiopians. Refugees. Boat people.'

'Where are their boats?'

'Boat. One.' Koert Jan directed my head with his hands. There was a dark speck in the distance out by the barrier reef. 'There are a hundred of them altogether.'

'That can't hold a hundred.'

'It did. At $300 a head.'

'Why did you go back?'

'It was too clean.'

'Koert Jan!'

'I met one who speaks English.'

'What're they doing here?'

'They didn't know where they are.'

'Jesus, the captain must know.'

'You'd like to think so, wouldn't you. Especially if you were paying for the ride.'

'Christ, where are they going?'

'Jeddah.'

'Why Saudi?'

'They seem to think they might find asylum there, and work. They sailed two days ago from Djibouti.'

'But that's incredible, boat people here.'

The Red Sea, split once by Moses with his rod so the Jews could pass out of slavery. And the Egyptians drown.

'Their first night the wind blew them off course. They washed up in South Yemen.'

'Uh-oh.'

'A farmer saved their lives. He let them sleep on his land. No lights. No talk.'

'Sounds perfect.' But my joke fell flat.

'That's why they were so scared when we came along yesterday. If they get caught, the authorities will send them back. And they'll be executed.'

'Who are they?'

'A grab bag. Gadi, the boy who speaks English, he has a BA in economics from the University at Addis Ababa.'

'Political?'

'He says he wasn't *against* the regime. He just wasn't for it.'

'Ethiopia's bad right now, isn't it?'

'Last week Gadi went to visit his family. They live in a village outside the capital. When he came back someone was waiting for him at the bus station. While he was away his friends had all been arrested. He didn't go home. He just set out and walked to Djibouti.'

'A hundred?'

'When they landed, they tried to buy food. The villagers had nothing over, only some crackers to sell them. So they caught those turtles.'

180

'Elso tells me when he surfs far out by the reef, if he looks down sometimes he sees a whole – what? – school of turtles dive away in front of him. They peel off, like parachute jumpers.'

'At first they thought they might be devils. On the west coast they don't have them. No one in the boat had ever seen a sea turtle before.'

'But hunger was stronger than fear?'

'Gadi says that after the first turtle was served up some of the group waited for three hours to see if any of those who ate would die.'

'What do they need? I didn't bring much money.'

'They're not poor. Not yet. They could've used that cake.'

'Come on, by the time you divided it into a hundred, the pieces would be pretty small.'

'Anything to take away the taste of turtle.'

'But what are they waiting for? This place has nothing to offer them, why are they still hanging around?'

'To travel on a Friday, especially with this wind, would be courting disaster,' Koert Jan said. '*Insh'allah.*'

'What about the head?'

'What head?'

'The turtle's. Was it still there in the sand? Don't tell me you didn't notice it yesterday?'

'No.'

'One hundred in that thing?' As we drew closer, the boat, tossing near the end of the spit, hardly seemed to grow larger. 'You've heard about the new Hyatt in Malaysia?'

'No.'

'The one on the east coast?'

'No.'

'It's got a cocktail bar made out of a Vietnamese refugee boat.'

'Shit.'

'Wait for it, it gets worse. When you come in there's a plaque that tells how the boat was found floating off shore with sixty-two bodies in it, no survivors. Maximum occupancy for the bar is thirty-five.'

'Sounds ideal for embassy parties. Come as you are. What kind of drinks do you suppose they serve?'

By now the sun was practically overhead. Underfoot there were colonies of blue starfish. Out of the water, their color changed.

'What's he like, Gadi?'

'Nice.'

'Would you hire him?'

Koert Jan laughed. 'No, he hasn't got the eyes. Gadi asked if we had – '

'Aha!'

'What aha?'

'Sorry.'

'Don't talk so much, listen.'

'Gadi asked if we had – '

' – a roll of film for him.'

'Film?'

'One of them has a camera, but no film. Gadi says it would be a pity, if they survive, not to have something to remember the journey by.'

'He said that – all of it?'

'The survival part, too, yes.'

'All we have is what's in my camera. One twenty. I think there are still six shots. Damn it.' My mind raced with the possibilities of photographs within the palm grove. 'Jacqueline has a camera.'

'Not a word to any of them, are you crazy?'

We nearly tripped over Hans sunbathing and masturbating. Despite ourselves we stood and watched too long to go away before his climax. It wasn't his intention to come, however. He was teasing himself, prolonging the tension. Unlike the rest of his body, there was something solid and real about his

182

sex organ, the shiny mushroom crown. His eyes were shut tight and he looked like he was frowning, as if there was something he couldn't quite remember. Do other of God's creatures know solo sex? I scooped up a handful of sand to toss on to Hans, Koert Jan knocked it out of my hand and we hurried on.

At camp Ulrike was still bashing away at jellyfish. 'They don't splatter,' she was saying, her accent more pronounced than I'd ever noticed it before, 'why don't they splatter?'

Crushed beer cans lay about everywhere in the sand. It took will-power not to make a show of collecting them to put in a garbage bag. Down at the water's edge Saskia had stretched out on a cot to read a Dutch news weekly. Puffs of wind were making it impossible. She tried to pin the pages with chin and elbows, but lying like that on her stomach, her eyes were too close to the page to read.

'You're so good,' I said to Hester who only now was beaching her surfplank. She wore a grin of utter satisfaction.

'It's a lot easier than it looks,' she said.

'You want me to kill myself, is that it?' Yes, if I have to, I can small talk with the best of them. And now, with all those photogenic Ethiopians waiting, I had to. I shouldn't overdo it though. Smile a little, growl a little. Too much friendliness could give the show away.

'Hey, where's Bert?' The motorcycle was gone.

'Headed back,' Jan Willem said. 'He had a barbecue at three.'

'Last time we came to Yachtule Bert brought Malvina,' Elso said. 'You never saw anyone drink like those two, never. Bert got so pissed he couldn't find his bed.'

'He had his mosquito net tied around his waist,' Saskia chimed in, 'like a ballet dancer.'

'"Hey, Malvina, bitch, where are you?" That's what Bert kept shouting.'

'She passed out early, so she wasn't much help.'

'Bert went from bed to bed. He would sit down on the edge and ask, real polite, if there was any room for him.'

'When he got to Elso, Elso panicked.'

'I didn't know what kind of a drunk he was.'

'He gave Elso a kiss and Elso started stuttering. "B-b-bert, I like you a lot, r-r-really, b-b-but this stretcher can't hold b-b-both of us."'

Jan Willem and Pim had moved their folding chairs down into the surf. They sat drinking beer, their backs to the waves. At times a big wave would engulf them. Then they'd fall out of their chairs laughing and the chairs would tumble up on to the shore. The sun above throbbed, casting stunted shadows. The stretchers and mosquito nets were in disorder. Fully dressed Jonathan sat in the protective shade of the Land Cruiser, his nose buried in an Agatha Christie. He was afraid of burning, but his precautions came too late. His nose at least was already bright red. Jacqueline crouched at the edge of the sea building a sand castle with half-hearted shoves of her massive arms.

Koert Jan had strolled on ahead. Casually I hunted up the Yashica from the glove compartment of the Toyota. Then after a swig of warm orange soda, I hurried, slowly, after him. Where last night the beach had swarmed, now it was bare. My heart pounded. From a distance there was no life visible in the palm grove. How different it felt to be approaching it now.

'Good old Bert,' Koert Jan commented at the tire tread in the sand. We had expected it to turn off sharply at the access wadi, but instead it kept going. 'Underneath he's sweet. Not the fascist diehard he wants you to think he is.'

'Besides which you have to work with him.'

As we passed the village half-way to the grove, the mythical fishnet lay folded neatly on the sand. Nearby a number of slim dugouts had been hauled up on to logs. Each could hold half a dozen men, no more.

'To be *asked* to take pictures!' Despite my best efforts, my excitement was showing. 'What a chance.'

'We'll see.'

Towards the far tip of the spit, Bert's trail veered away. Instead of cutting back through the desert you could also follow along the coast all the way to Moccha. Koert Jan kicked the sand and laughed. 'Bert got himself in trouble with security last month.'

'How?'

'He brought a video of *Fiddler on the Roof* back from leave.'

'And they thought it was porno?'

'Not exactly. On Malvina's birthday he asked Dr Sabeti, the head of the hospital, over for a showing. Sabeti's the local whiz kid. When he was eight, he'd already read more than all the rest of Taiz put together. Night and day the boy was driving his father crazy, begging for an education. Finally the man, a poor tailor, put Sabeti on a ship to Cairo with a pocket full of change. Years later Sabeti came back trained as a doctor, speaking French, German and English. He's a very charming, clever man with one unfortunate blind spot. For example, when the Minister was here, the Governor gave a dinner and Sabeti chose the occasion to enlighten the company on the fact that Freud was really a minor figure in the history of psychiatry, one whose importance has been blown up out of all proportion by the international Jewish conspiracy.'

'Which brings us back to *Fiddler on the Roof*.'

'At the end of the film there wasn't a dry eye in the house – except for Dr Sabeti's. He smiled and said goodnight. He thanked his host for a most enjoyable evening. Half an hour later, we were singing Happy Birthday at the time, the security police broke in. Not one or two, mind you, a dozen at least. They confiscated Bert's tapes. Three he didn't get back. *Star Wars*. *ET*. *Fiddler on the Roof*.'

'You're sure it was Sabeti?'

'No. Only last week when I had dinner at his house, afterwards we watched *ET* – with Dutch subtitles.'

185

'Was Bert invited?'

'Are you kidding? Sabeti's a snob.'

We arrived at the grove and skirted it, averting our eyes. Without breaking stride we passed beyond the shelf of beach where yesterday we'd come upon the men busy with the giant turtles. There was another turtle marooned there now, helpless on its back, life pulsing at the exposed throat. We lingered in full view, skimming stones out to sea.

' – three, four, five, *six*! Match that, maestro!'

When Gadi failed to come out to meet us, we circled back and headed in among the trees. In the grove men were seated in clusters. Many were holding small cardboard cracker boxes filled to the brim with greasy chunks of meat. The shell of a sea turtle was being used as a cooking vessel, flames from a pit fire licking up around the edges. Eerily, no one seemed to take notice of us. We were wearing our *futa*s. In the shade I saw for the first time how dark Koert Jan was after the morning's sun. A short distance beyond the back of the grove, in a small clearing, several men were doubled over in prayer, their foreheads pressed to hot sand. Mecca, I thought, was in an altogether different direction.

'Hello.' The man who greeted us was tall and thin, dressed in a white string vest and a blue and yellow checked *futa*. His face glowed, shiny black with perfect white teeth and pointed ears. He was one of Gadi's companions. Gadi himself was off bathing. Before Koert Jan could object, the friend ran off to fetch him. We sat. I was acutely aware of the camera on my hip, as if it were a deformity, or weapon. Men were staring at it, trying not to get caught looking.

A few feet away, stretched full length on the ground, two men, one fifty-five, I'd say, the other about thirty, were embracing and kissing and laughing. The younger man rolled free and fumbled among papers folded in his shirt pocket. He came up with a small photo. From where I sat I could see a woman's face. He gave it to the older man who, lying on his back, held it up over his eyes and nodded lewd approval. The younger man now took the picture back. He kissed the older one on the mouth and wasn't pushed away. Their tongues met and rowed. A third man was sitting with his back to them, knees pulled up to his chest. He looked down over his shoulder at the couple with a mixture of envy and amusement. He was holding one of the older man's hands.

'Hello.' This time it was a short, heavy-set boy who greeted Koert Jan and Koert Jan nodded back non-committally. The boy had a scraggy beard, a cataract in one eye, a broad, flat nose, fierce acne scars on his cheek and neck. 'You were looking for me?'

'Yes.' Koert Jan, as usual, covered well. Only someone who knew him as well as I did would have noticed his lapse. 'This is the friend I told you about, Gadi. The one with the camera.' We shook hands. A smile transformed Gadi's face, making it appetising. 'I didn't mean to disturb you.'

'So much waiting is making everyone nervous. Bathing's only an excuse to get away.'

'Your English is very good,' I said.

'I went to high school in the United States. Shaker Heights, Ohio. Ever been there?'

'No.'

'It's the pits. Nothing to recommend it, except the ice cream. Mint chocolate chip.'

We were attracting too much attention for comfort. Any outsider was a threat to the refugees, every new face. I tried to attach histories to separate men. Of the hundred, few I would say had known each other before stepping aboard the boat. The first time, had they gathered by night, illuminated by lanterns? Black faces flaring for a moment in lamplight as they backed down a short ladder and groped to a place on one of the rough thwarts. Paying in cash before they climbed from the jetty. The first small waves lapping at the hull in darkness, the rocking motion gentle but frightening still, for they knew, all of them, the Red Sea was deep and wide and the wind was rising. Or had everything been arranged coolly, clinically beforehand in some hotel, or even police station? Did embarkation take place in broad daylight, the fugitives turned invisible by bribes?

In any event I could imagine the first aboard hugging themselves with relief. With what feelings did they watch their numbers grow? And grow. Probably the first ten welcomed the second. Gave each other the once over, nodded, smiled, shifted belongings, made room. But then? Each man after fifty would have had to bear the hatred of more than a hundred eyes. How the ninety-nine must have loathed the hundredth. What tricks did the captain use to keep them docile? Or was flight, fear of capture, tranquilliser enough? Did they talk at sea? When the boat slipped from the harbor, with the known world receding, was each mumbling a separate prayer? How many jokesters were along? By night huddled together for warmth, in the heat of the day they would protect their heads with cloths, shift and strain to avoid contact. How fast the politics of their situation must have stamped their behavior. Allegiances, factions. Sharing cigarettes, keeping count. Swapping lies. How many had brought weapons, like the knife used to scour the turtle's entrails from its shell?

'No,' Gadi was saying as we moved through the grove, 'I can't swim, not a stroke. Will you teach me?'

Gadi took us to the captain. A condition accepted by all on the journey was that until they reached Jeddah, the captain's word was law. To shoot photographs without his consent would be asking for trouble.

The captain wasn't distinguishable by dress. Short and fat, with splotched skin, he reclined against a carved wood chest. He wore his headcloth like a dinner napkin tossed on to the table after a long meal. The whole time we stood over him, his eyes never once stopped moving. His hands, darker than his arms or face, were clasped around his furry belly, a fold of which oozed over the top of his purple sarong. The man's fingers were covered in rings, silver set with amber. Warning: this jewelry did not testify to vanity. The rings were magic. He navigated by those rings.

When Gadi introduced us the first thing the captain did was spit on to the sand and stare at the discharge. He then glanced up and prodded us between the ribs with his eyes. When he began to speak, which he did in Arabic and with great panache, his voice dripped honey. On and on he went.

'He is telling us about the family of man,' Gadi interpreted, 'and expressing his awe at the forces of destiny that have brought us together.' The captain paused, smiled – or rather his lips peeled back to reveal his teeth. 'What he really wants to know is who the hell you are and what the fuck you're doing here?'

'Here?'

'In Yemen.'

'Tell him we're tourists,' Koert Jan explained before I could give an honest answer. In his most ingratiating manner he went on, 'A small party come to enjoy the seaside attractions. Our camp is further up the beach.' Later than I should have, I realised that any kind of connection between us and the government would have alarmed the captain. By now a large number of men encircled us. Few were as young as Gadi. They crowded so close that when I crouched down the better to talk with the captain their legs were like the bars of a cage. Someone began to feel my hair between his fingers.

'Now I'm going to tell him how we met.' Gadi was self-assured. 'And how I asked if you had any film.' While he spoke, Gadi used his hands expressively. At one point he reached over and tugged at the shoulder strap of my camera. A shock rippled through the ranks of onlookers. An angry chattering broke out, shouts. A man stepped forward and began to harangue the captain whose small, tight smile remained unchanged – if anything it grew tighter. I thought I recognised the man as the scrawny leader of those we had watched disembowel the sea turtle yesterday. Something he said touched the captain who began to pull at his lower lip with ringed fingers. He really looked very funny. I had to pinch my leg not to laugh.

'They have a bad case of the jitters,' said Gadi. 'Their nerves want to snap. What makes them worry is what you would do with the photos afterwards.'

The captain nodded.

'Of course,' Koert Jan said. 'Tell them' – Koert Jan looked around at the gathered faces – 'after we finish making the pictures you want, we will take the film out of the camera and leave it with you.' A slight arch of Koert Jan's eyebrows was the only sign he saw me flinch. 'You will take the film with you and when you reach Saudi you can develop it, and send us copies. That way no one has to be afraid.'

Gadi translated.

'Very good,' the captain said in English, brightening. He cleared his throat, swallowed his sputum. In fact, Gadi told us later, the man understood seven languages. Of all the captains evacuating fugitives from Mengistu's reign of terror, he was the most trusted. And the most expensive.

'But he doesn't know where you are!' Gadi was not ruffled by my protest.

'What does that matter, as long as he brings us where we are going?' He had been told the captain was trustworthy and it suited him to believe it.

Koert Jan's proposal to relinquish the film settled the question in our favour. The captain dismissed us with a wave of the hand. Clearly, however, not everyone was happy with the outcome. I can't say I was overjoyed myself.

'What about the first six pic—'

'What about them?' Koert Jan silenced me sharply. He was right, of course, but what, I couldn't help thinking, would

Gadi, safe in Jeddah, make of Ulrike in her bikini mashing a jellyfish?

From the waistband of his swimming-trunks, Koert Jan produced a business card. The stinker, when had the idea of parting with the film first occurred to him?

'Taiz Solid Waste Disposal Project,' Gadi read. 'Public Health Consultant. Can you explain?'

Koert Jan smiled. 'I'm a garbage man.'

Bert's safety helmet! We hadn't taken much more than ten steps from the captain back towards the trees where Gadi's friends were sitting when, out of the corner of one eye, I saw Bert's helmet. One of the helpers who'd been carrying gobbets of turtle flesh the day before, shuffling stiff-legged through the sand, sat now with the motorcycle helmet clamped between his knees, drumming on it with the fore and index fingers of both hands. A black motorcycle helmet was hardly the kind of thing you took along on a life or death cruise. Oh, damn my heavy eyes: the drummer's hands froze in mid-air. And then he pulled the hem of his *futa* forward, down over the helmet.

'Six?' Gadi was asking.

'We have already taken six,' Koert Jan explained with his fingers, 'six more remain.' I handed Koert Jan the camera. He's a far more accomplished photographer than I. Free of the camera, moreover, I might have a look round. Gadi, unfortunately, chose to lead us clear of the trees down to the fringe of the sea. He walked hand in hand with a friend, a rather degenerate-looking, puffy figure with unkind eyes.

Standing, hopping really and almost falling, they stripped down to their undershorts. Gadi's were stretched too large for him and printed either with hearts or motorcars, I didn't want to squint. His friend's shorts were a spider web of rags. Together they waded past the carcasses of sea turtles several yards into the blue-green water. They turned, threw their arms around each other's shoulders and assumed serious,

191

self-important expressions. 'All right,' Gadi called to Koert Jan, 'shoot.'

This then was to be the gripping record of a once in a lifetime adventure? That patch of sea could have been anywhere. A crowd had drifted down to the beach behind us, including the scrawny fellow so black, openly antagonistic to our presence. I had no doubt he was a murderer. He had killed before and would do so again. He didn't try to justify his acts either, not to others, not to himself. If expedient, he struck, plain and simple. Just because a man was a refugee, didn't make him holy.

It took me more by surprise than it should have: the anticlimax of what we would be asked to photograph. In developing countries all over the world Koert Jan and I had seen photographers' studios. We no longer laughed at the rigid formal poses. Cliché pictures on the walls of mud huts in fancy frames, photo albums full of people eating or sitting and staring self-consciously into the lens. Oh, we'd been in similar situations before, yet now Koert Jan couldn't use one of his favorite tricks, to pretend to shoot and save his film for candids later. We had pledged to give the film away.

Koert Jan didn't take defeat lightly. He waded into the sea as well and wagging a finger at the sun managed to circle round the friends so that when he stopped to focus he at least had the fishing boat of their adventure bobbing in the background. How I wished I could photograph the taking of the photograph – especially the onlookers. Gadi and friend, splashed with spray, were delighted.

'Two.'

Knees pumping, Gadi thrashed back on to the beach and seated himself on the cream-colored underbelly of the decapitated sea turtle. He crossed his legs, leaned back to support his weight on one arm, propped up like a pin-up girl. The absurdity of the pose would have been delicious except for the sense of waste and the smugness involved. To take the picture Koert Jan went down on one knee. Surf wet his *futa*, tugged one edge free. I looked away. My eyes fell on the severed turtle head. It had pitched forward on to its beak. One eye socket had been picked clean by the birds. The effect was not unlike Gadi's milky cataract. I became aware of an increasing number of gulls standing on the sand spit or criss-crossing low overhead, screaming.

To think the severed head would be left out of the photographs made me wild. I wanted to rush in and set it down at Gadi's feet. Why not? What held me back? Fear? Not only: Koert Jan was always accusing me of carrying around too much melodrama I wanted to impart to the world.

Then I heard the girls. Low reassuring tones of idle female chit-chat. Hester and Jacqueline came rounding the point of the grove, beachcombing. The Ethiopians took an instinctive step back. No one looked amused. Both girls were in skimpy bathing-suits. Jacqueline was in the act of stuffing some found treasure into her briefs. Her exposed shoulders, belly, thighs were brick red, with filigree streaks of white where the flesh creased. Hester was walking with her gold cross pressed between her lips. The dark flesh of her large nipples showed above the sagging top of her suit. Our eyes met. I flashed a warning and turned away. Koert Jan did not look around. He stayed down on one knee, steadying the camera.

To their credit the girls did not call out to us or come closer. They laughed at something, admired the gulls. Hester turned a sea cucumber over gingerly with her toes. Then they retreated gracefully, no faster, no slower than they had been moving before. When their backs disappeared from view, shoulders broad, slightly stooped, bottoms sandy, I let out my breath. And there was a scuffle in the ranks of the Ethiopians. Two of them were holding the angry black who twisted to free himself, practically foaming at the lips, calling out angrily. They released him and he charged back to the grove, hands in fists, nearly falling in his haste. The laughter which followed him was uneasy, African laughter.

For Gadi's next photographs he led us back among the trees. I tried to slip away but, whether intentionally or not, spectators hedged me in. To break their ranks would have created a stir I chose not to risk. Gadi knelt and ransacked his belongings. He pulled on his good trousers – brown polyester flecked with points of red and yellow. He fought his way into a too-snug Rolling Stones T-shirt: red lips and tongue. Then from his knapsack he produced platform shoes with red, white and blue heels. Sunglasses provided a finishing touch, wrap-arounds in zebra-stripe frames. He rammed a wooden comb through his hair, too – leaving it standing straight up behind one ear.

For the third picture Gadi did his best to look earnest, and, I suppose, imposing. For the fourth, he relaxed, shoving his glasses up over his forehead on to his kinky hair and letting fly with a gigolo's smile. My eyes tried to scour the grove. My heart lamented missed chances. Gadi the gadfly. How had we become locked into this damn farce when, on all sides, there were such moving vignettes? In the refugees' situation how would I respond? I had to fight the suspicion my determination to survive would be undercut by wave after wave of self-pity.

And what of Bert? Was there any evidence lying about? Cruising the beach – vrroooom – could he have met up with some Ethiopians and maybe traded them his helmet for something? For old silver? Bert was always on the lookout for a bargain. I almost laughed out loud at the vision of Bert on his bike speeding back to Taiz, bareheaded, but draped with bright necklaces and breastplates.

'Koert Jan?' Koert Jan was busy. 'Hey!' I know he heard me. And I know he was ignoring me. In front of so many people he didn't want to exchange confidences. What he did want, I suspect, was to finish the photographs and go. Act normal, see the charade through, get out. Perhaps he had seen Bert's helmet himself, or more?

Photo five it was settled would be a group affair. Many crowded into shapeless rows. Gadi played the celebrity. He

194

waved people off, rearranged the position of others. Here, too, there was a pecking order. The arrogance on Gadi's face, the dismissive gesture of his hand were matched by haughty words spat out in Arabic. Oh cub of the Lion of Judah. I no longer liked Gadi, nor sympathised with his *emergency*. Were these people in any real danger, or was it only my runaway imagination? Except for Gadi's story, what did we have to go on?

No – it was true. The boat bobbed on the sea.

For the sixth and last pose Gadi was at a loss. He couldn't think of anything he wanted! We agreed on a repeat of the group. At the last instant two brown-skinned youths, slender adolescents Gadi had driven off earlier, edged back in and flopped down in front of the rest. If we were ever to receive copies of these photos, it would be their risking rehumiliation I would remember.

Only later did it strike me how odd it was, how very odd, we weren't asked to pose with the refugees. Not once.

True interest in the group revived when Koert Jan sat cross-legged at the base of a palm and began to remove the film from the camera. As he opened the Yashica, pulling the back free, the crowd sighed. Many were familiar enough with cameras but few had seen the insides of one. The emptiness! They huddled close, leaning on each other's backs, peering between legs as Koert Jan fiddled with spools. I seized my chance and drifted backwards towards the heart of the grove.

The drummer on Bert's helmet no longer sat where I had seen him. Beside a sputtering fire, however, some twenty yards further, half-screened by several men eating scraps of gleaming, fatty turtle, licking their long fingers, there was a body on the ground covered over with a frayed blanket. Short and broad it lay in a cramped, foetal position. It didn't move.

Ripple soles. What shoes were Bert wearing? When would I learn to be more observant! At any rate the figure under the

195

blanket was shod, and that in itself was unusual. Refugees with shoes had removed them and put them away, only to be taken out again upon arrival in the city.

The eyes of the eaters followed me, their lips in constant motion. 'Taste good?' I asked. Whose grin, starched and out-of-size, was I wearing?

I regained the fringe of the surrounding crowd just as Koert Jan was presenting Gadi with the film. Gadi offered him money. Tattered, dirty dollars. Koert Jan refused.

'Coming?' Koert Jan asked, moving past me briskly. He gave the empty Yashica back to me to carry.

'I hope Bert didn't run into any unexpected trouble on his way back,' I said, hitting separate words with unnatural emphasis. The non-sequitur I accompanied with an attempt to point with my eyes at the figure under the blanket. Koert Jan, out of character, seemed to notice nothing. To take our leave we didn't report back to the captain. Some spy would have had us under surveillance anyway. Koert Jan's haste, feet sinking in loose sand to jar the ankle, began to feel like flight.

'Koert –' As soon as we regained the crescent beach which arched back towards camp, I took Koert Jan's elbow and blurted out my fears about Bert.

'Show me,' he said. He turned and I had no choice but to follow. What made Koert Jan think he was invulnerable? We cut into the palm grove from a new angle, my disorientation complete. With no attempt to disguise our actions, we stalked through the grove. The blood rang in my ears. I didn't know whether to feel silly or scared, so I felt both.

Wherever sleepers lay Koert Jan paused to take a good look. No one seemed to care or notice. We were as insignificant as sand-flies. Finally I had to give up. The body was gone. No helmet anywhere either.

When we nearly stumbled over the captain, gorging on turtle, all he did was blink at us sleepily. At his feet, stretched out, lay the turtle butcher, a drugged, mysterious expression on his ebony face. Even dead to the world the man looked dangerous.

'Most probably they've just finished eating Bert,' said Koert Jan. I let him know I considered the joke in bad taste.

IX

Back at camp, without disclosing the true situation, we apologised to the girls for our rudeness. Their bikinis, we explained, might have set off a chain reaction. We mumbled something about Islamic standards of decency and left it at that.

'Of course I realised *something* was going on,' Jacqueline said. 'I *do* work at the embassy.' When we came up the beach, she was foaming at the mouth – chlorophyll – and waved to us with her toothbrush. I was happy to see she was safe. In penance I glowingly admired the most non-descript collection of seashells and tidbits of fossil and coral I ever hope to see.

By now the afternoon furnace was at full stoke and our party was on its last legs. I took to the sea but my tension and nausea refused to rinse away. I closed my eyes, dove underwater and imagined I was a sea turtle, hunted. Unlike the refugees, I could swim. If their boat capsized, they would go down like stones, bodies everywhere, clutching, churning, in each other's way. Their sleep on the sea floor would be final, uninterrupted. Bodies in a heap, a tangle – and in Gadi's pocket, our film.

When I surfaced Elso fluttered up on a surfboard and amiably offered another lesson. 'One last chance.' I wanted to touch him, stroke him, hug him. 'Wind's died down,' he said. 'Now or never.'

The unending awkward struggle was a comfort. Straining to haul the sail out of the water, I saw myself leading a hundred refugees – and one captain – on surfboards to Jeddah. When I gave up and came ashore – a glide of several seconds my best effort, enough to taste what wasn't to be – Hans came and sat next to me.

'You must think I'm crazy,' he said. After having stumbled on him spreadeagled with self-pleasure in the sun, it was hard to look him in the eye. He'd had such a different face then, like a frowning baby's. 'Three years in this god-forsaken country. So how'd things go in Dhamar?' The transition was so smooth it was almost seamless. Hans had a reputation for diplomatic intelligence. Because there was too much I didn't feel like saying, I resorted to questions about his work. He wasn't fooled. Still he was grateful to be asked about himself.

As we talked, sitting on the wet sand, scooping up handfuls and hurling them out to sea, my eyes kept returning to the far-off palm grove. Hans told me he was pulling strings to be transferred to a 'place where something happens'. His first post had been South Africa. 'They spoiled us silly. There's a lot of Dutch money at work down there. What're we doing in Yemen? A garbage project – ' With perfect timing a wave carried a crushed beer can up to our feet and we laughed. 'No, you can say what you like about South Africans, they're not hypocrites.'

When our group broke camp, I watched with admiration. They effaced every trace of our stay. Jan Willem skipped about, rounding up beer cans. He even raked them out of the coals of the fire.

'We bury them,' Hester told me. 'A time capsule! Two thousand years from now some archaeologist will prove there was a sect of Islam along the Red Sea coast that thrived on alcohol.'

'Wait a minute.' Jonathan tore a sheet off his notepad and tucked it into one of the beer cans.

'What'd you say?' Jacqueline asked.

'Nothing. I want them to have a sample of our paper, if it lasts.'

The Sana contingent were planning to drive non-stop back to

the capital, seven or eight hours in all, more if rain caught them, as was likely, in the high mountain passes. Jacqueline rushed about, a billowing shift over her bathing-suit, camera in both hands. 'I have to use up the roll,' she apologised. She'd been taking snaps of Koert Jan all weekend.

Humming, Ulrike toted a last jellyfish to the cemetery she had created at the edge of the grove. 'A mass grave,' she smiled. 'Serves the bastards right.'

Pim knotted the surfplanks on to the carrier rack of his Land Cruiser. Goodbye Red Sea. Inside a towel I shimmied out of my trunks and into shorts. Koert Jan stripped and changed in the open. It was possible, it was likely no one in the entire colony of refugees had ever stood naked in any wind, except perhaps stealthily, to bathe at night. Wardah had explained to us that was why the men of Taiz soon tired of their wives. Arab women never took their clothes off. Vietnamese were better. *Habibi, habibi*, they said. I love you. And they let you kiss them on the mouth.

'And Ethiopians?' I'd asked Wardah.

'Oh,' she shot back, 'the best of all!'

'Well, thank you, it was a pleasure.' Ulrike led off the farewells, extending her hand to me. 'I can't tell you how much I enjoyed myself, really.' When I looked closely, I saw relief in her eyes, as if a siege was over. 'Come see how we rescue paper.'

I would make the first part of the journey back with Jan Willem in his jeep. Pim, too. We were going to ride the sand dune.

'Okay, take everything out,' Elso told Saskia. The Suzuki looked full and the sand was still crowded with boxes and sacks and folding chairs.

'I've plenty of room,' Koert Jan offered. But Elso made it a point of honour that what came with them, went home with them. 'It's just a question of taking the trouble to do it right,' he said.

'No, it isn't,' Saskia contradicted him. 'You also have to be a real anal retentive.'

'Oh.' Jacqueline pointed at the last item Elso strained to fit into the car, a bulging canvas bag marked Property of the Netherlands Ministry for Foreign Affairs.

'I'd like a bathing-suit with that written on it,' Hans said. 'Or would I?'

The wind had all but died. Our vehicles assumed position in a line along the rim of the beach. The bay glistened. Our camp was spotless, pristine.

'Got your spoons, Saskia?' Hester asked hoarsely.

'And three extra,' she laughed.

Hans's vehicle in the lead had started to roll when a figure came gliding towards us, pushing back low palm fronds as he hurried through the shade of the grove, half-walking, half-running. Gadi.

'What do you want?' Pim snarled in Arabic. He was closest to the place where Gadi emerged into the afternoon sun, a puzzled smile on his face. Gadi shaded his eyes with one hand as he searched the party for our faces.

'We know him,' Koert Jan said. At the sound of Koert Jan's voice Gadi brightened. He looked somehow different. Perhaps it was simply that now he had detached himself from ninety-nine other black faces. Yet, no. As he went up to the Toyota I could see a gentleness, a softness to his features hidden before. After our last visit up the beach, I had decided I disliked Gadi. His high-handedness. His whole life he had been spoiled by privilege. Who could say what he had done to make flight necessary? But now, as he smiled at Koert Jan, I wondered instead what pressure he was under in the group, what demands did the other Ethiopians make on him.

Gadi was in his faded *futa* and Rolling Stones T-shirt. Next to the Toyota his chin barely came up to the bottom edge of the driver's window.

'You're going?'

'Yes.'

'I wanted to tell you how much I appreciate everything you have done for me.' Although Gadi spoke in a low, steady voice, I could still hear everything from the jeep. We all could. This was more than politeness. Gadi looked nervously over his shoulder and up and down the deserted beach. He had, no doubt, snuck away. Perhaps he was afraid he'd been followed. To come looking for us was risky. The captain might think Gadi was passing the film back. For an instant I thought Koert Jan might even have worked the whole thing out beforehand. 'I am truly grateful, thank you.' Gadi was trying not to let his fear, his loneliness show. 'And from Jeddah, Allah willing, I will send you a letter about the journey.'

With their long ride ahead, the Sana bunch began honking impatiently. Jan Willem pulled out from behind Koert Jan, jolting across ruts in the wadi. The last glimpse I had of Gadi was of his shaking Koert Jan's hand in both of his. How easily we could come and go. How tempting – to ask Gadi to climb aboard with us, to drive away from the sea, safe. But what then? The Mayor would throw a fit. Security would descend like vultures. Crazy world.

Suddenly Hans, in the lead, stopped. Jacqueline scampered down, and thongs flapping, ran back to us. 'Hey, what about the turtles? Before we go, don't you guys want to drive over and see them?'

'They're gone,' I lied. 'There's nothing left to see.'

'Oh damn. Did you take any pictures?'

'Yes,' I tapped the Yashica slung over my shoulder.

'Can I have a copy?'

'If they turn out.'

Jacqueline smiled. 'I'll hold you to that.'

'Who was he?' Pim asked after we were under way.

'A fisherman.'

'Who speaks English?'

'A smart fisherman.'

Navigation of the sand dune had, pardon the expression, its ups and downs. Jan Willem kindled with adolescent glee. He skidded and churned about, shrieking and hooting without very much idea of what might be going on under the wheels. 'Like a pig on a woman,' Pim put it. Our sudden dips and turns shattered the sky into pieces with overlapping edges and cost me what was left of my stomach. Jan Willem stalled out once, on the crest. He began spastically trying to bring the engine back to life when Pim laid a hand on his.

'Wait a sec,' Pim said. 'Look.'

We commanded a view that stretched to infinity in all directions, sand and scrub, the flatness pocked with brush and lengthening shadows. Riding the dune, tilted at steep angles, I was Gadi pitching between the salty tongues of the sea.

In the middle of nowhere we caught up with the others. The surfboards had worked loose, one sliding forward on to the hood, startling Hester at the wheel. Elso was now lashing them back in place with the blue cable.

'Good to be back,' I told Koert Jan as I slid in next to him. The rest soon outdistanced us, specks swallowed by space. 'Goodbye,' I called after them.

'Not yet,' Koert Jan said. 'They're coming to the house for coffee. And *cake*.'

'You're the glutton – for punishment.'

As we slithered and bucked through the desert, our gear clanging away in back, we were closer than we'd been in years.

'If Gadi doesn't write,' I broke the silence as we spurted up on to the Moccha road, 'we won't know what's happened, will we?'

'No letter means they didn't make it.'

'Do you think?'

Half-way back to Taiz it started raining and Koert Jan began to sing the *Actus Tragicus*. It was the music he wanted performed at his funeral. To hear better, I rolled up my window.

'Nice after the desert,' I said, mopping at condensation on the inside of the windshield. Koert Jan put a hand on my leg. With Taiz sprawled in the distance the rain stopped as suddenly as it had begun. Arching above the city were no less than two rainbows, one on top of the other. The far distance was still menacing, black with massive clouds, but these were radiant in outline. The fourteenth-century mosque near the heights of the old city was so white it appeared luminescent.

'St Peter once came down to earth,' Koert Jan told me, 'to Taiz. He had some business to do. When he was finished, and started up to heaven again, the mosque thought it would go too. It started to take flight after him. "No," St Peter said, "whoa there. You're still needed where you are." So the mosque sank down – and that's why it rests lopsided on its foundation.'

'Are they Sunites here,' I asked, 'or Shiites?'

'You're only asking because you think I don't know the difference. Well, I do.' Koert Jan drove under an arch at the edge of the city. Behind one of the uprights was a sprawling heap of trash. 'When I heard you were coming, I asked.'

'And?'

'We have both.'

'What's the difference – how do they perceive the differences?'

'Shiites pray with their hands folded on their bellies. Sunites keep them clasped behind their backs.'

'KJ, what time do you think they'll set out to sea? Does Friday end at sunset?'

'If it wasn't for the boat people,' Koert Jan was scrubbing my back hard, 'that would have been one wasted weekend. Sounds like the kind of nonsense you could say, I know, but it's true.'

The bell rang.

'Take your time' – Koert Jan squeezed the sponge out over my head – 'but hurry. I'll *entertain* them.'

As I finished my bath, tired social chatter echoed deep in the house. Pulling the plug I filled with sudden sympathy for the wife of the Chargé d'Affaires. Not so much for the desperate minute she had lived through when one of her little boys, or both, had squeezed her hand and looked at her with beggar's eyes and she knew she would have to be quick or they would soil their clothes. 'Mommy, why did you bring us here?' That's what their bodies turning inside out of their own accord were saying. 'Why?' No, my sympathy extended further. It reached to the present moment. It stretched past the event to include how what happened had passed into local history. She would have to burn that dress bright with flowers and even then that wouldn't do any good. She would only make more history, digging herself in deeper.

As I stepped over the edge of the tub, the bathwater belched and swirled in a vortex down the drain, leaving a deposit of sand on the bottom. High up one wall a small lizard scuttled into a corner and then, upside down, ran out to mid-ceiling where it froze motionless. The little boy in the house half-way up Jebel Sabar, Kassem's son, he would never wash himself, or clean himself after passing waste. Diarrhoea streaming down the inside of his leg would be a fact of life and the brusque, disapproving cluck of a sister or his mother wiping the leg clean. Sea flippers, he had, vestigial. And the face of an angel.

No, the child who had reached into his father's shoe and pulled out a grenade, he was better off. At least until the bitter day he grew sick of hearing his father rant and rave about how his son was such a hero.

When I came into the living room, drying my hair, everyone was slumped with exhaustion. Elso and Saskia had been home already to unload the Suzuki and sweep out Pim's Land Cruiser. Hans & Co. had pushed on. I sat on a small glass and chrome end table. Saskia was explaining to Hester why she felt she was through with physiotherapy: 'I'm not about to spend the rest of my life meeting people through their pain.'

204

Elso wanted to know why Koert Jan hadn't told them right away about the sea turtles on the beach. 'Why the big secret?'

Wardah's cake had been right where I'd left it, carefully set out to be taken to Yachtule. In our absence sun and heat had fused the multicolor sprinkles and vanilla icing. Now Koert Jan cut huge slabs studded with cardamoms still in their husk. He didn't want any left-overs.

I closed the windows. A stink of burning rubber was invading the room. Children burning old tires out back. Or it might have been the stench of a dead, bloated goat.

'How much beer did you buy, Pim?' Hester asked. 'Four crates or five?'

'A hundred and twenty beers,' Saskia exulted. 'How many people were drinking for Christ's sake?'

'Don't forget the wine.'

'And the Scotch.'

'Jesus.'

Koert Jan poured coffee, rich and dark, a gift from Mahyub's mother.

'I only had four,' Saskia said. 'What about you, Hester?'

'Last time there were seven crates.' Jan Willem spoke with his mouth full, spraying cake crumbs. 'Sorry.'

'But last time Bert came,' Elso interjected, 'that's a crate right there.'

'More.'

'Bert with a mosquito net around his waist. The buck-toothed bride. I'll never forget it.' Elso's tone changed. He grew earnest. 'Poor guy's had an accident.'

I stopped drying my hair.

Saskia giggled. 'Typical Bert.'

Koert Jan licked the cake knife slowly. 'Did he crash the bike – for the tenth time?'

'No, Bert got home all right. Then when they were getting ready to go to the barbecue, he had to take a shit. He has piles,' Saskia explained for my benefit. I was clearly the only one in the room who'd never heard Bert tell any of his piles stories. 'He was sitting there and the pain got so bad he passed out. Fell off and hit the floor so hard his teeth went through his lip. Blood all over the place. Malvina's driven him to the American dental hospital in Jiblah.'

'What were those characters doing anyway?' Elso persisted. Icing gleamed on his upper lip. 'Killing turtles for fun? That's the kind of thing a Yemeni would get off on.'

'They were eating them,' Koert Jan said.

'No.'

'Yes.'

'Disgusting.'

'There was nothing else. "Those characters" were refugees from Ethiopia, of course, fighting to stay alive.'

'While we were having a nice day surfing at the beach?' Only Pim seemed to take in fully what Koert Jan was saying. With two fingers sliding in opposite directions, he stroked his moustache. 'Was that their boat off the spit?'

'Yes.'

'God help them.'

'I still think it's a pity,' Elso kept on. 'Those poor turtles.' I realised then how deeply the image of the severed turtle head, erect on its chopped neck, the blood-filled eyes staring, had been burned into my brain.

'Yes,' Koert Jan said.

'They never hurt anybody.'

'What a prince you are, Elso,' Saskia said, shrewd eyes narrowing, 'always rooting for the underdog.'

Easy Come, Easy Go

I

Kisumu, western terminus of the trans-Kenya railway, was my first experience of a former British colonial town. The English had been gone for decades, of course, but like it or not, they had made a lasting mark. The sleepy main avenues were more pothole than pavement, still every road divider had its own flowerbed. The day Koert Jan and I arrived, birds of paradise, strident orange, thousands upon thousands, were out on parade to welcome us.

The heart of Kisumu is a scorched and sprawling park, like a piece of chewed burlap. Dappled light sifts down through a host of acacia trees and, falling on your skin, makes you itch. At the top of the park, due north, the Kisumu Hotel survives, a faded picture postcard of itself. You know the kind: semi-circular drive, elevated front porch, overhead fans like squashed spiders in the dining-room and bar. Next door, in front of the post office with its commemorative cornerstone and rusted iron shutters, three Masai sleep in a row under blood-red blankets, earrings for sale spread on the pavement, drinking gourds inlaid with beads and soapstone chess sets. There is even a supermarket in Kisumu, the Acme. In the unwashed window the equatorial sun bleaches hand-printed signs advertising last year's Rotary Club picnic or a gala paddle-boat cruise on Lake

Victoria. Inside the shelves are still stocked with a hundred and one dried breakfast cereals turning to dust inside their cardboard boxes.

A few minutes' winding drive downhill from the hotel towards the Lake Victoria shoreline brings you to the Kisumu Club. A tattered awning, blue and white, flaps in the lake breeze above the crumbling front entrance. The gaping mouths of ornamental stone lions have gone green with rot. It is something of a miracle, moreover, how despite so many cracks the club pool holds water. Nowadays there is a rather stiff daily admission fee. None the less black guests far outnumber the rest. But then, we soon found out, a hole in the fence lets them pass freely in and out. Swarms of spindly kids in torn-off trousers or sagging underwear, screaming and splashing and sailing through the air. Somehow death by drowning eludes them.

Whites from a wide catchment-area converge at the Kisumu Club to swim. Not the pure Anglican breed of colonial times though, no. Mongrel international development cadre. Some are volunteers without pay to speak of, others are experts in this or that with an obscene *per diem* to prove it. They – we – sport spotty tans. Faces brown, hands, and maybe forearms. A few have also criss-cross patterns burned on to the tops of their feet betraying the habit of sandals. As newcomers Koert Jan and I were welcomed over-cordially and questioned with polite disinterest about our mission. Wives especially tested us with various complaints. Would we close rank with those who kept themselves going by daily tirades against backwardness and corruption? Or would we prove silent, suffering types – laconic in our defiance of the odds stacked against changing the world one jot for the better?

Even before we laid eyes on Kisumu, however, Koert Jan and I had planned to pass through and leave it behind quickly. We had come to Western Province to do anthropological fieldwork among the Abaluhya, third largest of Kenya's tribes.

It was our first job. If we didn't often speak to each other of our excitement, it was the better to preserve it. Finding a home base, however, proved far from simple. Beyond Kisumu, north and west as far as the Uganda border, the country was densely settled, true. Overpopulated in fact. Everywhere clusters of huts and granaries. Yet 'suitable accommodation', as officials put it, was scarce. There were few 'permanent' or 'semi-permanent' houses to rent. And then from our point of view these squat, bunker-like cement buildings, painted one pastel tint or another and stained with mildew, had undesirable locations, fronting on a main road or standing in stark isolation on an abandoned school compound. What we wanted was to be part of a local community. Ask as many questions as we might, interview until hoarse, the information about the Abaluhya and their lives bound to mean the most to us, ultimately, would have to come from what we saw happening around us.

Our house search dragged on. We looked for weeks in vain. Finally Charles Hammer gave us a promising lead. Charles, Mr Cattle Dip, was a balding American veterinarian. We met in Kisumu in a back-alley Indian sweet shop. We walked in, he was sitting there gorging himself on pink and green and dripping delicacies. 'Go on,' Charles called over to us, 'live dangerously.' We stood peering through the glass counter, puzzling over our selection. 'The pumpkin halva isn't bad and I can recommend the Jalebi, those twisty things, with all my heart.'

There was a bulky bandage taped to the side of Charles's neck with red streaks like the points of a star emerging from under the edges. He had nicked himself shaving, so he told us, and the wound had gone septic. Now as soon as someone qualified to take his place at the cattle dip in Kakamega arrived, Charles would fly home to St Paul, Minnesota, for treatment. 'The World Bank doesn't take chances.' Charles was flip but worried, and in obvious pain. 'You've got to taste the cheese fudge here to believe it. See, as long as I can keep my mind on sweets, I forget that there's an infection seeping towards my heart.'

I liked Charles and hope he's on his feet again and up to good things.

'A house? Let me see. A house, a house, a house.' He licked the honey from his fingertips. 'No, I don't, but I'll ask around. You Dutch are fussy, aren't you?'

A few days later we ran into Charles outside the post office. There was powdered sugar on his chin and shirt front. 'Just sent off my last batch of Wish-you-were-heres,' he said. 'With any luck I'll beat them home.'

'Find anything for us yet?' Koert Jan asked.

'Depends how desperate you're feeling.' We laughed. 'Elizabeth Khaeri, behind the Catholic church in Mumias. She lets rooms – mostly for transients who harvest cane for Booker's Factory. She maybe could let you have one.'

We found the Catholic church on the fringe of Mumias all right. You couldn't miss it. It was part of a large complex which included a Mission hospital, a girls' secondary school and a school for the deaf. The church itself was an enormous affair with a chunky spire. Its original orange colour had faded almost to buff. The roof was steeply pitched, with terracotta tiles, some cracked, some slipping from place.

We parked our little Renault 4 in the shadow of the building, scattered the chickens that came brazenly to greet us and followed a footpath out back through a field of green maize. The path led to a compound where two round thatched mud huts, traditional Luhya houses, faced each other across a pounded dirt yard. In the middle, humming, a woman stood winnowing millet in a flat, woven tray. Her body swayed back and forth as she tossed the grain up in the air, caught it and flung it aloft again. She smiled when she saw us, gave a few more tosses to the millet, then came to offer us her firm handshake.

Koert Jan and I liked Elizabeth Khaeri instantly. She was a handsome woman, regal in bearing. The day we met she wore a blue-green wrapper knotted at one hip, a yellow tank top, and another blue-green cloth tied around a high bush of hair. Gold teeth flashed when she talked. Her high forehead furrowed with concentration when she listened to us.

'We are looking for lodgings,' Koert Jan explained. At that Elizabeth disappeared into the house and came back with a bunch of keys – and three daughters. Anna – who would become our closest friend in the family – large for her age, thirteen – with the blackest, and shiniest of faces, very round. Mary, eleven, definitely funny-looking, with a nap of coarse hair, projecting ears, an enormous slash of a mouth and a stick body. Mary was the cleverest of the Khaeri girls. And Rosa, only four, Elizabeth's last-born, the image of her mother, if anything more imperious in how she carried herself.

'Please follow us.' Anna spoke English but she was so shy with us that she never raised her voice above a whisper. Never. Her diction was precise and her good humor unfailing. Even when we began to whisper back to Anna to tease her, she didn't raise her voice.

Elizabeth led us some fifty yards by a twisting path back to a level clearing where a single long, narrow one-storey breeze block building caught the full weight of the sun on its sheet-iron roof. There were six doors spaced along the façade, no windows. The two doors farthest from where we reached the clearing stood open. In one doorway a man naked to the waist sat on a low three-legged stool shaving himself in a small hand-mirror, a basin of soapy water between his feet. I think he saw us in the mirror before he heard us. At any rate he stood instantly, a towel falling from his lap to the ground. He nodded with short, rapid movements of his head, smiling awkwardly. Lather on one cheek made him look like he had suffered a stroke and the halves of his face no longer quite met properly.

211

Without a word he disappeared inside. From the other open room the sound of hi-life music on a radio blared. Here even the sound of your neighbor's breathing would be impossible to escape.

Huge padlocks hung from all the remaining doors. Elizabeth opened the first of these and we stepped inside. The air was stale and dank. Mary pushed open a shutter in the back wall. Iron bars filled the square window. The room was unutterably empty, the lilt of hi-life ironic and painful as it throbbed through the walls. In one corner what looked like a pile of shit turned out to be corroded batteries when I bent to see. Behind the door was a calendar from four years back with a glossy portrait of Kenyatta wearing a smile and leopardskin cap. The calendar was a hand-out from a funeral parlor in Kitale. Beggars, I knew, couldn't be choosers but I held my breath and kept waiting for the sound of Koert Jan's voice saying, 'No, thank you' to this cell.

'How long do you want to stay here?' Anna asked, walking backwards, lifting bare feet to avoid roots she couldn't possibly see, as, single file, we retraced our path to the Khaeris'.

'A year,' Koert Jan said and Anna clapped her hands.

Back at the compound Elizabeth sent Anna and Mary into the house to bring out chairs for us. In the meantime two more Khaeri girls had returned from school, Anastasia and Beatrix. All in all, we were told, there were seven girls and one boy, Joachim, away at boarding school. Anastasia and Beatrix, fourteen and sixteen, were carrying hoes over one shoulder. They were about to weed the family gardens. Now I noticed how densely planted the area surrounding the compound was. Banana trees, sweet potatoes, sim-sim, cow peas, pepper and eggplant. Anastasia's and Beatrix's dresses had holes in them. Washing clothes on rocks, we learned later the hard way, did not add to their lifespan.

Mary was sent running into the second hut on the compound with instructions from her mother to make us some 'nice tea'.

Elizabeth appeared in no particular hurry to pursue the business at hand. She asked Koert Jan to explain our work to her. As he spoke every once in a while she turned to look quizzically at Anna who crouched at her side. In a burst of words Anna then explained what her mother hadn't been able to follow for herself. It was startling how different Anna's volume was from when she addressed us.

Mary came back with a round copper tray carrying a chipped porcelain teapot and china cups and saucers. She also brought a brown paper bag of coarse sugar and a new can of Carnation evaporated milk. Elizabeth shook the milk and then – it happened so fast I wasn't sure what I was seeing – she pierced the top with one of her teeth. Through the maize Anastasia and Beatrix were leaning on their hoes and looking at us. Our tea was poured out through a strainer which little Rosa held with both hands over each cup in turn.

'To tell you the truth' – after a few sips of tea Koert Jan looked up and spoke – 'that's where I'd really like to live.' He nodded towards the hut where Mary had made tea.

Elizabeth laughed.

'It's beautiful,' Koert Jan said and as he said it I saw it was true. Dense thatch came down to within a few feet of the ground, the roof supported by uprights all the way around creating a veranda under the straw eaves.

'That's our kitchen,' Anna whispered.

'Can we see?' I asked.

Elizabeth was looking at us differently now, with keen interest. I think she wasn't sure Koert Jan wasn't teasing. She raised her cup to her lips and took some sips without answering.

'Please.'

To pass through the low wooden door, we had to bend practically double. Inside, as I straightened up, I could hardly believe the vastness of the space. The hut, some eight meters in diameter, was one cavernous vault. Mary again skipped to the

213

far wall to open shutters. This time there were two, opposite each other – ears to the door's mouth. The unequal shafts of daylight that fell in nearly met at my feet. As our eyes adjusted to the darkness the first thing I noticed was a triad of cooking stones in the middle of the floor – and a mound of gray ashes and live coals. There were pots in profusion nearby as well – round earthenware and aluminum. Against the wall were large round water jars of clay balanced on straw rings and covered with conical lids. Under one window charcoal spilled from a burlap sack.

'It's very beautiful' – this time I said it. 'Look at the roof, KJ.'

The inside of the thatch was black from smoke. Smooth poles rose on all sides to meet overhead, re-enforced by slender branches lashed in place with long strands of grass.

'Yes, it is,' Anna agreed, 'like lace.'

Koert Jan walked slowly around the inside perimeter of the hut, running the fingers of one hand along the wall.

'We have bats living there,' Anna said and pointed up at the roof, 'but they hardly make a sound.'

Outside we trapped Rosa trying to guzzle down sweet milk from the can. Elizabeth called her name and, startled, Rosa dropped the can which rolled along the ground, leaking a sticky trickle. Elizabeth picked it up and laughed. Rosa, sobbing inconsolably, was swept up into Mary's arms and carried into the house.

'Mother agrees,' Anna told us in her whisper. 'She will write to father today. He works in Kabsabeti.'

With much rolling of her eyes and fluttering of fingers across her mouth, Elizabeth finally set our rent. It was trivial. For basic furniture she sent Anna with us to nearby Mumias to inquire at the carpenter's.

Mumias itself was nothing much to write home about. A crossroads with an ill-assorted smattering of buildings in disrepair. The largest edifice in town was a mosque, whitewashed

214

mud brick, set back off the road and surrounded by a low stone wall. Its dome seemed hammered out of ten thousand used tin cans. During the heat of midday women slept in the narrow band of shade cast by the wall, odd lots of fruits or vegetables which they would sell towards evening tucked under their heads to make a pillow. That first day in the trampled mosque courtyard children tore about, shoving each other and kicking a badly deflated ball.

Across the murram road from the mosque, a road with sharply sloping shoulders, on the crest of a low knoll, was a gallery of some half-dozen shops, cement, each cave-like, with crude double wood doors comprising the front wall. The town petrol station, a single roadside pump with a padlock, stood some yards east of the shops. Here we left our car while Anna led us down the road to admire Mumias police headquarters, neat and tidy, a flagpole in the middle of a square courtyard, officers in caps and short trousers and high socks, men from other tribes. Just next door was the plain reserved for the Saturday market and a short stroll beyond the edge of town Anna pointed out the *boma*, the premises of the local health dispensary, a red-brick building under the only beautiful old trees remaining in town.

As Anna led us back to the carpenter's workshed tucked up behind the row of shops, the afternoon Mawingo bus pulled in, setting up a dense swirl of fine dust. When the dust settled we saw a dozen children, at least, with trays of food on their heads hawking food to passengers leaning out of the bus windows. The Mawingo buses were the town lifeline to the world beyond. Battered, maroon relics they were held together by wire, and made deafening rattling noises in motion. In the middle of the day a flurry of *matatus*, private group taxis, served Mumias as well. Erratic mosquitoes, these unstable, tinny vehicles, low to the ground, had pens in back for shuttling local passengers short distances through the thickly settled bush country. Death traps really, hardly a week passed without a lurid account of some gruesome *matatu* disaster.

The carpenter Anna took us to see had gray hair, a pencil behind one ear, a cigarette behind the other. His main business, to judge from what we saw on the premises, was making coffins. Small ones. Anna explained what we needed. Elizabeth had beds of local make for us, which left a work table, chairs and a cupboard. Koert Jan also wanted a pair of planks with holes in the ends. These we could rig up with sisal rope and hang from roof poles to make shelves. The carpenter nodded and nodded. He made a sketch of a table and chair, breaking the pencil point more than once in the process and fastidiously sharpening it again with a razor blade held close to his eyes. His helpers crowded close, pointing at the sketches, laughing. One man stealthily reached out and stroked my arm, feeling the hair.

After brief, comic haggling we agreed on a price for the order. With great formal ceremony the carpenter drew up a receipt. Koert Jan paid in advance, settled a delivery day. We shook hands with everyone, waved and were gone. Maybe a slow way to do business but, I felt like I glowed, it was certainly personal.

'Father is a carpenter, too, for the Ministry of Works,' Anna told us in her shy whisper as we walked back towards the petrol pump. 'He lives there, in Kabsabeti.' Anna pointed far to the north.

Before we reached the car we ran into trouble. There was a ruckus in the road, people shouting, running from all sides to join a growing crowd. Anna hung back, Koert Jan, of course, pressed forward. The first thing I saw in the middle of the road, surrounded by jeering, taunting men and women, was a naked man with a wild matted thicket of hair. Chest, thighs, hair – all were powdered red from dust off the murram road. The man, blinking, held something in one hand. I just had time to identify it – raw meat, I think – when he began to tear at it with his teeth, shaking his head back and forth. He had a powerful, hairless body with enormous genitals that dragged in the dirt. There were deep cracks in the soles of his feet.

The crowd was in a nasty mood but the naked man – his eyes were vacant, his mannerisms those of a self-preoccupied child – seemed to think he was alone. What made them so angry? (I thought perhaps it was because he held a mirror up to them, one in which they saw too plainly where they, too, had come from. Despite the jeans, the sun-glasses, the Coca-Cola. Like the Jews in America who burned the only surviving photographs of life in the Polish ghettos. Maybe.)

From the back ranks someone threw a lump of earth that struck the madman on the chest. He dropped his meat and roared. Then a stone grazed his head from behind. He spun around, rose to one knee. His eyes looked hurt.

I shudder to think what would have happened next if a young man hadn't stepped forward into the closing space and lifted both hands over his head. He himself was short and had a large plum-like head. He wore a short-sleeved white shirt buttoned all the way up to the neck, baggy trousers shiny with wear and too short for him, a pair of pointy black shoes with no socks. First he raised his hands, then he lowered them and spoke calmly. As he spoke, sweetly, he turned in slow circles so he could see everybody.

'What's he saying, Anna?' I asked.

'"Go home," he says. "It is God who chooses who must suffer. And – emotion is a bad thing."'

A few in the crowd continued to murmur, spoiling for action, but through the boy's poised intercession the momentum of public meanness had been lost.

The peacemaker's eyes met Koert Jan's. I saw it happen. The boy even seemed to nod and smile faintly, just for a fraction of a second before he carried on with dispersing the crowd. The naked man subsided in the dust. He picked up his meat – it might even have been only a piece of red cloth – wiped it against his chest and wandered away.

'That, you see, was a mad man,' Anna told us on the way back. 'There are so many here. They run wild in the country.' Madness, we would learn, was the illness people in West Kenya feared the most. *Lilalu*, it was called – the melody of the name capturing the nonsense syllables that flow from the lips of the insane. 'If you're mad you can even kill your mother or father. Or' – Anna's eyes were enormous as she clued us in – 'you can run so far from home that you lose your way. Then you can die and be buried in some strange place where nobody knows you.'

II

Early the next week we were ready to move in. I dropped Koert Jan off at the Khaeris' with our few belongings. He would await the promised delivery of our new furniture while I drove into Kakamega for provisions and had our little, pale blue Renault 4 serviced. As a first happy surprise we found the Khaeri women had cleared a road through their maize all the way to the compound so we didn't have to leave the car by the church. And their kitchen – our home – had been cleaned out completely and was spotless. Meanwhile behind their other hut they had put up a small, temporary kitchen.

My solo drive to Kakamega was shattering. There was no choice, I had to take a dreadful road with washboard corrugations. The light Renault shivered with fits the whole way there. Still, I was so exhilarated I could almost convince myself I enjoyed the bumps. Was this then deepest, darkest Africa? Land at the farthest reaches of my imagination? How often had I fallen asleep in my father's arms listening to his soothing voice describe my adventures as a legendary explorer in the equatorial jungles, never dreaming how easily one day I would demystify the continent by the simple act of going there in person. Perhaps that's sad – how a place never stays strange long once we bring ourselves to it. We work more transformatory magic on our surroundings than they on us.

And if in my boyhood fantasies darkest Africa had been primarily a place of night, still the 'darkest' was most of all surely an allusion to the faces and bodies of the natives.

Eyelids heavy, fluttering, on the brink of sleep, I would see savages lurking, pointed teeth, the whites of their wild eyes gleaming out from beneath the deep shade of lush, sinuous overlapping vegetation. No fear – my pith helmet and elephant gun protected me from all danger. No feat was too daring, no risk too great. Hero was my middle name.

By mid-afternoon I couldn't wait to get back to Mumias. On my own in Kakamega, I felt alien. How much nodding and smiling I did to strangers, whose eyes and voices were not always so friendly. And I saw what I took to be another madman, rags so shredded and torn he was as good as naked. He had waded into a garbage heap and was poking through it while children, feasting on mangoes, stood watching.

At the sight of the stubby church spire my spirits lifted again. How lucky we were to have found the Khaeris. Then Koert Jan had a habit of making his luck happen. For the next year we would be part of a fine family. Anna and Mary, beaming friendliness, rushed to help carry in my purchases. The compound was the picture of domestic peace. Anastasia sat braiding Beatrice's hair into hundreds of tiny pigtails. Elizabeth was hanging up the wash – worn khangas and school uniforms – between two papaya trees. Rosa was helping her by handing up clothespins. But there was something wrong: I saw that as soon as Koert Jan came out of the hut to greet me. Despite a hand over his eyes to shield them from the glare of the sun, I could make out a sadness that didn't belong there. And, incredibly, fear.

'You took your time,' he said and went straight back inside.

I followed, and admired the furniture and how he'd arranged it. 'Rough and ready,' I said, picking out a splinter after I'd run one palm across the top of the table, 'but not inelegant.'

When Anna and Mary cleared out, I started putting our supply of tinned goods away, waiting for Koert Jan to speak. He pumped life into our cooking primus and made a pot of tea. We sat on our new chairs drawn up to our new table. It wobbled a bit under my elbows. Koert Jan took a bite out of one of the vegetable samosas I'd brought home – then he laughed, spraying bits of food.

'I've been robbed,' he said. He used the voice he always did to make light of things that deeply bothered him – and which was a warning – woe unto me – if I let myself get upset by whatever the trouble was.

'Tell me.'

Koert Jan drew a deep breath and blew several times across the top of his tea. 'The stuff came not long after you left. Three men were carrying it. One stayed behind. He wanted more money. I showed him the bill, rubber stamp and all. He wanted much more. It was ridiculous. I wasn't having any of it and sent him packing.'

Table and chair were simple slam-bang things. Rough planks, crude joints.

'Well – then a teacher came from the Mission School for the Deaf. Zakayo. Nice boy. Wears a pointed beard and a rainhat. He heard we were looking for an interpreter.'

'And?'

'His English was hopeless – at least I think it was English. Very friendly though – wants to show us around the school.'

Koert Jan shook his head, gave another short laugh like a snort, and finished off his samosa. Telling the story seemed to relieve him. 'Anyhow I walked Zakayo to the edge of the Khaeris' maize. Good manners, right? Then I came straight back to the hut. When I entered, it was like the air inside was still in motion. I'm not sure – I may even have seen a leg disappear out the back window. On the table – there – my shoulder bag lay open with all my stuff dumped out.'

For the first time I realised how odd it was that all the things Koert Jan always carried with him in his bag were set out in neat little piles on the table.

'What's missing?'

'My wallet. And my watch.'

The watch hurt most, I knew. From Koert Jan's grandfather, a man who had helped to dig the Grand Canal du Nord. It had stopped working years ago, but Koert Jan seldom took it off.

'What did Elizabeth say?'

'I haven't told her.'

While we finished tea, it grew dark. Not another word fell about the robbery. Outside we heard the children running, laughing, chasing each other no doubt. I kept up a false stream of small talk. What I'd seen along the road: a handless, legless beggar under an umbrella; a bus loaded to twice its height with bales and bulging parcels, even a trussed goat, and the bus gave off clouds of exhaust black as any ink fish could ever squirt; a marching band of Legio Maria, twelve strong in white uniforms, red crosses, their big drum booming long after I'd turned the bend and left them out of sight.

'Did they know anything about cars at the garage?'

'Not much, no.'

On reflection I could understand Koert Jan's reluctance to report the theft. For starters we were in Kenya without the proper working papers. The politics of launching an aid project such as ours with a research arm often meant a costly and frustrating wait for official permission to enter the field. A common ploy, the one we had adopted with the tacit approval of the concerned ministry officials, was to enter the country on a tourist visa and press ahead with preliminary work until the vital approval at last was extracted. Any hue and cry over stolen wallet and watch would call too much attention to us for comfort. Still I thought Koert Jan was wrong not to say anything about the theft to Elizabeth, and after tea I told him so.

Elizabeth was horror-struck at Koert Jan's story. '*Polé*,' she kept repeating. '*Polé*. I'm sorry.' Then she called her girls and barked orders to them. They scattered in the bush surrounding the compound. There they raced back and forth, calling to each other, searching for signs of the culprit's trail. In a few minutes it would be night. Here darkness fell abruptly – as if the day, tired, lowered its eyelids.

Anna was the first to run back into the clearing where we stood waiting. She was carrying Koert Jan's wallet in the palms of her outstretched hands – like a wounded bird. On Anna's heels, Mary ran in with Koert Jan's watch.

'On the path, there,' the girls showed us. Koert Jan strapped the watch back on his wrist. He examined his wallet.

'Only the money is missing,' he grinned.

'How much money?' Elizabeth asked.

Although Koert Jan lied by more than half, still you could see the amount sounded enormous as it fell into the women's eager listening ears. Anna gave a low whistle. It was the act itself, however, even more than the sum involved, that required an answering action. The carpenter who had carried on, demanding extra payment, was a lodger of the Khaeris', one of four Tesos who shared a rented room out back. He'd been there, Elizabeth explained, two months and she was always seeing him sneaking around.

'Come.' Elizabeth led us directly to the man's quarters. It was clear she felt that her honor was at stake. We were amazed by her dispatch, impressed by the determination she showed to fix the guilt.

We found two of the Tesos in. One was sewing a button back on to his shirt. His chest was badly scarred – from fire, I guessed. The other lay on his back sharpening a knife with a whetstone. As soon as Elizabeth appeared and greeted them, they stood and showed proper respect.

'Gone, Mama.' The one with the needle in his hand said our man had entered some hours ago, quickly packed a few things together and without a word about where he was going or for how long, had disappeared.

'He left his radio.' The other Teso pointed with his knife.

'Why, Mama?' the first man asked. The shirt he was holding had many patches.

'We are looking for him.'

Indeed what the thief had lifted from Koert Jan's wallet, our salaries for the month and project expenses, was far more than he could hope to earn making tables and chairs – and coffins – for a year or more.

Koert Jan had then tried to persuade Elizabeth to let matters rest there. She shook her head, no. No, she stamped. 'If you don't report it, other thieves will come.' Mob justice in Kenya could mean stoning and bludgeoning a thief on the spot. We'd seen the bloody aftermath of such a ghastly spectacle in a sunny Nairobi park.

That evening, about an hour after nightfall, Anna came to our hut. '*Hodi*.'

'*Karibu*.'

She entered carrying a dish of leafy green vegetables cooked with 'African salt', a viscous substance that looked like raw egg. While we tasted the gift, Anna announced that she was going to work for us. 'Fetch water, make the fire, sweep the house.' And we were not to pay anything because we had been 'stolen' while living in their home. Koert Jan didn't even pretend to try to say no.

'I know what you're thinking,' Koert Jan said, his voice filling the dark before we fell asleep, 'but you're wrong.'

In fact I was simply lying there feeling vulnerable. 'What?'

'That we deserve to be robbed.'

'As a matter of fact, no' – I turned on my side and peered across at Koert Jan but all I could make out was the drapery of his mosquito net – 'that hadn't occurred to me. But now that you mention it.'

'Imagine if it had happened to either of us out here alone.'

In the morning Elizabeth put on her good clothes to visit the local chief: Skin and Bones he was called. She took a large papaya for him, and a chicken. This last gift Mary caught, not by chasing it, but by imitating a chicken herself, crouching low and engaging the gullible bird in conversation as she edged closer and closer.

Less than an hour later Elizabeth was back, empty-handed. 'Chief Ndegi knows the man's identity and even the village he is coming from. He's left his job. He took his box of tools.' Elizabeth sighed and seemed to diminish. There was a mischievous gleam in her eye though, relief that the drama was over. She smiled a small smile. 'The Chief promises he will send word to that man's home place and have him apprehended.'

'I don't think so,' Anna spoke softly, from behind her hand.

III

Twice a week early in the day there was fresh meat for sale in Mumias. *Very* fresh. Elizabeth sent Mary with me the first time I visited the butcher. For a city boy it was an experience. In front of the butcher's an iron wheelbarrow stood with a stone wedged back under the wheel. In it the head of a newly slaughtered black cow sat upright on a rosette of banana leaves. It was an enormous thing. Wherever you stood the great staring eyes with their long lashes followed you. Drops of moisture stood out on the black nostrils, as if the cow were still perspiring.

The fat black butcher wore high black boots. His arms and chest were bare under a white apron smeared with blood and gore. Whack! His cleaver flashed down, chopping and trimming bright slabs of beef on a broad tree stump. Whack! Huge hunks of meat hung from hooks in a cage surrounded by wire screening. The door of the cage didn't quite shut so that a busy population of flies added black patches to the red and white marbling of the beef. The butcher walked on bones and waste fat. A bruised, honey-colored mongrel bitch slunk around his feet, limping, a long, steady low growl pouring from her throat. Now and then the butcher would plunge his arms up to the elbow into a bucket of water and then shake his dripping hands at the dog. She fell all over herself trying to retreat.

There was a small queue. Those in front of me bought tiny quantities of meat. 'Too expensive,' Mary explained. People did not eat meat every day. By our standards even prime cuts were a giveway. Yet our fear of parasites made us cook the meat so thoroughly it turned to leather.

Back at the Khaeris' I found Koert Jan sitting on the veranda holding hands with a stranger. Not quite a stranger. The boy's face, almost purple in the shade, like a ripe plum, looked familiar. By the time I'd ducked into the hut to put down my package – the beef wrapped in leaves had begun to leak blood – I had placed him. It was the lunatic's knight errant, the boy who had met Koert Jan's eyes.

When I came outside Mary was explaining how the butcher had asked my help. 'He was having pain in his eyes,' she said, imitating the man. ' "Don't you have something to give me?" '

'I told him I wasn't a doctor,' I said. And I still felt guilty, knowing the portable pharmacy I had in my bag: vitamins, chloroquine, eye drops, ear drops, nose drops, aspirins without aspirin, pills against worms, against heartburn.

'Then he said he had headaches,' Mary continued.

'I told him I thought he looked perfectly healthy.'

'Then he took one foot out of his boot and all the flies, a great cloud, came to sit on the wound.'

Peter Ohundo sat there laughing, enjoying Mary's perform-ance and my discomfort. He was what you could call a fast worker. Through news of our having been robbed he tracked us down at the Khaeris'. 'Sir, please, can I work for you.' Later Koert Jan described Peter's direct approach. 'Anything. No satisfaction, no pay.' Peter's features beamed good nature. Yet there was always a latent gleam of shrewdness in his eyes, the tell-tale alertness of a hustler who lived by his wits. And not only Peter lived by Peter's wits. He supported a brother, an old mother, a wife and the wife's sister.

'People say that man's leg is turning into meat. He has killed so many cows.' Peter's English was archaic, and mellifluous. He could talk the skin off a snake. Let me get it off my chest at once that I took an instant dislike to Peter. His too perfect, spotless teeth. In the coming months he turned into our most precious asset. His loyalty, his kindness, his open intelligence and curiosity were proven over and over again beyond doubt. And yet I never quite overcame my initial reaction. Why? Surely it was more than the sight of his black fingers laced with Koert Jan's resting on Koert Jan's knee? No, what appalled me immediately, what I never grew used to, was how ingratiating Peter was, how humble with us. A willing servant, anything but our equal. By knowing his place he kept us in ours.

'We are cursed with our black skin,' Peter could say most matter-of-factly. 'We are the children of Ham.'

Peter was born in Amin's Uganda. When his father, a small farmer, was detained on suspicion of sympathising with enemies of the government, Peter's mother had decided to return to the land of her birth. She took her two young boys and with her life-savings knotted into a rag, together they walked back to Kenya. 'My mother is a Luo. These Luhya here cheated her when she bought our land.' The owner of the land had sprinkled a thin layer of topsoil on the rocky hectare Peter's mother paid too much for. By the end of the first rainy season it had all eroded. Whatever grew there now, grew grudgingly.

'Because I am short,' Peter grinned, 'I could not continue further with my schooling, even though I was the number one in this whole province.' It was some months before we

226

understood Peter was not talking literally in referring to his shortness. He was rather a man without family or connections or the cash to bribe his way further in life. So he was obliged to scramble a living together from odd jobs and opportunities. Peter told us his story without a trace of rancor. He seemed amused by his hardships, superior to them.

Peter invited us to visit his home and we accepted. It was small. You could fit two of his huts inside our one. The area surrounding his hut was planted with flowers. Bougainvillaea swarmed up over the door and covered the thatch. On our first visit Koert Jan admired a purple flower, a kind of thistle. Peter presented him with seeds. The gift pleased Koert Jan immensely.

Inside Peter's house he had built some thin, crumbling walls to create privacy. You could count his possessions on the fingers of one hand. These were on display in a small cabinet with glass doors that locked. A pile of schoolbooks. A harmonica. A wedding photo. At our arrival Joachim, Peter's brother – he wore a sweatshirt with a hood so that during our first visit we never had a good look at his face – ran to the neighbor's to borrow two small folding wood chairs. We sat outside and Peter's mother, and his wife, Berlita, clearly pregnant, prepared *ugali* for us.

I did like Berlita. Koert Jan found her an insufferable shrew and a she-devil, but I admired her sass and spirit. She was very quick, very observant. Peter's mother on the other hand looked like life had chewed her up and spat her out. She was all fluster and cringe.

Before our meal Peter led us in prayer. The prayer went on and on. Mother dropped a lot of hallelujahs, rolling her eyes to heaven.

'We are pentecostals, sir,' Peter said immediately after *amen*. 'What are you?'

'Nothing,' was Koert Jan's answer. Peter's smile slipped, but only for an instant.

'In Europe many people are nothing, sir, aren't they?'

'Yes,' I said.

'Here nobody is.' Peter looked thoughtful. 'Here it's mostly a question of how you want to be buried.'

It was then I realised how dangerous Peter could be for us. On the surface so familiar, so many words, expressions the same as ours. Any lull in concentration and we might forget that nothing could be taken for granted as understood between us.

'Whatever happened to divining and good old animal sacrifice?' I wanted to ask, but didn't.

When we began to eat *ugali* with our hands, Berlita shrieked with laughter. The boy scouts of the world once voted *ugali* the best food in the world. Well, they are welcome to it. A porridge from maize and cassava flour, at times with a mix of millet, too, it sets in the stomach like cement. During our fieldwork there would be days we might be served *ugali* at every hut we visited. Somehow Koert Jan developed a technique which made it look like he ate a lot, his hands moving steadily back and forth between his mouth and the pot – I was always the one our hosts urged to go on eating.

'What is your mother saying, Peter?' Koert Jan asked.

'Guests walk with angels,' he smiled.

The curse of Peter's life, his poverty notwithstanding, was that he had no children. Berlita was a teenager and he himself only twenty-six but they were way behind in the family sweepstakes. Berlita had already lost three 'wombs' after the foetus was whole. Three times at work in other people's fields she had dropped her hoe, laid down between rows of sugar cane, and given premature birth to slithery death.

'How many children do you want?' Koert Jan asked Peter.

'We'll have to see, sir.'

'How many wives?'

Peter laughed. 'Berlita married me on the pentecostal condition, sir. One wife.'

228

'I've never been anywhere with so many children.' True, the neighbor's children had all come to stare at us from a respectful distance from behind bushes or branches, but from Koert Jan's tone I knew he was fishing. Some argued that people in Peter's situation wanted as many children as possible to be sure in their old age one or more might survive to care for them. Procreation as social security. Others argued each extra pair of hands produced more than the extra mouth consumed. It seemed unlikely to us that people were so calculating.

'Don't people here know how *not* to have them?' Under the circumstances, Berlita's history of loss and her present condition, I thought Koert Jan's question a trifle indelicate but I filled my mouth with *ugali* and swallowed.

'They know, sir – but you see' – here Peter looked straight at Koert Jan and grinned mightily, ear to ear – a symptom I would come to diagnose as indicating he was about to say something which pleased him because he knew it was clever and would please us – 'we have no television.'

'What?' I laughed.

'We are poor, backward people. There are no theatres, no concert halls, no televisions here. Children, sir, they are our number one entertainment.'

Everything Peter told us about himself seemed to confirm that he was disaster prone. Not long ago he had bought a cow, for example, and then, before it could calve, 'she caught leprosy, sir'.

'Sad,' was Koert Jan's comment. 'All these things that happen to you.' Koert Jan was himself the son of a Protestant minister. His father had died of overeating when Koert Jan was a baby. 'What do you make of it?'

'Sir?'

'So many set-backs.'

Peter laughed. He ate with us. His wife and mother had withdrawn. His brother stayed hovering in the doorway to the hut, pulling on the drawstrings of his hood so that it stood straight up, and only a small part of the center of his face, features squeezed together, was visible.

'Nothing that happens can surprise us, sir. It is God who decides. Life is hard, but we will be free in the end.' Then he flashed one of his here-it-comes-get-ready smiles. 'Besides which, now I have met you. That is good luck.'

IV

In the middle of our first week with the Khaeris, late one afternoon, Joseph, Pater Familias, arrived on foot, unheralded. He carried a tool box, blue aluminum, and a small, neat rattan suitcase. Rosa practically knocked him over as she came running and jumped into his arms. Joseph was our age, but, typically, he looked old enough to be our father. He was not quite Elizabeth's height, and of slight build. His nose was flat and broad, his eyes large and sparkling. His movements were slow. His voice deferential. Elizabeth and his daughters treated him with great respect, almost with a formality reserved for strangers.

'Hello. Pleased to meet you. You must know the Bishop of Kisumu?' These were practically Joseph's first words to us. 'Little chap, like a dwarf. Has a hunchback. Enormous ears that stick out, like this, from his head. Nose like a vulture.' On the spot Joseph became the man he described – a grotesque.

'No,' Koert Jan said.

'He's my best friend,' Joseph said. More Christianity! It was beginning to feel like Koert Jan and I had stumbled on to the set of a religious epic – with an all-black cast.

Joseph Khaeri had come home, surely, to inspect his wife's bold addition to the household. Although he never mentioned our being robbed, his acts and words left us no doubt that he knew, was grieved, and wanted to make amends. During his very first conversation with us, Joseph Khaeri shared the secret of his fondest dream. He wanted to be rich enough to build a 'safe house'. 'One so designed, with a door sufficiently strong, that while the enemy is delayed battering his way in, the family can escape out a second door, here, in back.' He drew a plan of this house in the earth with a stick. His hands – large, wrinkled, steady – were the oldest part of him. 'Glass in the windows, and bars. Locks from Czechoslovakia. And a fire extinguisher that the children can lift.'

The following morning Joseph presented us with a key to the *cho* – the pit latrine with mud walls and thatch we had been sharing with Elizabeth and the girls. 'I have hired workers to dig a new *cho* for my family,' he explained. As Koert Jan predicted, however, these workers never came. After Joseph's departure, we had duplicate keys cut for the family. This remained a secret between Elizabeth and ourselves.

Before Joseph left again we came to understand his ties with the church. 'My father was eaten by a wild animal. My mother drowned in a flood when she tried to cross the Nzoia in a poor craft. The fathers adopted me. I was still a boy, one of six children. When the man who is now the bishop, Ngeresca, saw I was a serious worker, he looked after my schooling.' With Joseph we wandered into the ungainly Catholic church. He himself had been one of its original builders – out of gratitude for the unflagging kindness of the priests. Indeed Joseph Khaeri was a man driven by gratitude, the victim of it.

The interior of the church was filled with prayer stools in meticulous rows. The floor was poured concrete – with large cracks in it, the kind that appear in ice when the surface can no longer hold weight. Up front, mounted on the wall, a large crude crucifix, two rough slabs of wood with a giant, white plaster cast of Christ spiked in all the familiar places, bathed in scorching sunlight. The way he looked made me think of my dentist, who handed out miniature busts of Beethoven and Mozart, pure white, to children who stood the drill without cries of pain. All the churches I knew were dark and rich with shadows. Yet I felt happy inside this bright, clean space with so many open windows.

'Some day we will have a proper cathedral in Kenya,' Joseph told us. 'My friend the Bishop of Kisumu is collecting the money. Then I will make a cross.'

At that moment a belled goat walked into the church. He moved slowly and with great dignity down 'the nave' and towards the altar. Later Koert Jan admitted he had imagined one of Bach's preludes playing as the goat, hind quarters swaying slightly, came forward. Before the animal started nibbling the flowers in front of the altar, however, Joseph came alive and shooed him away. The clatter of hooves on the cement was a welcome, real sound. And the spray, a fusillade, of waste pellets, made Joseph laugh warmly.

When we strolled back to the compound after our tour of the church, we found our chairs and table had been carried outside. Joseph spent the rest of the morning improving them. It was a delight to watch him with his tools. Each nail that he picked up he would squint at, lips moving in some dim incantation. Then neatly, tap, tap, tap, he would sink the nail, drive it home with absolute confidence, and no waste of effort.

'Our problem, as a people,' Joseph confided to us while Anna and Mary were ferrying our furniture back inside, 'is a simple one. No forward vision. In Christianity, you see, it is the future which dominates.' Was it Joseph's upbringing in the shelter of the skirts of the Bishop of Kisumu which filled his head with tags of philosophy – or was it the solitary life he led, solitary nights far from his loved family in one or another of an endless series of Ministry of Works barracks? 'Our traditional African way of life faces backwards. How fast can a man walk down a road facing backwards? How long until this man crashes into a tree? As Africans' – Joseph pointed at his chest – 'we are prisoners of yesterday. As Christians,' – again he pointed – 'we are speculators about tomorrow.

'In our own Luhya language, to make my point clear, there are no verbs for future time.'

'Really?'

'True. But we can distinguish so many different tenses for the past. Speaking about the past that we can still remember, for example, we use a different form than for the past that stretches back beyond memory. You can say we are a people living in a confused state without a present. At least our present seems to be shrinking all the time.'

Who did Joseph remind me of? So much so that my brain kept ticking over loud with the blocked connection. The man seemed to leak goodness, like sawdust from a doll. The longer we were in Kenya, days turning into weeks, weeks sluicing into months, the more often I began to recognise old friends, neighbors and family among the people I met and saw – at markets, schoolyards, during our excursions to the field, in hospitals. By that I mean their blackness lifted, turned transparent – eyes, noses, mouths, bearing, movements, voice, humor – these emerged – with a powerful, unsettling, reassuring sense of familiarity. Elizabeth, for instance – she was the living twin of the mother of one of my closest friends, the wife of a rather aloof, distinguished cello player, a handsome, aristocratic woman, whose pleasure to be alive, whose ease with people, the speed with which she discharged a hundred household responsibilities effortlessly, were intimidating. And like this woman Elizabeth occasionally had splitting headaches, through which she smiled bravely.

'She's nothing like Lisa,' Koert Jan insisted when I pointed out the uncanny resemblance, 'nothing.'

'The lips then?'

'What's the matter? Homesick already?'

Although I couldn't pin a name, an identity on Joseph, he seemed familiar from the moment we met. Patient, never hurried. His stay didn't last longer than a day and a half. Were so many children conceived then on such lightning stops at home?

'You call this a cradle, I believe? All my children first slept in it.' Among Joseph's many repairs, he sanded and varnished anew a cradle of which he was very proud. It was made of Elgon Teak. No nails were used, but tongue and groove construction, and wooden pins. We didn't pause to consider the implications of his work on the sturdy box. He made us rub our palms up and down the smooth sides. Suddenly Rosa, the smallest Khaeri, came running in tears, chased by Mary, brandishing a switch through the air.

'She keeps getting in the way. Do you want to lose a leg, silly girl?' Mary, Anna and Anastasia were weeding the maize fields behind the house, using hoes, too, to turn the soil.

Joseph balanced his brush on the edge of the cradle. He lifted Rosa in his arms and dried her tears with his fingers. Then he went and snapped off a branch from a young eucalyptus. With a pocket knife he whittled a point on it and showed Rosa how to use this digging stick to loosen the earth without doing any damage to the roots of crops. Armed against idleness, Rosa went skipping jubilantly back to her sisters.

'When I go' – Joseph picked up his brush and smiled, looking each of us in turn in the eyes – 'I am entrusting my family to your care, gentlemen.'

'What did he do,' I asked Koert Jan when Joseph Khaeri went back inside his family hut, 'before we came along?' Oh, I was flattered by the gesture all right, but also annoyed by the heavy imposition of responsibility. It sat like *ugali* in my stomach.

'Don't worry,' Koert Jan said, 'Elizabeth can take care of herself.'

V

Joseph Khaeri's income from his carpentry job with the government was only modest, nevertheless because he practised self-denial and lived so soberly in a Quonset hut on the workshop site of the moment, he managed to save something each month to help feed and clothe his family. The Khaeris also owned several not inconsiderable plots of land, scattered throughout Kakamega District by typically aleatory patterns of inheritance. On these holdings the family raised food crops. Some surpluses – sesame seed, banana and sweet potato – were marketed. A few cattle we never saw were tended on rocky pastureland by poor Pokot herdsmen brought down from the north. Still, to pay for her children's education, Elizabeth found herself obliged, twice a year, to turn bootlegger.

In Mumias, back from the main road, there were three *pombe* shops, local beer joints, dank one-room affairs. The No Name Bar. The Friendly Bar. And, yes, The Pink Elephant. By mid-morning the first customers came drifting in. Soon after noon there were crowds, sitting on logs or stones out front, radio music manic inside, low cement brewing vats bubbling out back. Peter, puritanical about drink, called these establishments a curse to the country. This was a drawback in our work. We felt there was a lot to learn from the gossip in *pombe* shops. The steadiest drinkers were transients, known locally as 'locusts'. Once they started to drink they kept going until they fell down. Fights were not uncommon. Then the music would be turned off for half an hour and the bar girls would sulk inside, looking out the windows and speaking to no one.

Since time immemorial beer has been an integral part of ceremonial life among the Abaluhya. Beer was made locally from charred millet – and later maize – left to soak with raw sugar, then filtered and served before it had time to cool. On ritual occasions, at weddings, birth celebrations, and funerals, a round-bottomed clay pot full to the brim with warm beer was set in the midst of a circle of guests who took turns drinking from several long reeds. The pot and snaky drinking stems looked like a giant upside-down spider with its feet in the guests' mouths. People would sip, stand up – usually the eldest first – shout, shuffle in place, do some gentle singing, sip again, and pass on their reed.

'Never step over a reed,' Anna once told us in her slow whisper. 'That way the devil can enter the beer. No,' she mimed, ducking her head, 'always go under.'

Me, I couldn't get used to the taste. And Koert Jan compared it to licking ashtrays.

It wasn't *pombe* Elizabeth brewed, however, but *changga*, Nubian gin, pure poison. To make it you tossed some 'yeast' – germinating grains of millet – into *pombe* and allowed it to ferment further, gaining in potency. Then distilling, highly illegal, took place so that the final product was clear and transparent. Step by step we watched the process on the compound. No one told us what was going on. We were slow, I admit, to catch on.

First an iron sheet riddled with holes was set on top of half an old oil drum laid on its side and filled with glowing charcoal. Here the necessary ingredients were slowly roasted, the girls all taking turns under their mother's watchful eye to rake the grain on top of the iron with special long bamboo staffs the tips of which had been hammered flat. For days the work went on – all other normal activity came to a halt. The whole time Elizabeth wore a look of intense preoccupation.

Khaeri *changga*, we learned from Peter, was famous. Pour a few drops into a hollow in the earth and you could set it on fire! At last even we were implicated in its manufacture. 'Mother would like you to save your Tree-top bottles,' Anna told us. So we did. These tapering containers held the killingly sweet syrups – red and orange – we used to enliven our drinking life. From all over the neighborhood in fact the Khaeri children scrounged bottles, from the Mission, from the kitchen of the school for the deaf, even from the local dispensary. Peter, too, donated a few. Koert Jan wouldn't let me tease him about it.

After the hard work of distilling *changga*, came the still harder labor of selling it. Elizabeth's first clandestine customers were none other than the District Commissioner and Chief Skin and Bones. We happened to be sitting outside when the chief came. He scratched in his beard – a stubble of gray curls – nodded, and looked through us. Soon other dignitaries wandered in as well, arm in arm. They greeted each other, chatted, and ducked into Elizabeth's hut. Such was the pulling power of her gin. When they left afterwards, looking no worse for the visit, here a swerve and there a swerve gave them away. Paying customers came later. Schoolteachers, male nurses – it was a strictly sex-segregated clientele – even imams came to call. Elizabeth, dressed in her best, welcomed riff-raff too if they paid. All was for school fees, uniforms, books. As hostess she displayed a contrived conviviality foreign to her – at least to my idea of her. All the girls seemed to shrink into themselves.

Early one evening Elizabeth and the children crowded into our hut bringing a precious half Tree-top bottle of *changga* for us. Koert Jan took a careful sip and spat it out. Elizabeth and the children split their sides laughing. I swallowed my taste and it burned all the way down. Then suddenly I pretended to go blind – to instant hilarity.

We really only realised how frenetic the *changga* season was once it ended. The long nights were still again. We could hear dogs barking far off. Elizabeth, too, was clearly relieved it was over – to the last inflammable drop.

Before long each of the Khaeri girls turned up wearing something new. Workmen came to make certain small repairs to the homestead, too – window latches replaced, thatch reinforced. We missed another clue to the future at this time. Anna sat out on the veranda by our door nursing a doll. Pink plastic. The doll's eyes clicked open and shut depending on the angle you tipped her at.

'For baby,' Anna whispered when she saw us staring. She tugged at blonde curls stitched to the scalp. 'With washable hair!'

Koert Jan and I laughed. When we first saw Anna sitting there and talking to the doll wrapped in cloth, we both had thought it real.

VI

We settled into something of a routine. Happily so. The rapid succession of passing days was so relentlessly rich, eventful and varied that sticking to schedule was like some kind of rudder to cling to. As if by waking and sleeping at regular hours we could keep a grip on reality! To stay alive back home, to sustain any sense of discovery, you had to make the effort. You were the one who had to dredge up the will from deep inside. Sit and wait for the phone to ring and you'd be dead before you knew it. Here the world did all the work. All we had to do was wake up and step outside.

Nor were we nagged by the suspicion we didn't deserve our delight, we hadn't really earned our pleasure. It was all so simple. Witness and enjoy. If Koert Jan and I didn't talk about such feelings or ideas, we were, I'm sure, both acutely aware of making an effort not to talk about them. I know I was. Whatever was happening agreed with me utterly and I wanted it to go on and on as long as possible undisturbed. If I had to hold my breath to cherish my luck, that was fine by me.

Of course looking back now I think our being outsiders, our being, literally, exceptional, had everything to do with the experience. All that tireless deference mixed with affection. The security of impassable distances. No one knew our weaknesses, or cared to. No one dreamed our pasts, too, like theirs, were littered with human failure. No one questioned our motives. At least no one seemed to. Indeed, maybe the Luhya treated us like madmen – with a special dispensation to keep our clothes on and trim our hair. Koert Jan with his grandfather's watch that didn't tick. Me with a solemn oath to learn five new words a day.

Our routine began in darkness. The first sound I heard would be Peter Ohundo riding his bike on to the Khaeri compound. When he started to work for us, Peter had walked from his home. It took him more than an hour. So Koert Jan bought him a bicycle. Black with footbrakes. To Peter it was a treasure. He practically burst with pride of ownership. To ride the bike, Peter had to stand on the pedals, otherwise his legs wouldn't reach. At every root or bump in the road, the bicycle bell would ring.

It was, I'm sure, to save food at home that Peter timed his daily arrival at the Khaeris' to coincide with the break of dawn, and our simple breakfast – tea, bread and devastatingly sweet orange marmalade from a tin. At first he made a face, but forced it down. Soon, however, it became the more marmalade the better.

'*Hodi*,' Peter called each morning from the doorway, his infallibly cheerful greeting chasing the last wisps of my sleep.

'*Karibu*,' Koert Jan would answer. He was always up before me, reading through field notes, lighting the primus on its tripod to boil water for tea.

'Good morning, sir.' Peter would come in, carrying his school briefcase, shirt buttoned at his thick neck, his sleeveless wool pullover patched in a dozen places with colors that didn't quite match.

'Morning, Peter – 're you?' Still in my long cotton nightshirt, heavy-eyed, I would stumble out to the *cho* to enjoy a few quiet and reflective moments alone as the sun rose. Squatting over a hole in the ground, a spider web over my shoulder glistening with dew, a runnel in the clay at my feet criss-crossed by giant ants, the sounds of my internal organs startling a snake or lizard into motion, the rhythms of my body shuddering back to life, my eyes fixed at the level of the brilliantly lit slit between the tin *cho* door and its thatch roof – it was a fine way to start each day.

The day's end conformed to pattern, too. We would be back at the Khaeris' half an hour before sundown, to give Peter time to cycle home before dark. Although he would never admit to the slightest fear, he wasn't happy to be abroad late alone. His wife and mother, he assured us, they were the ones who grew nervous if darkness came and he had not returned.

'Good night, sir.' Peter would hang his briefcase over the handlebars, roll up the bottom of his trousers, ring his bell and set off. Anna would light our charcoal stove, bending over low to blow on the coals until they caught. We would eat something. Then maybe we would write letters or read a few pages of a book. At times we were asleep even before the moon was up.

Then one day the Khaeris' first-born, Jenifa, came back home. We returned from work and found Joseph Khaeri's crib outside, tented with mosquito netting. Anna and Mary waved us over to see. Staring up from a clean white sheet with borders of lace was a coal-black baby, fat and sleek.

'Sister is home,' Anna whispered. On cue Jenifa, secretary for a firm in Nairobi, glided out of the hut to give each of us a hand. She was chewing gum, fashionable, shy. Why did Jenifa's unexpected arrival seem such an invasion of our privacy? She was a beautiful young woman, supple and graceful. Nothing of her father was visible in Jenifa except for a slight, playful sadness in her eyes.

'How do you do?' Jenifa said. 'I'm Jenifa.'

Elizabeth came running out of the house. She clucked her tongue, kicked up dust, dancing around and around. Her speech tumbled out at a great clip. When she held up her index fingers, on each there was a tiny white baby shoe.

'Mother says' – Anna held a hand to her mouth – 'that now she is a grandmother. What an old woman!'

'Mayende is his African name,' Jenifa told us. She unbuttoned the top of her city dress with nonchalance, and lifted one breast free. As the baby sucked, his cheeks went in and out.

'But he has been baptised' – Mary, too, danced in circles with her mother – 'with the name of Joseph.'

In the weeks that followed Koert Jan and I had ample chance to see for ourselves what Peter had told us about the entertainment value of babies in a Luhya famiy. The Khaeri children were constantly quarreling whose turn it was to carry Mayende in their arms, or soon, on one hip. At feeding time Jenifa stepped in. She gave Mayende the breast only briefly, switching in less than a month to the bottle. Mayende seldom cried. He would pout, make a fist, frown, but not cry. At times he seemed a fruit dropped from a tree – a shiny black, serene melon, dark lips almost purple, fingers tiny worms, so many soft wrinkles and folds.

'Do you want to hold him?'

Mayende seemed more at ease with me than any of his sisters. That's what Elizabeth said. He liked to play with my lips, pulling them, and to clasp handfuls of my hair.

As for Peter, he was always bringing Mayende small surprises, presents he would unpack out of his briefcase. Feathers, stones, reeds his mother wove into tiny baskets. The doll with pink rubber flesh just seemed to have disappeared after Mayende came. And no one spoke a word about the baby's paternity.

Jenifa was the only one of the family who didn't work in the garden. She drifted about in her fancy dresses cut above the knee, idle and bored. Sometimes she would sing to the baby but if she thought anyone else was listening, she would stop. She also kept more of a distance from us than the others did. The tension set up between us the moment of our initial meeting continued to crackle, like distant lightning. Sometimes early or late we would pass along the path to the *cho* and then the unwritten rule was to pretend the other didn't exist, even when we brushed shoulders – not by accident.

In time, however, the tedium of maternity and exile in the bush, prevailed over Jenifa's reticence. When at the end of the afternoon our little dent-scarred Renault negotiated the dirt rut carved through the ripening Khaeri maize, Jenifa too would drop what she was doing and come running with the other children to welcome us and ask questions about our day. And an evening didn't pass without my having a short man-to-man talk with the baby before retiring to our hut.

One afternoon we were about to turn into the Khaeri compound when Jenifa jumped in front of the car and waved her arms to make us stop.

'You must leave the car here. Anna's repaving,' she said. Baby Mayende, in a sailor suit, blinked at us from her arms, a bubble on his lips. Where some of his clothes came from – they could be so absurd – was a mystery.

We locked the car and walked the rest of the way. The trampled earth of the compound yard had been swept clean of all twigs, husks of grain, pebbles and leaves. Out near the center Anna was on hands and knees. There was a winnowing fan on the ground next to her heaped with sludgy, wet cow dung which Anna was busy smearing on to the soil with broad swipes and strokes of her palm. The odor was far more overpowering than any paint back home.

'When it turns hard, it keeps away insects. Then you can just spread your grain out on the ground to dry,' Peter explained. He watched Anna admiringly. 'Anna's a good worker,' he said. Berlita, we knew, well into pregnancy, was not allowed to tire herself. Apparently she was keeping Peter's mother busy with an order a minute.

As Anna worked she crawled backwards slowly. Most of the compound, spread already with its new surface, was far darker than the shrinking portion that remained for her to cover. As soon as Anna saw us coming, she waved. Her raised hand and arm up to the elbow flashed in their coat of liquid shit. While we walked around the edge of the Khaeri yard, feet sinking into the turned topsoil of sweet potato ridges, Anna rose and ran with her brisk, straight-legged shuffle to our hut. Then kneeling next to the wall, with the fingers of her hands spread apart as wide as possible, she left a careful handprint. First one print, then another. The imprints – spaces at the joints and lines in her palms reading white – were sharp.

With glad yells Anastasia, Mary and even the little one, Rosa, raced to copy Anna, dipping their hands up to the wrist into the basket of dung, running back and forth to our hut, pressing hand prints at regular intervals.

'Watch me!' For once Anna's voice was full. Dipping one bare foot in the dung she hopped from the source to the wall and holding on to an upright under the eaves for support, lifting her leg high, while the rest watched squealing, she left her footprint cocked at an angle near the window. How festive it looked, the one foot among the growing number of hands. Black hands, black prints. By the time Elizabeth came outside to see what the girls were making so much noise about, wiping her hands which were coated with flour on her apron, the house had been transformed.

Elizabeth shaded her eyes, frowned. 'Anna!' She shooed her daughters down to the communal bathing place, a stream among the stand of trees at the bottom of the hill which, lumpy and gashed by erosion, sloped away behind the nearby Mission school kitchen. The setting sun, a fierce orange, reflected from the drying coat Anna had smeared on to the earth of the compound. Every ripple shimmered visibly like some tiny inland pond.

'Peter,' Elizabeth said, and pointed to a basket full of dung that stood next to his bicycle, left for the work day under the banana trees.

'Thank you, Mama.' Peter's pleasure was evident. 'Good

243

night, sir.' In next to no time he was gone, the basket balanced on the luggage rack behind him, short legs pumping in a race to reach home before Elizabeth's gift could solidify and turn useless.

'Peter!' Elizabeth shook her head laughing, then went back to grinding grain. If it hadn't been for us, tribal snobbery would have made any friendship between Peter and the Khaeris unlikely at best. Oh, he was amiability itself, but he knew his place. The invisible bars of a cage could seem to vibrate around him and his smile.

'How do you like it?' Jenifa asked, nodding at the new decorations on our house. She laughed and handed Mayende to me. Then slowly, in high-heeled shoes, her hair done up in intricate, twisting vines, she advanced to the now abandoned winnowing fan piled with dung. Crouching down she stuck in one finger and wormed it around good. She pulled the finger out dripping, pretended to stick it into her mouth, and laughed. Then, looking at us, she slinkily tottered to our hut where, choosing a place between the blots of her younger sisters, she printed a series of small dots with her finger tip. She pressed and pressed until the top dried.

'Why are you here?' Jenifa asked us. 'Why would anyone from your country want to come to *this place*?' Was it bitterness asking, or curiosity? Koert Jan avoided looking me in the eye. Jenifa held out her arms for Mayende. When I'd surrendered the baby, my arms felt so light they wanted to lift of their own accord.

'Are you married?' Jenifa looked at each of us in turn.

'No,' said Koert Jan. 'Not everyone in Holland marries.'

I knew the formula. We had used it before and would use it again.

'This would be a hard life for wives,' I added, blushing at intruding even more falsity than necessary.

'You wear a ring,' Jenifa said to me, pointing with her eyes.

'She died,' Koert Jan spoke up for me.

Jenifa nodded quietly, her cheek pressed to Mayende's, offering and absorbing warmth.

VII

There'd been no sign of Jenifa around the compound for almost a week. At last one night when Anna came to bring us drinking water, I asked if Jenifa was ill.

'No, the health she is having is just all right,' Anna said. She put the bucket down she was carrying on her head without spilling a drop. Then she rubbed her hands back and forth across the crown of her skull. Looking at me, her eyes narrowed. 'Tom's back.'

'Tom?'

'Thomas.' Anna looked left and right, careful to see we were not being overheard. 'Before father sent Jenifa to Nairobi, that boy was always chasing her.'

'What do you mean, he's back?'

'Tom works in Mombasa unloading the ships. People have been noticing him lately in Mumias and came to tell mother. So she is keeping Jenifa in the house until Tom's leave is over.' Anna made a face. 'I don't like him.'

'He knows about Mayende?' Inside on his bed Koert Jan shifted position. He would, I knew, be listening through the open window. And Koert Jan disapproved of direct questions. If you want to gain someone's confidence, he said, direct questions work about as well as bullets.

'Yes, Tom knows,' Anna replied, pullling out some tangled debris that floated on the water in the bucket. 'Of course he must. People will have told him.'

'Mayende is his baby?'

'Yes, sister told father.'

And what, I couldn't help wondering, did the Bishop of Kisumu make of that?

245

'Tom even wanted to marry Jenifa.'

'But?'

'He's not good enough.'

And the next morning, Peter, too, without our asking, told us that Jenifa's old boyfriend was back in town. 'He's in the *pombe* shops, talking big and buying people beer. With a different pair of shoes on everyday.'

I'm no longer a hundred per cent sure, but I'd be surprised if it was anybody but Anna who told us not to open the door if we heard knocking at night. 'It can be an *omulosi*, a thief prowling abroad while at home his wife turns *sim-sim* seeds over the fire to keep him invisible while he is out raiding the country.' When Anna spoke of the world she only half-inherited, whispering stories about old beliefs, her eyes gleamed and grew enormous. 'And if the wife is careless, say she lets even one seed scorch, then the *omulosi* will have to materialise, naked, and you can capture him.'

The night we heard pounding at our door, however, the forceful blows did not sound like they came from the fist of any invisible spirit. It was raining hard, even for Kenya. In a few places the thatch of our hut leaked. Wet spots, small puddles gathered on the round earth floor. Koert Jan sat at our rickety table with only a small, flickering oil lamp to see by. The lamp in the shape of an airplane, complete with propellors, was made by a local smith using old tin cans. With two forefingers Koert Jan hunted and pecked at our lightweight portable typewriter – the one where half the letters always stuck. I was already in my sleeping-bag, poor torn mosquito net tucked around my wobbly canvas cot. It was only nine but I could hardly keep my eyes open.

The clatter of the typewriter keys and Koert Jan's muffled curses, the thump of the machine as it hopped about on the table, wind rattling our wood shutters and door – the mix of sounds was soothing. I was almost asleep when the wild knocking began.

'Hey, wait!' My fears only drew a tush from Koert Jan. After all this was Kenya, not Rhodesia or Uganda. Here there were no terrs, no risk of our being dragged outside by 'the boys', humiliated, mutilated, shot. We were part of an African household, a stone's throw from one of the oldest Catholic churches in the country – and from a school for the deaf. 'At least let me put some clothes on.'

What local violence there was, was pretty small-time. Co-wives smashing each other's skulls, scratching each other's eyes out. Drunks at *pombe* shops carving each other up. School children at exam time tearing their classrooms to pieces in waves of hysteria. But until that pounding – boom, boom, boom – I'd never had a moment's unrest.

'*Hodi.*'

By the time Koert Jan slid back the bolt and swung the door open, I had pushed aside the mosquito net, sat up and pulled on my jeans. The legs were clammy and chill. A dark figure burst into the hut, bent double to pass through the door. Only when she stood, I saw it was mother Elizabeth, drenched to the skin. Anna followed, and Mary, dripping, shivering in their school dresses. Elizabeth had the panga with her that she used to hack firewood. Her handsome black face, regal, was drawn and haggard. She stood staring at the oil lamp, the thin flame rising out of the wick from the cockpit. In the quavering light her face was like a skull.

I was pulling on my shirt when Anna whispered, 'He took the baby.' Anna's response to our stunned silence was to repeat the statement again, more slowly. 'Thomas has taken the baby.'

Wind blew rain in at the door.

'Where's Jenifa?' I asked.

'She's following them,' Elizabeth spoke in a small voice.

'Where?'

'I don't know,' Elizabeth wailed, tossing her head.

As I raced to tie my boots, the laces broke in my hand. Anna and Mary huddled next to their mother, holding on to her wet dress. The flame of the oil lamp cast large, dancing shadows on the hollow insides of the thatch. Up there somewhere was a nest of bats with young.

'All right, let's find them.' Koert Jan led us out into the night. Rain obliterated every trace of light from stars or moon. To my body, still warm from sleep, the air was shockingly cold. I had our flashlight. Typically it didn't light.

'Koert Jan?' But he was gone, dashing into the dense bush behind the hut, swallowed by the vegetation. 'Koert Jan?'

'Aaaiyeee.' As soon as Koert Jan's scream split the night, I gave one of my own, an echo, only louder and longer. Then silence. Just as Koert Jan covered in mud came limping into the clearing, finally I managed to fumble the damn flashlight on.

'What happened?'

'What're *you* screaming about, idiot?'

Anna pressed both her hands over her mouth.

'Are you all right?'

Koert Jan simply turned his back on me. 'I thought I heard someone out back,' he said to Elizabeth, spitting out a leaf.

'No,' Elizabeth said. She extended her arm and pointed with the panga. 'He took the baby to town to wait for the bus.' I kept my flashlight pointed at the ground. The cracked nails on Elizabeth's toes looked very old.

'He wants to be going to Mombasa,' Mary added.

'He was convincing Jenifa to go with him' – Anna again in determined whispers – 'but she wouldn't.'

My heart still hadn't slowed from the vision I'd had of Koert Jan as a casualty in the bush – stepping on a snake, or in a hole, his back snapping, spine wrenched. The night was immense as we huddled together.

'Jenifa told Thomas to leave.' Elizabeth was trembling as she spoke. How long had they been out looking on their own already? 'So he moved to the door like he was going, then he snatched up the baby and ran out with it.'

'Mayende's blanket' – despite her tight monkey's face, prominent ears and hardly a nap of hair, tonight Mary didn't look foolish. She showed us the corner of the baby's blanket, yellow with satin trim. She held it bunched under her dress in an effort to keep it somehow dry.

'Did you hurt yourself?'

Koert Jan was rubbing his shoulder. He ignored my question. He seemed camouflaged by earth and twigs and scraps of leaf that stuck to him, even to his hair.

'Thomas doesn't want the baby,' Anna explained, 'only Jenifa.'

'What time does the bus go?' Koert Jan asked.

'Tomorrow morning,' Mary said, 'at six o'clock.'

'Won't he go home first,' I said, 'to his parents?'

'He has no parents,' Mary spoke harshly. 'Only an old uncle who never wants to see him again.'

'We have to be careful' – Elizabeth's teeth were chattering. 'Thomas is drunk.' The rain meant we had practically to shout to be heard. 'Can we go with your car?' Elizabeth said. 'Please.'

'Mother is asking' – Anna never took her eyes off the weapon her mother was holding – 'if you'll drive us to Mumias to get Jenifa and the baby back.'

The oil lamp was almost out when I ducked back into the hut to dig up the keys, and pull on a sweater. Then we piled into the Renault which stood parked among the sweet potatoes. Anastasia and Rosa stayed behind. 'Lock the door,' Elizabeth told her daughters. 'If anyone tries to get in, start beating the pots together.'

The rain was too hard for the windshield wipers. I felt like an animal that had only hearing and scent to rely on, not his eyes – but my hearing and sense of smell, I well knew, weren't up to the challenge. As we drove, veils of water streaked and sluiced down the window. The headlights dissolved into weak clouds of light, more blinding than revealing. If there was anything out there in front of us, alive or dead, I wouldn't see it until too late. Any moment I expected a dark shadow to loom up, then fall like a hammer against the front window.

Slowly we pitched ahead, slithering, jolting past the church towards the murram road which turned and sloped away towards town. Our breaths were fogging the inside of the window. With pages wadded up from old *Daily Nations*, Koert Jan next to me did his best to wipe the glass clear.

'Mother went to the chief to ask him to send Thomas away, and the chief promised to oblige her.' An edge crept into Anna's voice. 'But he is a foolish man, and too easy about giving his word.'

Where the access road joined the main asphalt artery, I couldn't make the uphill turn carrying such a full load.

'Everyone out.' With branches shoved under the back tires, wheels spinning, I came free. Then with a spurt of speed I plowed through a not unsizeable river that raced and frothed in the roadside gulley. This time Anna's teeth were chattering loudest when the Khaeris climbed back in. Then, just in case our hearts weren't racing fast enough already, there was a frantic clap of thunder.

But with the report of thunder still resonating in our ears, the rain seemed to relent and the storm wandered off like some grazing animal. As at last we neared the intersection of Mumias, through a light, fine drizzle pinprick stars appeared.

'We must find them,' Elizabeth said. Her breathing sounded like a whimper.

We entered a ghost town. Huddled back among sleek trees, the mosque crouched, a pale, chalky apparition. The slapdash white of the petrol station, too, glimmered in our headlights, flimsy and insubstantial. Skeins of puddles in the road caught light beams shining from the car and hurled them back at the sky.

'It's quiet,' said Anna, her face pressed forward over the front seat between Koert Jan's shoulder and mine. Thunder

250

rumbled now in the distance – an old sot turning his back on his wife. 'Too, too quiet.'

We scanned the main intersection. There were no signs of life. Vision became still easier with the moon nibbling away hungrily at the edge of inky clouds. After so much darkness, the cold wash of moonlight seemed eerie. And the beauty of it all was no distraction for fear.

On foot the walk from the Khaeris' to Mumias, the descent really, was far shorter than our roundabout route by road. The narrow track though was full of rocks and trees and shrubs that pressed in at the sides. Not a pleasant thought: drunk Tom with Mayende lurching ahead through the punishing cloudburst, Jenifa hurrying to keep up with him – straining to keep the shifting badge of his back in sight.

'Nothing,' Elizabeth exhaled in despair as we finished our first pass through the village. Near the entrance gate to the market square, grinding gears, I turned us around to head back up the main street. We startled a wild dog drinking from rain water pooling in tire ruts. His woebegone eyes flashed and he slunk away. Koert Jan opened the car window on his side, I on mine. Cold air shot through, seeming to pierce us like a wire and leave us dangling.

'There's Jenifa.' Mary's small voice over my shoulder was clear. It wasn't really necessary for her to point straight ahead. In the glare of the Renault's lights Jenifa stood near the skirt of the road, slowly waving. Her dress was soaked and clinging. Her western underclothes were all outlined distinctly. Jenifa's knees were visible, one leg streaked with mud, a gash down her shin, fresh blood. She waved to us without any display of emotion. No surprise, no alarm. The way she stood there it was as if she'd been expecting us for a visit and we were a little bit late. Once she was sure we'd seen her, she began to hug herself against the cold. We drove close, stopping at an angle. My windshield wipers were still whipping back and forth, screeching now against the dry glass. I groped all over the

251

dashboard before Koert Jan leaned over and turned them off.

Everyone scrambled out of the car. A few steps apart Elizabeth and Jenifa spoke to each other in an excited burst of words. Jenifa met her mother's eyes directly. There was a strength of character in her face I'd never seen before.

'Tom's crazy' – Jenifa turned her attention to us.

'Where is he?' Koert Jan asked. Jenifa faced about and shielded her eyes with one hand as if she were staring up into the full sun instead of into total darkness.

'The mill.' She pointed up at the row of shops. I climbed back into the car, and reversed, gouging a new rut in the mire. Then I swung the Renault around so the headlights caught the low concrete front porch of the Mumias shops. The third shop to the left was the miller's. Even at night he left his huge iron scale out hanging from an overhead beam. Here he weighed the loads of grain women brought to feed his machine. Seated on the scalloped lip of the scale was a young man in a white shirt. He looked so boyish! He was holding Mayende, but absent-mindedly, like a child with other things on his mind dragging a doll along behind him.

Koert Jan started to climb the short, slippery bluff to the shops, but Jenifa caught up to him and put a restraining hand on his arm.

'Don't,' she said.

We were maybe five or six yards away from Tom but he was above us, his face in shadow. When he spoke there was alcohol thickening his voice.

'What's he saying?' Koert Jan asked.

'If anyone comes a step closer, he'll swing Mayende's head against that post.'

'Jesus, nice fellow.'

'And he will.' Jenifa didn't flinch. 'He's crazy.'

Tom had leaned forward and smiled – like someone who knows people are talking about him, but can't hear what they're saying.

'Jenifa, what does he want?'

'He wants me to go to Mombasa with him.' Then Jenifa called up to Thomas – a mocking tirade, but at the same time seductive. She stood with one hand on her hip. He gave no answer.

'Jenifa, do you want to go?' I asked.

Slowly she turned her back to Tom and said, 'No.'

'Tom?' Koert Jan called. His voice seemed to expand in the darkness. His tone was friendly, conversational. 'Thomas, we want to talk with you. Talk things over.'

Jenifa stepped forward and sharply, firmly repeated Koert Jan's words. Her voice stayed low, musical. Her head was cocked to one side, arms crossed over her breasts. Tom stood unsteadily. He took a tentative step forwards towards the edge of the paved concrete stoep. Indeed baby Mayende just dangled from his father's grip, Tom's fingers tight around the baby's chubby upper arm. Mayende hung limp and didn't let out a sound.

'Oh Mayende!' Anna's whisper was full of terror.

'Aaaeeiyeh.' Just at that instant, like a bat swooping down out of the dark branches above, Elizabeth came dashing forwards from the shadows behind Tom and grabbed hold of the baby.

'Mama!' Anna called aloud, for once her voice at full strength. Anna had the panga! She lifted it now and started swinging it high in the air over her head. Elizabeth gave the startled Thomas a hard shove and crossed in front of him – a shade with wings, clutching Mayende to her bosom. Tom let go of the baby. Elizabeth with her prize hurried along the gallery, past the hotelli barred and shuttered, past the Asian's, too, honeyed sweets and bright plastics locked away for the night.

Tom staggered back into the miller's scale and sat heavily, setting the iron swinging, clanking on its heavy chain. Empty-handed, he seemed to shrink, no longer a menace but a bewildered uncoordinated boy. Unloved, outwitted. He, too, was soaked to the bone. Under his white shirt, his black chest heaved.

'Mama, wait,' Mary called and swiftly took to her heels. A corner of the baby's fluffy blanket shone for a moment in the Renault's lights before Mary, too, was swallowed by the night. 'Mama.'

'Tom?' Koert Jan's voice still betrayed no excitement. By now though I was ahead of him, close enough to touch Tom if I reached out my hand.

'Take the family home,' I turned to tell Koert Jan, speaking as calmly as I could. 'Drive them. I'll talk to Tom. I'll – '

'Be careful,' Jenifa called.

'He is my son. Why do you help them to steal my son?' Now that I was close enough to see Tom's face, I had a shock in store. It was Koert Jan – oh not the kinky hair, and the broad lips – but the eyes, the chin, the tone of his voice, speech slurred slightly by *pombe* but gentle, sweetly insinuating. The similarity was striking – under the skin, hung on the skeleton – that arm reaching up and holding on to the chain of the scale, the hand of fine fingers. 'Why do you interfere? You don't know what you're doing. You don't know anything about us? Why?'

I turned back for a reassuring look at the original, but Koert Jan was busy helping Elizabeth and Mary into the back seat of the Renault. They were all shadows, far away, hunched, urgent, and up on the miller's veranda, I was alone with Tom – and my doubts.

'*My* son.' Tom thumped his chest. '*My* rights.' He seemed deeply baffled by what was happening. The night, the storm, the vigil waiting for the morning Mawingo bus – for him perhaps these were not the drama, not the drama they were for us. His eyes – Koert Jan's eyes in that young face – were accusing me, bemused.

'We can talk about it,' I said, wanting to reach out and place my hand comfortingly on his shoulder. 'Come back and sleep in the hut with us.'

Tom heaved himself up out of the scale awkwardly. It banged against the back of his knees so he tottered forward. I helped him keep balance.

'We can go,' Koert Jan called up to us.

'I'll take the footpath. You drive.' I didn't take my eyes off the face gleaming in front of mine. Younger than Koert Jan, more dissipated – lines of meanness, perhaps, around the mouth.

'Be careful,' Jenifa repeated from the car window. 'You come with us. Don't walk with him. He's dangerous.'

Tom put an arm around my shoulder, smiling. I tried not to stiffen.

'Be careful, he's carrying a knife.'

Talking non-stop, reassuring Tom that, no, we weren't taking Mayende from him, that Jenifa wasn't our 'wife', explaining that, look, it was bad for such a young child to be exposed to the cold, to be out in the damp of the night, promising Tom that we would stick up for his rights, we would discuss the whole thing very thoroughly, we were friends, step by step I backed down the slippery mud slope towards the car.

'You, Jenifa!' Tom called but she didn't answer him. He jumped from the porch, arms wide like wings, and skidded down the slope. 'You're stealing *my* child.'

I was pulled into the front of the car on top of Anna, my knees pressed against my chest, shins grating against the dashboard. The door closed, but didn't lock. The window was open anyway! Tom had stooped out of the headlights and when he rose again he was grasping a stone the size of a mango. He came moving slowly, but purposefully towards us. He looked small now, smaller than Anna even. Behind me I could hear Elizabeth crooning to the baby. A voice I will never forget, a gentle charm of love.

Koert Jan gave gas, but he'd put us by mistake in reverse. Tom now stood on the road, arm raised high with the stone.

Jenifa and Mary too began screaming abuse at Tom as Koert

Jan wrestled the gears into first – punching me twice painfully in the side as I wriggled to get out of the way of the gear shift.

Night blind, Koert Jan swerved past the man tottering in mid-road. My last glimpse of Tom's face bore no resemblance to Koert Jan at all, no, but to Mayende instead.

The Khaeris, grateful and in a celebrating mood, made tea for us. We had never been invited inside Elizabeth's hut before. Photographs of her wedding, studio prints, hung on the wall. She and Joseph were so plump they almost weren't recognisable. Next to me, on top of a low table stood a Tree-top bottle, the cap off, and a number of empty glasses. What filled the bottle half-way might have been water, or *changga*.

Anna sat rocking Mayende in her arms, sunk in a reed chair. As soon as we went inside, Jenifa disappeared behind a blanket hanging from a cord stretched between two radial roof poles. A few seconds later her wet dress appeared, slung over the blanket, dripping steadily on to the floor. But we saw nothing further that night of Jenifa.

'Try again,' I joked, crawling back into my sleeping-bag, pulling the mosquito net into place. How long ago the pounding on the door seemed now. 'What did he mean, do you think, when he said we were denying him his rights?'

'As a father,' Koert Jan's voice came from the table. He was writing in his journal. 'A father has a claim on all male children.'

The worst hadn't happened, yet I couldn't blot out of my mind the sight of Mayende dashed against one of the cement uprights in front of the miller's, brains splattered, blood more black than red in the spreading light of the headlamps. As my head sank in the pillow, behind my eyes rain fell heavily again, on the roof of the hut, on the windshield of the Renault, but the rain was blood.

'At marriage, I know,' – I rolled on to my stomach, a position so uncomfortable on the local bed I couldn't hold it for long –

'the groom pays a cow to the bride's parents to purchase any fruit produced in her womb. That I know. The cow even has a special name.'

'I've forgotten it too.'

'But what's that got to do with Tom and Jenifa? They never married.'

'Even without marriage, male children are different.'

In the dark now it felt like I had my fingers closed around one of Mayende's ankles and I couldn't put him down safely. Instead of being heavy though, Mayende was light – a balloon – one that threatened to drift up over the moon, tugging my black heart up and out of my body.

'Koert Jan? Koert Jan, did you notice anything about the way Tom looked?'

'You're not seriously going to tell me he looked like our garbage man in Amsterdam, or our tax consultant?'

'Where do you think he is now?'

'Our tax consultant?'

'Tom.'

'Face down in a puddle somewhere like he deserves – face up if he's lucky.'

For once Koert Jan fell asleep without trouble. I lay awake for hours listening to his breathing. Mosquitoes kept me company. As always in Mumias, after rain, they seemed to spring out of the ground like blades of grass.

VIII

Next morning I had a hard time waking up. The climb back was a stop and go affair up a slippery ladder with missing rungs. When at last I opened my eyes and kept them open there was a tapering shaft of sunlight through the open front door that reached right to my chin. Outside I heard Koert Jan laugh. He was playing with the children. We were late! What had happened to Peter then? Had I slept right through his bell?

It was a brilliant, cloudless morning. The kind of day only God could make. The leaves of trees, bushes and crops hung weighted down with moisture, glinting where drops caught the early sunlight. By the time I came back from my squat on the *cho* – the little cabin steamy and damp from the night's rain – Koert Jan and Anna had carried our table outside. A full, elegant breakfast lay spread in readiness.

'Hungry?'

We sat to a feast of roasted maize, globs of Cowboy margarine melting on crisp chapatis, chunks of papaya sprinkled with lime.

'Mama,' Anna called out as soon as I took my place at the table. At once Elizabeth came around from the cooking stones behind her hut. She carried a deep dish of sweet potatoes bursting through their charred skins.

'Good morning.'

Elizabeth looked radiant, years younger than when we'd parted last night.

'*Oolimoolamoo.*'

Elizabeth laughed even more than usual at how I grew entangled in the Luhya greeting ritual, my tongue tripping over the simple words.

'How's the news?'

'The news is good.'

'How are your chickens? How are your goats? How are your wife and your children?'

This then was our victory party. Only Mayende seemed not to share in the mood. He was out of sorts, crying most inconsolably. Jenifa, wearing one of her flashiest Nairobi dresses, carried him back and forth, clucking at him.

'He has a fever.' Jenifa stopped near our table and held the baby out towards me. When I laid a finger in his hand, the fingers curled weakly and his crying stopped. Then Anastasia and Mary came carrying Mayende's teak crib outside. Together they lifted it on top of our Renault and began lashing it in place. Up there, bad luck to think so but it looked like a coffin.

'When you finish stuffing yourself,' Koert Jan told me, 'we're taking Jenifa and Mayende to her Aunt Mary's.'

'Near Kitale,' Anna whispered. Anna was soaping her legs. She stood bent at the waist, legs straight, at her feet a basin of water. Up and down she rubbed a cake of soap against her black skin to make it shine. 'Aunt Mary is father's sister. She's very' – Anna spread her arms – 'fat.'

'What's happened to Peter,' I said with my mouth full.

'I sent him home.'

'What did you tell him about last night?'

'I didn't. Elizabeth did.'

Now Anastasia came out of the family hut carrying a bulging suitcase of tattered cardboard trussed with local sisal rope. This she pummeled and kicked until it fitted on to the back seat of the Renault. Of course Jenifa's and Mayende's safety had to be vouchsafed, but I would miss them.

'Mama,' Jenifa called, 'look.'

'Rosa!' At the far side of the compound Rosa, wearing only a white slip, was trying to cultivate the garden with a hoe that was bigger than she was. Elizabeth, laughing, went to pick up her little girl. With water from Anna's basin she rinsed the soil off Rosa's face and hands.

'Take your time,' Koert Jan said to me, rising, 'but hurry.'

All in a row the rest of the family waved us off. Mary and Rosa ran right alongside the Renault making funny faces at the baby until we reached the pavement near the driveway to the school for the deaf. At the very last minute Elizabeth had tried to force Koert Jan to accept money for petrol. Deftly, but warmly, he had refused. I drove. I don't think I've ever had to yawn so much in my life. Koert Jan sat in back – he insisted – scrunched in next to Jenifa's belongings. Up front Jenifa held Mayende on her lap, fending off bumps with one hand on the dash-board.

'He likes it,' Jenifa said, merrily. Indeed Mayende's bad humor had lifted. He sat drinking in the world with visible glee. Last night seemed long ago.

'What's Peter going to do?' This expedition would cost a day's work. 'Did you ask him to do any interviews?' I said as we left Mumias behind.

'No.'

'No?' I stole a look at Koert Jan in the rearview mirror.

'His mother wasn't well. He was going to look after her.'

Jenifa laughed. Perhaps she was just laughing then at a private memory or thought, something that had nothing whatever to do with our conversation?

'Peter asked if he could have the day free,' Koert Jan went on. Despite the low key of his voice, he, too, I could tell, suddenly was extra alert.

As we drove past barren mudflats along the Nzoia, only Jenifa broke the silence, chanting pretty nonsense to Mayende, bouncing him on her bare knees. As the sun grew hotter by the minute I became aware of the heat of Jenifa's slim body next to me – and her faint, penetrating scent. The road was largely empty. Once I swerved to pass a tractor, a swollen insect pulling a flat trailer heaped with sugar cane – the articulated rods of cane strapped down in unruly bundles, ends sticking out in all directions. There was almost no room to pass. The outside wheels of the Renault veered off the paved surface. A rapidfire burst of small stones rang out against our car bottom. Mayende laughed, clapped hands in his mother's arms.

Near the top of the next hill a squashed dog lay in the road. It took three blasts on the horn to scatter scavenging birds. As soon as we left the carcass behind, the dark cloud reconvened. Then as we came over the crest, we startled a row of local women and girls with tins of water on their heads, wending their way barefoot down the faded white stripe painted in the middle of the road. In their hurry to get out of the way, some moved left, some right. A number of containers, bright as mirrors, toppled and splashed.

'Sorry,' I said, although the angry women couldn't hear me.

'What's wrong with Peter's mother?' I asked. Jenifa laughed again. She was using a tissue to wipe clots of milk from Mayende's tiny, purple rosebud lips.

'That woman is fine,' Jenifa reached out and touched my elbow. She shifted in her seat to be able to speak more easily with Koert Jan. 'It's Peter's wife.'

'Berlita?'

'Yes, she has been dreaming.' Her eyes were bright with a story. She paused to see if we knew it. 'In her dream their late neighbor came back, the one who hanged herself when her husband took a junior wife.'

'Hanged herself?'

Koert Jan put a hand on my shoulder to restrain the parrot in me.

'First she lit the candles and put the Bible on a chair. Then she climbed up there, wrapped her husband's good belt around her neck and tied it to the roof. Peter's wife was the one who found her.'

'When?'

'Oh it was happening some time ago. But then last night the dead woman came back in a dream. There was such a mark on her neck. Berlita woke up screaming. For the rest of the night she was afraid to sleep again. Then early this morning for the first time the child in her womb started kicking.'

When we drove up in front of her house, Jenifa's Aunt Mary, Joseph Khaeri's youngest sister, ran out to greet us. 'Welcome, welcome, welcome.' She even shuffled her feet in a small dance, raising a cloud of dust. Anna had not been exaggerating. Her aunt was an enormous woman. It took only a few seconds to see how irresistibly good-natured she was as well. What a devouring smile! Seated on a tree stump, black brow furrowed with concentration, Aunt Mary listened to Jenifa's laconic account of last night's events. 'My, my, my, my.' When Jenifa was through, Aunt Mary rose, bulk quivering, to embrace us with effusive gratitude. All we could do was stand there and be hugged.

Aunt Mary lived in a large permanent house with glass windows and cement floors. The many square rooms opened on to each other without any hallways. They were crammed indiscriminately with city furniture in lurid, clashing fabrics and caramelised formica. Religious prints in fancy carved wooden frames hung from nails driven into the walls. St Sebastian. The Last Supper. The Annunciation. While we were inside a crash on the sheet-iron roof made me jump a mile.

'Mangoes,' Aunt Mary laughed, and two, three, four fell in a salvo.

Everywhere inside the house and out there were chickens and goats underfoot. And Aunt Mary owned a dog so persecuted by fleas that when he sat to scratch behind his ear, his leg kept propelling him round and around in circles.

Jenifa herself supervised the removal of Mayende's crib from the roof of our car. It was duly installed on top of a blanket in the lush shade of a loquat tree. Here we sat to drink coffee – locally grown, roasted and ground. Aunt Mary had a set of fine bone china cups decorated with roses. You could see your fingers through the sides when you held a cup up to the light, the way Koert Jan did.

An indefinite number of naked babies and small children went crawling, creeping or tottering about, twin streams of green snot leaking from their small, flat noses, disappearing into their mouths, down their throats. Many had sores, too, on their scalp or knees, angry with pus. As for Mayende, Aunt Mary herself took charge of him. He made no secret of his pleasure in her bulging, spongy breasts. He pushed and pulled and pummeled them.

The priests who had provided Joseph Khaeri's education, had arranged a marriage for Mary. Her husband was a powerful man, a farmer who was also active in national politics. He was seldom at home. The family homestead was seventy-odd miles north of Mumias in the direction of Mt Elgon. A high wire fence surrounded the premises. Most of the men around, and there were many, were hired workers. All the time we were drinking our coffee, I could feel Aunt Mary's eyes on us, weighing, judging. At least part of her joviality was a mask for shrewdness. Even if Tom should learn of Jenifa's whereabouts, it was unlikely he would be rash enough to attempt a visit. If he did, I had no doubt he would soon be sorry. This house was as safe as any in Joseph Khaeri's mind.

When we left Aunt Mary, she gave us three splendid speckled chickens with rainbow tail feathers. For good measure she ordered one of her 'boys' to load a burlap sack full of freshly pulled groundnuts into the car.

'Thank you,' Jenifa said and shook our hands, 'very much.' I squeezed her fingers before I let go. For luck.

Heading back, we lost the way. Koert Jan did. He was singing and missed the turn-off. Then on an awkward incline in the middle of nowhere we had a flat.

'Aha, the Tire Pirate strikes again!' This odd, unsavory fast-talker sat by the petrol pump in Mumias patching tires. He had a monopoly and in the way he did his work made sure his customers would be back soon. At his mercy, we tried to enjoy his treachery.

It took us half an hour, laughing and calling each other names, to find stones to prop under the wheels and to work the mystifying jack. It was an odd, intense moment of love, reminiscing about all the flat tires we had shared together. Then dumping the flat among our tools in the back of the

263

Renault we found a carton of tins of evaporated milk that Jenifa forgot to unload.

'Poor kid,' Koert Jan said, 'now they'll probably feed him *ugali*.'

IX

Without further mishap we reached the outskirts of Mumias. Instead of turning towards the Catholic church, Koert Jan headed east towards Akero, Peter's village. 'Let's see how Peter's mother is doing,' he said.

A massive clump of bamboo – home of a hundred snakes, to hear Peter tell it – marked where to cut off the main road inland. The feathery bamboo showed black against the pale sky. From this point on we had to follow what really was no more than a footpath to Peter's compound. Our first visit, we had walked in. Later Peter and his brother had hacked away the long grass, black jack and weeds to make it possible for us to drive closer. Everything grew back so fast here, however, that already we could feel thick tufts and sprigs raking the protective plate, the hard belly screwed to the bottom of our Renault.

'Lookee there.'

Less than half-way we came face to face with Peter himself at the head of a small family procession. He was pushing his bicycle. On the carrier rack behind the saddle Berlita sat perched on a blanket folded small to make a cushion. Berlita had wrapped one cloth, blue, into a turban and had drawn another, yellow and green, across her face. Peter's old mother came hobbling along in back. She was as thin as Aunt Mary had been fat. And last of all, silent, hooded as always, came Peter's younger brother.

At the sight of us, delight, surprise, concern mingled on Peter's face. We climbed out of the car and stretched.

'Good afternoon, sir. Did you travel well?' Peter asked and gave us the slightest of bows. Berlita, he went on to explain, was having such sharp pains in her womb. All day the pains were only growing worse.

At this point Peter's mother began to sputter and speak compulsively. Peter listened to her with a mixture of respect and a tight-lipped smile of toleration. When she finished her narrow chin kept nodding like an accusing finger.

'My mother is asking you to persuade me to do as she says,' Peter laughed nervously. His shirt was open at the throat. He was not his usual self. His skin that normally gleamed was ashen gray. He was distracted.

'Which is what?'

'To fetch one of our traditional doctors, sir.'

'A midwife?'

'No, sir. A doctor who knows magic.'

Berlita had pulled aside her veil. She sat and listened intently but she said nothing. The whole time she was biting down hard on her lip, one hand with the fingers spread lying on her enlarged belly, the other holding on to the bicycle saddle.

'My mother is thinking that someone jealous is trying to witch my wife.'

Peter now put his hands on his mother's shoulders and spoke to her in soothing tones. She nodded vigorously. 'I have asked her if she is a good pentecostal believer,' he told us. 'As such we must leave behind all our ignorant foolishness.'

Now Peter's mother actually went down on her knees and was wringing her hands in our direction.

'Sir, she is afraid for Berlita's life.'

'Where are you going?'

'To Namulungu, the health center there. I am hoping the doctor can give her a medical examination.'

As carefully, as gently as possible, Koert Jan and Peter lifted Berlita off the bicycle and helped her into the Renault. Her eyes were brimful of fear. Aunt Mary's chickens, silent the whole journey until now, set up a dreadful squawking. Peter's brother stroked them still again.

Peter told his mother to guard his bicycle which he left leaning against a craggy termite's nest and we reversed along the narrow trail. At times I couldn't help lurching or hit an unexpected bump. Berlita would cry out. Her tongue and teeth showed green. Surely then she'd already swallowed local medicines? What would the pentecostals say to that?

When the clump of bamboo that served as our landmark came in view again, Berlita broke her silence. Her voice was shrill and charged with anger.

'Those people are the ones' – Peter pointed to a group of three huts where a woman and a man, shading their eyes, watched us pass – 'who are practicing magic against her. Berlita has been listening to my mother.' Peter's admission seemed to come reluctantly. How his voice turned harsh. Berlita's only reply was a covert smile, and she sank again into a shell of quiet. Not for long, however. As we gathered speed she looked over her shoulder at Peter again, laughed and with a toss of her head said something which made him laugh as well.

'My wife has never been in a motorcar before, sir. She says she's surprised it hasn't chewed us all up.'

We reached the Namulungu Health Center at least an hour before Peter could have hoped to by pushing, or even pedaling his bike. It was one of the oldest clinics in the district, breeze blocks with a peaked roof set among tall evergreen trees. When I pulled back the emergency brake, it made a dreadful wrenching sound as always. Berlita recoiled in fright.

Koert Jan and Peter hurried off directly to try to find somebody, leaving me behind to cope with Berlita. The place looked deserted. It took some coaxing, but finally Berlita trusted me and began to climb, slowly and in pain, from the car. Her breath was uneven and whistled faintly through her clenched teeth.

'It's closed.' Koert Jan was back quickly.

'Shouldn't be,' I said stupidly.

'Is.'

Berlita whimpered and clutched at her belly.

'We're going to check at the doctor's.' Koert Jan pointed to a series of low white buildings behind the health center. Peter was running already in that direction. 'Wait up on the porch.'

Easier said than done. We'd driven as close to the health center as possible but there was still a steep gully I couldn't pass. Now with Berlita holding tight to my arm, leaning heavily against me, we set off towards the clinic building. After every few steps we had to stop. In places the ground was still slick from last night's rain. There were bones and twisted bits of wire, broken bottles, half-burned waste in the gully, pulp and skins and medical waste. The ground swarmed with insects. To go around, however, was out of the question.

When we gained level ground again, I tried to encourage Berlita. 'Good girl, now only a little bit further.' I was sweating like a pig. My eyes stung with salt and rubbing them only made it worse. So close, Berlita was more child than woman. I wanted to force a smile from her, but didn't have the faintest idea how. Instead I concentrated on how to help her climb the front steps to the clinic porch. Backwards was the best way – I was pretty sure I'd read that somewhere. God help me if I ever have to treat snakebite or stop a bleeding artery!

As I demonstrated to Berlita how we were going to go up the stairs backwards, I saw she was crying, silently. Then voices, like the gnashing blades of scissors, rose behind the health center. Berlita let go of my arm. She took a step backwards, then another, and another. What followed was dreamlike, a total distortion of time – unutterably slow, over with in an instant. It felt like I was floating, watching everything as it happened from a remote distance. All in total silence, dear

God, and the whole time the invisible squabble went on, the querulous voices behind the useless white building.

Berlita removed the cloth from her shoulders and dropped it on the grass. She leaned forward and lifted her wrapper. Underneath she had on plastic panties. These already sagged, distended by some distorting weight. With one hand Berlita began to claw at them, to try to free herself from their elastic cling. The waistband, the leg openings were both elasticised and dug into her smooth flesh. I knelt and helped rip the stretched and shiny fabric. As the panties gave there glided free a slippery mass that drifted, splashed down on to the cloth spread out on the ground, even as Berlita crouched low, knees spread, and averted her eyes.

Peter's baby, a son, premature, lay there, still. It was perfect, complete, miniature. White – the infant, slick in a caul, roped in bloody, clotted afterbirth, was so pale, so puzzlingly peaceful.

This was no birth, it was death. An easy evacuation, relief – almost a sensation I could share from my morning squats over a dark, stinking hole in the earth.

'Wait here,' I said pointlessly to Berlita, reaching out a hand to her even as I moved away. My legs were weak and I was afraid I was going to be sick. Berlita was kneeling now – still connected to her dead fruit by the twisted umbilical cord. She was looking down at the foetus curiously, bending over it. Next thing, for all I knew, she would start to nuzzle it with her nose, lick it.

Christ! I wanted to go for help, but I couldn't leave her alone like that. And I couldn't call out. It was like a seam in the day had ripped open, and there the two of us were, stranded. Even breathing seemed an absurd thing to be doing. I came back and took Berlita's hand between mine. We passed a long few moments together, not moving or speaking. Berlita had reached back and removed the worn rubber thongs from her feet, then curled her legs under her. She folded the corners of her wrapper on the ground over the dead child – leaving an opening for its dismaying, clenched face – and she picked the child up and held it – not tightly, not against her body, but loosely, on her lap. And the bloody squiggle that joined her to the corpse, hung down across her one bare knee. Her heart was still pumping blood into this rapidly shriveling icon.

I couldn't have been more useless with my hands tied. The shredded panties lay nearby obscenely. I didn't want to have to touch them. Berlita followed my eyes and laughed. If she had delivered at home, a midwife would have sawed the umbilical cord through with a sharp blade of vernal grass.

More laughter from Berlita made me look up – and drop the grass I'd been snatching from the earth in tight fistfuls. Koert Jan and Peter were running back towards us. In the distant doorway of the doctor's house, a man was now standing, smoking a cigarette.

Koert Jan took the scene in quickly. He came up behind me and let me lean, for a precious second, against his shoulder. Peter helped Berlita to her feet. She spoke to him rapidly, lightly, and laughed again, rolling her eyes towards us, then blushing and looking away. Where the miscarriage had lain the grass was flattened.

'What is she saying?' Koert Jan asked Peter quietly.

'She says it's one of the silliest looking things she's ever seen. No,' Peter corrected us, 'she means me – with you. When we were running, she says I look ridiculous because you're so tall and I'm so short.'

We drove Peter and Berlita to the Mission hospital. While the young Dutch doctor there examined Berlita and nurses packaged the baby for burial, Koert Jan and Peter described to me what took place out back behind the health center.

'The doctor's from another tribe. They've broken all the windows in his house. The local people accuse him of not helping them in a good way.' Peter seemed his old self again.

'Someone started a story that one day the doctor was

delivering a baby – ' Koert Jan looked at Peter who took up the account.

' – the head was out and one arm, but it happened that this doctor looked at his wristwatch and saw it was time for the workday to end. So he pushed the baby back in again – '

'No,' I said – my mouth filling with the taste of papaya and sweet potatoes.

' – and told the mother to come back the next morning.'

'Now the doctor's living under siege, waiting for a transfer,' Koert Jan said. 'In the night people come and throw things on the roof.'

Broken windows hadn't been unusual enough for me to notice. Only the solitary figure of the doctor, smoking, in his doorway.

'The doctor refused to come to look at Berlita because there were no females nurses on duty at the *boma*,' Peter said. 'He was afraid what people would say later.'

The whole time we waited at the hospital, Peter sat quietly holding Koert Jan's hand. The three of us took up a bench on the long veranda. Slowly it dawned on me more nurses kept passing than was normal. They came in pairs, greeted us, and stared at the black and white clasped hands. And who would comfort Berlita, and how?

'I am sorry, sir,' Peter said when finally we could all go. 'We've been so much trouble.'

We found Peter's mother asleep next to his bicycle leaning against a tower of the termite's nest. As we approached Berlita scolded her mother-in-law through the open car window. The baby wrapped in cloth fastened with pins lay on the seat next to her. All the way along the inland track, each time the chassis of the Renault shivered on our worn shock absorbers, Jenifa's forgotten cache of evaporated milk cans gave a noisy bounce.

Before we parted, Koert Jan handed Peter Aunt Mary's three chickens. Some consolation prize. Peter's mother clutched the stillborn child in its hospital shroud to her sunken chest and keened. Berlita's features twitched with annoyance at this display but she didn't comment.

'You see, sir.' Peter ran his finger down the smooth worn rubber of his front bicycle tire. Every trace of a tread was gone. 'Twenty-five shillings, sir. Each.'

Again I drove. I wasn't happy with the silence. Koert Jan lay his head back against the seat, eyes closed, one of his hands pushed between my thigh and the seat.

'What about Berlita's dream,' I said. 'Did you ask Peter about it?'

'Of course not.'

'But he told you?'

Without opening his eyes, Koert Jan smiled. 'First I had to make up a dream and tell it to him.'

'You crook. What was in it?'

'You don't expect me to remember.'

'Someone back from the dead?'

Now Koert Jan had turned his head to one side and sat looking at me. 'Peter knew what I was up to, I think. "Sir," he said, "in many ways we are ignorant people. But as for dreams, you can even find people in the Bible believing in them."'

'Koert Jan, it was horrible.'

'Don't be so dramatic.' He took his hand away.

'You weren't there.'

'Berlita's still healthy.'

When we could see the thatched roofs of the Khaeri compound, I spoke again. 'What about that doctor?'

'His eyes weren't bad. He was scared, though. They've been giving him a bad time.'

'*Polé* for Peter,' were Elizabeth's first words. When it became later and later and still we hadn't returned, the family had begun to grow uneasy. At last Mary had seen our Renault pull up in front of the hospital. Quickly she had learned our business there from the nurses, then rushed at once to tell her mother. 'I am sorry for him.'

Koert Jan gave Elizabeth the sack of Aunt Mary's ground-nuts. With Jenifa and Mayende gone the compound seemed larger and emptier. Rosa was the youngest again and now Antastasia carried her little sister on one hip the way I hadn't seen her do the whole time the baby was with us. Koert Jan went inside right away. He sat and began to write in his journal. I felt dizzy and lay down.

A few hours later as we were finishing our dinner, there was a knock on the doorpost.

'*Hodi*,' Anna whispered.

'*Karibu*.'

The girl came in carrying a bowl full of fresh-roasted nuts, the odor irresistible. We had to be careful eating them not to burn our mouths.

'Mother says' – Anna stood at the end of the table, eyes cast down; with one finger she traced a crack between the planks – 'you are good people.'

Her voice was all but inaudible.

"What?"

Anna looked up. "Mother says you are good people."

X

Brrring, brrring.

Next morning Peter was right on time for breakfast. We hadn't expected him. In fact Koert Jan and I had agreed we didn't feel much like working. We would drive instead to Kisumu. We'd have the buffet luncheon at the Kisumu Hotel with trifle for dessert, and kiwi-cheesecake and chocolate mousse. Then we'd lie in the sun next to the swimming pool at the club. If we were lucky someone might have a recent copy of *Time* or *Newsweek*.

When I came outside, Elizabeth, Peter and Koert Jan were standing and talking in the yard. The button was buttoned at Peter's neck again.

'Before Jenifa, I lost four,' I heard Elizabeth say as I headed for the solitude of the *cho*. Then she laughed. When I looked back she was holding up four fingers. Then she held up two more. 'And later two were born dead.'

This time Peter laughed. I didn't look back.

We spent the day working hard. The landscape we visited, flat but at a tilt, was largely barren. Once morning clouds lifted, we had to walk exposed to the sun. Koert Jan had forgotten his sunglasses. He carried Peter's briefcase on his head to shade his eyes.

Koert Jan was able to apply himself to interviewing with enviable concentration. Good for him. As for me, I felt unwell, absent. I just watched people's shadows.

By mid-afternoon we were back in Mumias. We took a break for tea and *mandasi*. In the depths of the blue hotelli next door to the miller we crowded around a small table. Under the table Koert Jan and Peter sat pressing knees. Through the wall the mill throbbed.

'So, Peter. How's Berlita?' I asked.

'She is well, thank you, sir.' Come, Peter, how well could she be?

Koert Jan signaled for more tea from the huge aluminum kettle kept ready on a fire of embers, a kettle so heavy that the man who poured had to hold it with two hands. Women finished at the miller's filed past the front of the hotelli. Their faces and bare arms were dusted with a fine white coat of flour. They might have been photo negatives of themselves.

'Last night my brother-in-law Jacob came to our place, sir, with my sister and some members of our church. Their purpose of coming was to bury the baby, Juma.' Peter laughed. 'My wife was in favor of giving a name.' To focus the pain no doubt, like a magnifying glass. 'We marked the grave with a cross, sir, two sticks, so, and I planted purple flowers all around. You should see it, sir, how nice the grave looks.

'Don't eat these, sir. They are stale.' Peter called for a fresh plate of *mandasi*. When they came, crispy, he dunked his in his tea until soggy bits fell away. He didn't miss a single crumb.

'Jacob is our minister, sir. So it had to be up to him to decide the rules for this funeral. It was even Jacob himself who chose to make the sermon, sir. Of all speakers he is the best, number one, but as it happens this time I couldn't agree with him. He was for telling about Job. All that Job was having to suffer because of God's plan. The loss of too many precious things, one right after another. Sir, I told Jacob that of all the stories in the Bible, he was wrong to be choosing this particular one.'

'Wrong?'

Peter concentrated on a careful, deliberate choice of words. In the dark hotelli he seemed to glow.

'Job, he was being tested by God, sir. He was even one of God's very favorite followers. To this good man's trial there was a purpose, a reward, an end. But' – Peter leaned forward, smiling – 'if Job was not innocent, if Job knew he was a guilty man, then the whole story would lose its meaning.'

'You've lost me now, Peter,' Koert Jan said. Peter's smile turned sad.

'Job in the Bible was a white man, sir.'

'Oh Peter!'

'But who am I? Only a poor black African, one of those who must pay unto the seventh generation for the sins of my ancestors.'

Koert Jan upset his teacup. It was empty though and only a small trickle dribbled over the edge of the table.

'God's will be done.'

It was a relief to step back outside. The afternoon was cooling off and Mumias was stirring again to life. Koert Jan and Peter walked back to the Renault several steps ahead of me. About

274

one thing Berlita was right: their difference in height made them a comic duo. I almost collided with Tom before I saw him.

'Tom!' With a smile that went as deep as my skull I stepped forward. Here on the crowded front stoep of the hotelli and town shops, with men lounging and laughing, the miller's boy weighing loads of grain in the iron scale, the street alive, too, battered *matatu*s honking, children throwing stones at a bottle set on the wall in front of the mosque, a bargirl in the road below with a radio balanced flat on her head, blaring – the whole world full, animate, light – Tom looked vital, and anything but vulnerable. For the first time I saw he had a scar, nothing tribal but a slash down through his one eyebrow narrowly missing the corner of the eye. He was very well dressed. Striped trousers with a crease sharp as a knife, polished shoes – platform heels, of course – a checked sport shirt open at the neck, and a fine gold chain around his throat.

'We meet again!' This chance meeting made me happy. To be honest Tom hadn't been out of my thoughts for a minute – together with feelings of guilt, and loneliness. The rest of us, we had people to comfort, console and support us. Even to hide us if necessary, or forgive us. But Tom – the poor black African – we had left him alone, bereft.

'Excuse me, sir.' The boy whose path I blocked looked at me with puzzled eyes. 'Mistaken identity?' He grinned and put a friendly hand on my shoulder.

'Sorry. I thought you were someone else.'

XI

When we reached the Khaeris' Anna was there waiting to greet us with a baby tucked into the crook of her arm. More asleep than awake the baby blinked docilely as Anna held one of his hands up and coaxed him to wave. Mayende!

I simply sat behind the wheel and stared. Koert Jan leaned over and took the key from the ignition. Jenifa came gliding out of the family hut and opened the car door. We got out and shook hands.

'Hullo there,' she said and suddenly lost her battle not to smile.

Mary came running now with Mayende's bottle. Jenifa took it from her and tested the temperature of the milk by squeezing a few drops on to the inside of her wrist – then lapping them up like a cat. Anna surrendered Mayende to his mother and Jenifa staggered back a step under the baby's weight.

'Mayende's growing so fast,' Anna whispered, and blew away a fly walking on the baby's cheek. 'He'll soon be as big as Aunt Mary.' The baby gurgled.

Peter pinched Mayende's cheek. Then he lifted the back of the Renault and unloaded Jenifa's carton of evaporated milk cans. We had never said a word to him about them. In fact we had forgotten all about them.

'Sister got bored,' Anna whispered, 'so she came home.'

'Not bored,' Jenifa said. 'There were too many men in that place.'

Peter came back wheeling his bicycle. He didn't say anything but lifted the front tire in the air and gave it a spin. While Koert Jan counted out money for new tires, I went into our hut.

'Shhh, shhh, shhh.'

Noise under our back window brought me outside again. Anastasia and Rosa were down on their hands and knees. They were rigging up a framework of twigs to arch above a small hole in the ground. Mary came running with Mayende's yellow blanket to stretch across the twigs.

Soon the air was aflutter with hundreds, thousands of winged ants, tricked into believing they could come out and forage safely under the protective cover of night.

Koert Jan sat on our earthen veranda, dark handprints and one crooked footprint spangling the wall behind him. Peter was gone. Exhaustion showed on Koert Jan's face. Rosa shyly brought him a winged ant to pop into his mouth. He pretended to do so and to chew it thoroughly while I saw him release the insect from a cupped hand behind his back.

Anna saw, too. She laughed and shook her finger at him. Then she hurried to bring Koert Jan a whole handful of ants and to make sure he swallowed them all.

I crossed the yard to Jenifa and the baby – thinking I was walking over hollow ground, a vast cave where the air was never still, but frothy from the motion of an infinite number of wings. Jenifa sat on the ground with her back against one of the uprights supporting the family hut. Mayende lay across her lap. I crouched down and closed a hand around one of his bare feet. He just kept on drinking. His eyes were clamped shut and he was draining the bottle for all he was worth, gasping as he sucked.

'And Tom?' I asked softly, hoping Koert Jan wouldn't overhear. Jenifa shrugged, cocked her head and didn't answer. 'Jenifa, what about Tom?'

'Next time Mother will kill him.'

Deep down I knew though there wasn't going to be a next time. Tom was through. He'd played his part out. He'd done enough, just, to guard his wounded honor. He had made his bluff and probably was relieved to have had it called. If we hadn't come along, it might have been all the more awkward for him. Morning light, a crowded bus, a hangover – Jenifa and the baby on his hands.

Now as things had worked out, back in Mombasa Tom could move among the *pombe* shops and complain about the whites who seduced his faithless wife and stole his child. What powers of magic might he not impute to us? One day he was sure to marry and tell his wife so many wild stories that not long after she would dream a frightful dream and wake up screaming: two white men would come for her children, one tall, one short, one

277

fair, one dark, they would walk closer and closer holding out their arms to her.

And Mayende? The rubber nipple twisted in his mouth now. Milk was spilling over his lips, on to his round chin. How long would he keep his laughing eyes? Pampered with even more ferocity than most Luhya sons he would grow up with seven mothers – and no father. '*Musungu*s saved your life.' How often would he have to hear the story of the white heroes who came to his rescue? Had we?

Or was our part carefully orchestrated? Had we performed, as dutifully as Tom, in a drama with a foregone conclusion?

XII

For years now we have continued to receive, at fitful intervals, letters from Peter Ohundo. The day we left Western Province we presented Peter with a book. He burst into tears.

'Oh sir, I know what it is!' My heart sank. 'The Bible!' He tore the wrapping paper open and laid bare our choice – a dictionary. Typically, he recovered in a heartbeat. 'Oh thank you, sir. Now all the words of the Bible will be having their own clear meaning.'

Peter has had his ups and downs. With the cash bonus we paid him upon our departure he started a small business at Akero market. Soap, matches, safety pins, candles. He wrote letters for people, too – 'some romantic, some official' – and he read the replies for them. Peter also used part of his savings to pay a lawyer to bring a court case against one uncle who had stolen some hectares of land from his father. And Peter won.

Only a few days later, however, Peter was struck down by a serious illness. His family agreed at once this must be poison and blamed the uncle's grown sons. They swore on the Bible they were innocent. Peter was carried to the hospital where for eight days he 'lay dead'. 'On the ninth day I began to see the world again, sir, and slowly, slowly recovered.' From Peter's description of his symptoms we diagnosed cerebral meningitis.

To meet the expenses of his hospitalisation cost Peter all his remaining capital. His little business went broke. And his bicycle was stolen. 'If only you were in the country, sir, I know I could start my trading enterprise again so easily.' True to form, Peter never asked a direct favor.

On the 'domestic front', Peter's own phrase, he took a second wife. He wanted to marry Anna Khaeri and when that proved no go, his choice fell on Mary. Elizabeth, Peter explained, wanted the girls to finish their schooling first. Besides I suspect Elizabeth and Joseph had higher ambitions for their children.

Indeed, as Anna herself wrote – even her tidy printing seemed only to whisper on the page! – soon after we left, Jenifa 'married four hundred acres'. The other young Khaeris are pitching in to help Kenya's development effort, training as midwives, teachers, inspectors for the extension service. The toddler Mayende, Anna insists, looks like Koert Jan – an avowal which he admits fills him with irrational pride. The notion of their looking alike makes me smile: I never told Koert Jan how much Tom had reminded me of him that dark and rainy night of the baby's abduction.

In the first year of Peter's marriage to his new junior wife, she bore him a daughter. The baby girl was named Webster, 'after the dictionary, sir'. Then, before the next television season in the west began, she gave him a son – promptly named Koert Jan. Berlita, now Peter's 'senior wife', didn't take matters lying down. She produced a healthy boy who was named for me – with Reagan as an extra middle name. We sent gifts. I don't know what the American President did. With every new letter it seems there came news of another son, another daughter.

Then, although Peter's cheerful writing style never faltered, instead of so many reasons for celebration, he began to report tragedies. Koert Jan died. 'We pray he is drinking angel's milk, sir, with a face as white as their wings.' The cause of death was whooping cough. Not long afterwards my namesake died as well. 'I am sorry to have to tell you, sir, this child was too badly bitten by our local monkeys when he was guarding the ripe maize. He was having a big stick but they took it from him and so many were just attacking him like flies on a piece of red meat. My senior wife took him to the Mission Hospital. He was fighting there for his life for ten days until finally despite all they could do he died. He has left us such a big bill behind. If you were here, sir, perhaps I could ask you to explain why God chooses to let one child live and another die. All I can do is praise him in my low ignorance.'

Why indeed? In Zimbabwe Shona and Mbdele are killing each other – pardon the expression – wholesale. In Uganda since Amin's expulsion tribal murder has diminished no jot. Bodies clot the streams. Crops in Ethiopia fail and famine spreads – but Mestingu's terror spreads further and faster, claiming countless lives. In Kenya politicians hoard maize to make a killing on the market.

Every time I read the paper it seems the pounding at the door grows louder and louder. I scratch at my cheek and wonder what ever happened to Chief Skin and Bones?

And through it all Peter's unruffled letters keep arriving – with postage stamps that bear the image of a flower, a rock crystal, a wild animal. I save the stamps for nephews and nieces. I save the letters. All begin with the very same salutation: 'To my everlasting boss.' All end with the identical valediction: 'Begging to pen off, I am your all-weather friend, Peter Ohundo.'